FreeBSD Porter's Handbook

A catalogue record for this book is available from the Hong Kong Public Libraries.

Published in Hong Kong by Samurai Media Limited.

Email: info@samuraimedia.org

ISBN 978-988-8406-75-3

Table of Contents

List of Tables

List of Examples

Chapter 1. Introduction

The FreeBSD Ports Collection is the way almost everyone installs applications ("ports") on FreeBSD. Like everything else about FreeBSD, it is primarily a volunteer effort. It is important to keep this in mind when reading this document.

In FreeBSD, anyone may submit a new port, or volunteer to maintain an existing unmaintained port. No special commit privilege is needed.

Chapter 2. Making a New Port

Interested in making a new port, or upgrading existing ports? Great!

What follows are some guidelines for creating a new port for FreeBSD. To upgrade an existing port, read this, then read Chapter 10, *Upgrading a Port*.

When this document is not sufficiently detailed, refer to /usr/ports/Mk/bsd.port.mk , which is included by all port Makefiles. Even those not hacking Makefiles daily can gain much knowledge from it. Additionally, specific questions can be sent to the FreeBSD ports mailing list.

 Note

Only a fraction of the variables (*VAR*) that can be overridden are mentioned in this document. Most (if not all) are documented at the start of /usr/ports/Mk/bsd.port.mk ; the others probably ought to be. Note that this file uses a non-standard tab setting: Emacs and Vim will recognize the setting on loading the file. Both vi(1) and ex(1) can be set to use the correct value by typing :set tabstop=4 once the file has been loaded.

Looking for something easy to start with? Take a look at the list of requested ports and see if you can work on one (or more).

Chapter 3. Quick Porting

This section describes how to quickly create a new port. For applications where this quick method is not adequate, the full "Slow Porting" process is described in Chapter 4, *Slow Porting*.

First, get the original tarball and put it into DISTDIR, which defaults to /usr/ports/distfiles .

Note

These steps assume that the software compiled out-of-the-box. In other words, absolutely no changes were required for the application to work on a FreeBSD system. If anything had to be changed, refer to Chapter 4, *Slow Porting*.

Note

It is recommended to set the DEVELOPER make(1) variable in /etc/make.conf before getting into porting.

```
# echo DEVELOPER=yes >> /etc/make.conf
```

This setting enables the "developer mode" that displays deprecation warnings and activates some further quality checks on calling make.

3.1. Writing the Makefile

The minimal Makefile would look something like this:

```
# $FreeBSD$

PORTNAME= oneko
PORTVERSION= 1.1b
CATEGORIES= games
MASTER_SITES= ftp://ftp.cs.columbia.edu/archives/X11R5/contrib/

MAINTAINER= youremail@example.com
COMMENT= Cat chasing a mouse all over the screen

.include <bsd.port.mk>
```

Note

In some cases, the Makefile of an existing port may contain additional lines in the header, such as the name of the port and the date it was created. This additional information has been declared obsolete, and is being phased out.

Try to figure it out. Do not worry about the contents of the $FreeBSD$ line, it will be filled in automatically by Subversion when the port is imported to our main ports tree. A more detailed example is shown in the sample Makefile section.

3.2. Writing the Description Files

There are two description files that are required for any port, whether they actually package or not. They are pkg-descr and pkg-plist . Their pkg- prefix distinguishes them from other files.

3.2.1. pkg-descr

This is a longer description of the port. One to a few paragraphs concisely explaining what the port does is sufficient.

 Note

This is *not* a manual or an in-depth description on how to use or compile the port! *Please be careful when copying from the README or manpage.* Too often they are not a concise description of the port or are in an awkward format. For example, manpages have justified spacing, which looks particularly bad with monospaced fonts.

A well-written pkg-descr describes the port completely enough that users would not have to consult the documentation or visit the website to understand what the software does, how it can be useful, or what particularly nice features it has. Mentioning certain requirements like a graphical toolkit, heavy dependencies, runtime environment, or implementation languages help users decide whether this port will work for them.

Include a URL to the official WWW homepage. Prepend *one* of the websites (pick the most common one) with WWW: (followed by single space) so that automated tools will work correctly. If the URI is the root of the website or directory, it must be terminated with a slash.

 Note

If the listed webpage for a port is not available, try to search the Internet first to see if the official site moved, was renamed, or is hosted elsewhere.

This example shows how pkg-descr looks:

```
This is a port of oneko, in which a cat chases a poor mouse all over
the screen.
  :
(etc.)

WWW: http://www.oneko.org/
```

3.2.2. pkg-plist

This file lists all the files installed by the port. It is also called the "packing list" because the package is generated by packing the files listed here. The pathnames are relative to the installation prefix (usually /usr/local).

Here is a small example:

```
bin/oneko
man/man1/oneko.1.gz
lib/X11/app-defaults/Oneko
lib/X11/oneko/cat1.xpm
lib/X11/oneko/cat2.xpm
lib/X11/oneko/mouse.xpm
```

Refer to the pkg-create(8) manual page for details on the packing list.

Note

It is recommended to keep all the filenames in this file sorted alphabetically. It will make verifying changes when upgrading the port much easier.

Tip

Creating a packing list manually can be a very tedious task. If the port installs a large numbers of files, creating the packing list automatically might save time.

There is only one case when `pkg-plist` can be omitted from a port. If the port installs just a handful of files, list them in `PLIST_FILES`, within the port's `Makefile`. For instance, we could get along without `pkg-plist` in the above `oneko` port by adding these lines to the `Makefile`:

```
PLIST_FILES= bin/oneko \
    man/man1/oneko.1.gz \
    lib/X11/app-defaults/Oneko \
    lib/X11/oneko/cat1.xpm \
    lib/X11/oneko/cat2.xpm \
    lib/X11/oneko/mouse.xpm
```

Note

Usage of `PLIST_FILES` should not be abused. When looking for the origin of a file, people usually try to grep through the `pkg-plist` files in the ports tree. Listing files in `PLIST_FILES` in the `Makefile` makes that search more difficult.

Tip

If a port needs to create an empty directory, or creates directories outside of `${PREFIX}` during installation, refer to Section 7.2.1, "Cleaning Up Empty Directories" for more information.

The price for this way of listing a port's files and directories is that the keywords described in pkg-create(8) and Section 7.6, "Expanding Package List with Keywords" cannot be used. Therefore, it is suitable only for simple ports and makes them even simpler. At the same time, it has the advantage of reducing the number of files in the ports collection. Please consider using this technique before resorting to `pkg-plist`.

Later we will see how `pkg-plist` and `PLIST_FILES` can be used to fulfill more sophisticated tasks.

3.3. Creating the Checksum File

Just type `make makesum`. The ports make rules will automatically generate the file `distinfo`.

3.4. Testing the Port

Make sure that the port rules do exactly what is desired, including packaging up the port. These are the important points to verify:

- `pkg-plist` does not contain anything not installed by the port.

- `pkg-plist` contains everything that is installed by the port.

- The port can be installed using the `install` target. This verifies that the install script works correctly.

- The port can be deinstalled properly using the `deinstall` target. This verifies that the deinstall script works correctly.

- The port only has access to network resources during the `fetch` target phase. This is important for package builders, such as ports-mgmt/poudriere.

- Make sure that `make package` can be run as a normal user (that is, not as `root`). If that fails, `NEED_ROOT=yes` must be added to the port `Makefile`.

Procedure 3.1. Recommended Test Ordering

1. `make stage`

2. `make check-orphans`

3. `make package`

4. `make install`

5. `make deinstall`

6. `pkg add` *package-filename*

7. `make package` (as user)

Make certain no warnings are shown in any of the stages.

Thorough automated testing can be done with ports-mgmt/tinderbox or ports-mgmt/poudriere from the Ports Collection. These applications maintain `jails` where all of the steps shown above can be tested without affecting the state of the host system.

3.5. Checking the Port with `portlint`

Please use `portlint` to see if the port conforms to our guidelines. The ports-mgmt/portlint program is part of the ports collection. In particular, check that the Makefile is in the right shape and the package is named appropriately.

> **Important**
>
> Do not blindly follow the output of `portlint`. It is a static lint tool and sometimes gets things wrong.

3.6. Submitting the New Port

Before submitting the new port, read the DOs and DON'Ts section.

Once happy with the port, the only thing remaining is to put it in the main FreeBSD ports tree and make everybody else happy about it too.

Important

We do not need the `work` directory or the `pkgname.tgz` package, so delete them now.

Next, build the shar(1) file. Assuming the port is called `oneko`, `cd` to the directory above where the `oneko` directory is located, and then type: `shar ` `find oneko` ` > oneko.shar`

A diff created from a Subversion checkout of the ports tree is also acceptable. Add all the files with `svn add`. `cd` to the base of the ports tree so full paths to the changed files are included in the diff, then generate the diff with `svn diff`. For example, `svn diff games/oneko > oneko.diff` .

Submit `oneko.shar` or `oneko.diff` with the bug submission form.. Use product "Ports & Packages", component "Individual Port(s)", and follow the guidelines shown there. Add a short description of the program to the Description field of the PR (perhaps a short version of `COMMENT`), and remember to add `oneko.shar` or `oneko.diff` as an attachment.

Note

Giving a good description in the summary of the problem report makes the work of port committers a lot easier. We prefer something like "New port: *category/portname short description of the port*" for new ports. Using this scheme makes it easier and faster to begin the work of committing the new port.

After submitting the port, please be patient. The time needed to include a new port in FreeBSD can vary from a few days to a few months. A simple search form of the Problem Report database can be searched at https://bugs.freebsd.org/bugzilla/query.cgi.

To get a listing of *open* port PRs, select *Open* and *Ports & Packages* in the search form, then click [Search].

After looking at the new port, we will reply if necessary, and commit it to the tree. The submitter's name will also be added to the list of Additional FreeBSD Contributors and other files.

Chapter 4. Slow Porting

Okay, so it was not that simple, and the port required some modifications to get it to work. In this section, we will explain, step by step, how to modify it to get it to work with the ports paradigm.

4.1. How Things Work

First, this is the sequence of events which occurs when the user first types make in the port's directory. Having bsd.port.mk in another window while reading this really helps to understand it.

But do not worry, not many people understand exactly how bsd.port.mk is working... :-)

1. The fetch target is run. The fetch target is responsible for making sure that the tarball exists locally in DISTDIR. If fetch cannot find the required files in DISTDIR it will look up the URL MASTER_SITES , which is set in the Makefile, as well as our FTP mirrors where we put distfiles as backup. It will then attempt to fetch the named distribution file with FETCH, assuming that the requesting site has direct access to the Internet. If that succeeds, it will save the file in DISTDIR for future use and proceed.

2. The extract target is run. It looks for the port's distribution file (typically a gzipped tarball) in DISTDIR and unpacks it into a temporary subdirectory specified by WRKDIR (defaults to work).

3. The patch target is run. First, any patches defined in PATCHFILES are applied. Second, if any patch files named patch-* are found in PATCHDIR (defaults to the files subdirectory), they are applied at this time in alphabetical order.

4. The configure target is run. This can do any one of many different things.

    1. If it exists, scripts/configure is run.

    2. If HAS_CONFIGURE or GNU_CONFIGURE is set, WRKSRC/configure is run.

5. The build target is run. This is responsible for descending into the port's private working directory (WRKSRC) and building it.

6. The stage target is run. This puts the final set of built files into a temporary directory (STAGEDIR , see Section 6.1, "Staging"). The hierarchy of this directory mirrors that of the system on which the package will be installed.

7. The package target is run. This creates a package using the files from the temporary directory created during the stage target and the port's pkg-plist .

8. The install target is run. This installs the package created during the package target into the host system.

The above are the default actions. In addition, define targets pre-*something* or post-*something*, or put scripts with those names, in the scripts subdirectory, and they will be run before or after the default actions are done.

For example, if there is a post-extract target defined in the Makefile, and a file pre-build in the scripts subdirectory, the post-extract target will be called after the regular extraction actions, and pre-build will be executed before the default build rules are done. It is recommended to use Makefile targets if the actions are simple enough, because it will be easier for someone to figure out what kind of non-default action the port requires.

The default actions are done by the do-*something* targets from bsd.port.mk. For example, the commands to extract a port are in the target do-extract. If the default target does not do the job right, redefine the do-*something* target in the Makefile.

Note

The "main" targets (for example, `extract`, `configure`, etc.) do nothing more than make sure all the stages up to that one are completed and call the real targets or scripts, and they are not intended to be changed. To fix the extraction, fix `do-extract`, but never ever change the way `extract` operates! Additionally, the target `post-deinstall` is invalid and is not run by the ports infrastructure.

Now that what goes on when the user types `make install` is better understood, let us go through the recommended steps to create the perfect port.

4.2. Getting the Original Sources

Get the original sources (normally) as a compressed tarball (`foo.tar.gz` or `foo.tar.bz2`) and copy it into `DISTDIR`. Always use *mainstream* sources when and where possible.

Set the variable `MASTER_SITES` to reflect where the original tarball resides. Shorthand definitions exist for most mainstream sites in `bsd.sites.mk`. Please use these sites—and the associated definitions—if at all possible, to help avoid the problem of having the same information repeated over again many times in the source base. As these sites tend to change over time, this becomes a maintenance nightmare for everyone involved. See Section 5.4.2, "`MASTER_SITES` " for details.

If there is no FTP/HTTP site that is well-connected to the net, or can only find sites that have irritatingly non-standard formats, put a copy on a reliable FTP or HTTP server (for example, a home page).

If a convenient and reliable place to put the distfile cannot be found, we can "house" it ourselves on `ftp.Free-BSD.org`; however, this is the least-preferred solution. The distfile must be placed into `~/public_distfiles/` of someone's `freefall` account. Ask the person who commits the port to do this. This person will also set `MASTER_SITES` to `LOCAL/username` where *username* is their FreeBSD cluster login.

If the port's distfile changes all the time without any kind of version update by the author, consider putting the distfile on a home page and listing it as the first `MASTER_SITES` . Try to talk the port author out of doing this; it really does help to establish some kind of source code control. Hosting a specific version will prevent users from getting checksum mismatch errors, and also reduce the workload of maintainers of our FTP site. Also, if there is only one master site for the port, it is recommended to house a backup on a home page and list it as the second `MASTER_SITES` .

If the port requires additional patches that are available on the Internet, fetch them too and put them in `DISTDIR`. Do not worry if they come from a site other than where the main source tarball comes, we have a way to handle these situations (see the description of PATCHFILES below).

4.3. Modifying the Port

Unpack a copy of the tarball in a private directory and make whatever changes are necessary to get the port to compile properly under the current version of FreeBSD. Keep *careful track* of steps, as they will be needed to automate the process shortly. Everything, including the deletion, addition, or modification of files has to be doable using an automated script or patch file when the port is finished.

If the port requires significant user interaction/customization to compile or install, take a look at one of Larry Wall's classic Configure scripts and perhaps do something similar. The goal of the new ports collection is to make each port as "plug-and-play" as possible for the end-user while using a minimum of disk space.

> **Note**
>
> Unless explicitly stated, patch files, scripts, and other files created and contributed to the FreeBSD ports collection are assumed to be covered by the standard BSD copyright conditions.

4.4. Patching

In the preparation of the port, files that have been added or changed can be recorded with diff(1) for later feeding to patch(1). Doing this with a typical file involves saving a copy of the original file before making any changes using a .orig suffix.

```
% cp file file.orig
```

After all changes have been made, cd back to the port directory. Use make makepatch to generate updated patch files in the files directory.

4.4.1. General Rules for Patching

Patch files are stored in PATCHDIR, usually files/, from where they will be automatically applied. All patches must be relative to WRKSRC. Typically WRKSRC is a subdirectory of WRKDIR, the directory where the distfile is extracted. Use make -V WRKSRC to see the actual path. The patch names are to follow these rules:

- Avoid having more than one patch modify the same file. For example, having both patch-foobar.c and patch-foobar.c2 making changes to ${WRKSRC}/foobar.c makes them fragile and difficult to debug.

- When creating names for patch files, replace each underscore (_) with two underscores (__) and each slash (/) with one underscore (_). For example, to patch a file named src/freeglut_joystick.c, name the corresponding patch patch-src_freeglut__joystick.c. Do not name patches like patch-aa or patch-ab. Always use the path and file name in patch names. Using make makepatch automatically generates the correct names.

- A patch may modify multiple files if the changes are related and the patch is named appropriately. For example, patch-add-missing-stdlib.h.

- Only use characters [-+._a-zA-Z0-9] for naming patches. In particular, *do not use :: as a path separator*, use _ instead.

Minimize the amount of non-functional whitespace changes in patches. It is common in the Open Source world for projects to share large amounts of a code base, but obey different style and indenting rules. When taking a working piece of functionality from one project to fix similar areas in another, please be careful: the resulting patch may be full of non-functional changes. It not only increases the size of the ports repository but makes it hard to find out what exactly caused the problem and what was changed at all.

If a file must be deleted, do it in the **post-extract** target rather than as part of the patch.

4.4.2. Manual Patch Generation

> Note
>
> Manual patch creation is usually not necessary. Automatic patch generation as described earlier in this section is the preferred method. However, manual patching may be required occasionally.

Patches are saved into files named `patch-*` where * indicates the pathname of the file that is patched, such as `patch-Imakefile` or `patch-src-config.h`.

After the file has been modified, diff(1) is used to record the differences between the original and the modified version. `-u` causes diff(1) to produce "unified" diffs, the preferred form.

```
% diff -u file.orig file > patch-pathname-file
```

When generating patches for new, added files, `-N` is used to tell diff(1) to treat the non-existent original file as if it existed but was empty:

```
% diff -u -N newfile.orig newfile > patch-pathname-newfile
```

Do not add $FreeBSD$ RCS strings in patches. When patches are added to the Subversion repository with `svn add`, the `fbsd:nokeywords` property is set to `yes` automatically so keywords in the patch are not modified when committed. The property can be added manually with `svn propset fbsd:nokeywords yes` *files....*

Using the recurse (`-r`) option to diff(1) to generate patches is fine, but please look at the resulting patches to make sure there is no unnecessary junk in there. In particular, diffs between two backup files, `Makefiles` when the port uses Imake or GNU `configure`, etc., are unnecessary and have to be deleted. If it was necessary to edit `configure.in` and run `autoconf` to regenerate `configure`, do not take the diffs of `configure` (it often grows to a few thousand lines!). Instead, define `USE_AUTOTOOLS=autoconf:261` and take the diffs of `configure.in`.

4.4.3. Simple Automatic Replacements

Simple replacements can be performed directly from the port `Makefile` using the in-place mode of sed(1). This is useful when changes use the value of a variable:

```
post-patch:
 @${REINPLACE_CMD} -e 's|for Linux|for FreeBSD|g' ${WRKSRC}/README
```

Quite often, software being ported uses the CR/LF convention in source files. This may cause problems with further patching, compiler warnings, or script execution (like `/bin/sh^M not found`.) To quickly convert all files from CR/LF to just LF, add this entry to the port `Makefile`:

```
USES= dos2unix
```

A list of specific files to convert can be given:

```
USES= dos2unix
DOS2UNIX_FILES= util.c util.h
```

Use `DOS2UNIX_REGEX` to convert a group of files across subdirectories. Its argument is a find(1)-compatible regular expression. More on the format is in re_format(7). This option is useful for converting all files of a given extension. For example, convert all source code files, leaving binary files intact:

```
USES= dos2unix
DOS2UNIX_REGEX= .*\.([ch]|cpp)
```

A similar option is `DOS2UNIX_GLOB`, which runs `find` for each element listed in it.

14

```
USES= dos2unix
DOS2UNIX_GLOB= *.c *.cpp *.h
```

The base directory for the conversion can be set. This is useful when there are multiple distfiles and several contain files which require line-ending conversion.

```
USES= dos2unix
DOS2UNIX_WRKSRC= ${WRKDIR}
```

4.5. Configuring

Include any additional customization commands in the `configure` script and save it in the `scripts` subdirectory. As mentioned above, it is also possible do this with `Makefile` targets and/or scripts with the name `pre-configure` or `post-configure`.

4.6. Handling User Input

If the port requires user input to build, configure, or install, set `IS_INTERACTIVE` in the `Makefile`. This will allow "overnight builds" to skip it. If the user sets the variable `BATCH` in their environment (and if the user sets the variable `INTERACTIVE`, then *only* those ports requiring interaction are built). This will save a lot of wasted time on the set of machines that continually build ports (see below).

It is also recommended that if there are reasonable default answers to the questions, `PACKAGE_BUILDING` be used to turn off the interactive script when it is set. This will allow us to build the packages for CDROMs and FTP.

Chapter 5. Configuring the Makefile

Configuring the `Makefile` is pretty simple, and again we suggest looking at existing examples before starting. Also, there is a sample Makefile in this handbook, so take a look and please follow the ordering of variables and sections in that template to make the port easier for others to read.

Consider these problems in sequence during the design of the new `Makefile`:

5.1. The Original Source

Does it live in `DISTDIR` as a standard `gzip`ped tarball named something like `foozolix-1.2.tar.gz` ? If so, go on to the next step. If not, the distribution file format might require overriding one or more of `DISTVERSION` , `DISTNAME`, `EXTRACT_CMD`, `EXTRACT_BEFORE_ARGS`, `EXTRACT_AFTER_ARGS`, `EXTRACT_SUFX`, or `DISTFILES`.

In the worst case, create a custom **do-extract** target to override the default. This is rarely, if ever, necessary.

5.2. Naming

The first part of the port's `Makefile` names the port, describes its version number, and lists it in the correct category.

5.2.1. PORTNAME and PORTVERSION

Set `PORTNAME` to the base name of the port. Set `PORTVERSION` to the version number of the port unless `DISTVERSION` is used (see Section 5.4.1, "`DISTVERSION/DISTNAME` ").

>
> ### Important
>
> The package name must be unique across the entire ports tree. Make sure that the `PORTNAME` is not already in use by an existing port. If the name has already been used, add either PKG-NAMEPREFIX or PKGNAMESUFFIX.

5.2.2. PORTREVISION and PORTEPOCH

5.2.2.1. PORTREVISION

`PORTREVISION` is a monotonically increasing value which is reset to 0 with every increase of `PORTVERSION` , typically every time there is a new official vendor release. If `PORTREVISION` is non-zero, the value is appended to the package name. Changes to `PORTREVISION` are used by automated tools like pkg-version(8) to determine that a new package is available.

`PORTREVISION` must be increased each time a change is made to the port that changes the generated package in any way. That includes changes that only affect a package built with non-default options.

Examples of when `PORTREVISION` must be bumped:

- Addition of patches to correct security vulnerabilities, bugs, or to add new functionality to the port.

- Changes to the port `Makefile` to enable or disable compile-time options in the package.

- Changes in the packing list or the install-time behavior of the package. For example, a change to a script which generates initial data for the package, like ssh(1) host keys.

- Version bump of a port's shared library dependency (in this case, someone trying to install the old package after installing a newer version of the dependency will fail since it will look for the old libfoo.x instead of libfoo.(x+1)).

- Silent changes to the port distfile which have significant functional differences. For example, changes to the distfile requiring a correction to `distinfo` with no corresponding change to `PORTVERSION`, where a `diff -ru` of the old and new versions shows non-trivial changes to the code.

Examples of changes which do not require a `PORTREVISION` bump:

- Style changes to the port skeleton with no functional change to what appears in the resulting package.

- Changes to `MASTER_SITES` or other functional changes to the port which do not affect the resulting package.

- Trivial patches to the distfile such as correction of typos, which are not important enough that users of the package have to go to the trouble of upgrading.

- Build fixes which cause a package to become compilable where it was previously failing. As long as the changes do not introduce any functional change on any other platforms on which the port did previously build. Since `PORTREVISION` reflects the content of the package, if the package was not previously buildable then there is no need to increase `PORTREVISION` to mark a change.

A rule of thumb is to decide whether a change committed to a port is something which *some* people would benefit from having. Either because of an enhancement, fix, or by virtue that the new package will actually work at all. Then weigh that against that fact that it will cause everyone who regularly updates their ports tree to be compelled to update. If yes, `PORTREVISION` must be bumped.

Note

People using binary packages will *never* see the update if `PORTREVISION` is not bumped. Without increasing `PORTREVISION`, the package builders have no way to detect the change and thus, will not rebuild the package.

5.2.2.2. PORTEPOCH

From time to time a software vendor or FreeBSD porter will do something silly and release a version of their software which is actually numerically less than the previous version. An example of this is a port which goes from foo-20000801 to foo-1.0 (the former will be incorrectly treated as a newer version since 20000801 is a numerically greater value than 1).

Tip

The results of version number comparisons are not always obvious. `pkg version` (see pkg-version(8)) can be used to test the comparison of two version number strings. For example:

```
% pkg version -t 0.031 0.29
>
```

The > output indicates that version 0.031 is considered greater than version 0.29, which may not have been obvious to the porter.

In situations such as this, `PORTEPOCH` must be increased. If `PORTEPOCH` is nonzero it is appended to the package name as described in section 0 above. `PORTEPOCH` must never be decreased or reset to zero, because that would cause comparison to a package from an earlier epoch to fail. For example, the package would not be detected as out of date. The new version number, 1.0.1 in the above example, is still numerically less than the previous version, 20000801, but the .1 suffix is treated specially by automated tools and found to be greater than the implied suffix .0 on the earlier package.

Dropping or resetting PORTEPOCH incorrectly leads to no end of grief. If the discussion above was not clear enough, please consult the FreeBSD ports mailing list.

It is expected that PORTEPOCH will not be used for the majority of ports, and that sensible use of PORTVERSION can often preempt it becoming necessary if a future release of the software changes the version structure. However, care is needed by FreeBSD porters when a vendor release is made without an official version number — such as a code "snapshot" release. The temptation is to label the release with the release date, which will cause problems as in the example above when a new "official" release is made.

For example, if a snapshot release is made on the date 20000917, and the previous version of the software was version 1.2, do not use 20000917 for PORTVERSION. The correct way is a PORTVERSION of 1.2.20000917, or similar, so that the succeeding release, say 1.3, is still a numerically greater value.

5.2.2.3. Example of PORTREVISION and PORTEPOCH Usage

The gtkmumble port, version 0.10, is committed to the ports collection:

```
PORTNAME= gtkmumble
PORTVERSION= 0.10
```

PKGNAME becomes gtkmumble-0.10.

A security hole is discovered which requires a local FreeBSD patch. PORTREVISION is bumped accordingly.

```
PORTNAME= gtkmumble
PORTVERSION= 0.10
PORTREVISION= 1
```

PKGNAME becomes gtkmumble-0.10_1

A new version is released by the vendor, numbered 0.2 (it turns out the author actually intended 0.10 to actually mean 0.1.0, not "what comes after 0.9" - oops, too late now). Since the new minor version 2 is numerically less than the previous version 10, PORTEPOCH must be bumped to manually force the new package to be detected as "newer". Since it is a new vendor release of the code, PORTREVISION is reset to 0 (or removed from the Makefile).

```
PORTNAME= gtkmumble
PORTVERSION= 0.2
PORTEPOCH= 1
```

PKGNAME becomes gtkmumble-0.2,1

The next release is 0.3. Since PORTEPOCH never decreases, the version variables are now:

```
PORTNAME= gtkmumble
PORTVERSION= 0.3
PORTEPOCH= 1
```

PKGNAME becomes gtkmumble-0.3,1

Note

If PORTEPOCH were reset to 0 with this upgrade, someone who had installed the gtkmumble-0.10_1 package would not detect the gtkmumble-0.3 package as newer, since 3 is still numerically less than 10. Remember, this is the whole point of PORTEPOCH in the first place.

5.2.3. PKGNAMEPREFIX **and** PKGNAMESUFFIX

Two optional variables, PKGNAMEPREFIX and PKGNAMESUFFIX, are combined with PORTNAME and PORTVERSION to form PKGNAME as ${PKGNAMEPREFIX}${PORTNAME}${PKGNAMESUFFIX}-${PORTVERSION} . Make sure this conforms to our guidelines for a good package name. In particular, the use of a hyphen (-) in PORTVERSION is *not* allowed. Also, if the package name has the *language-* or the *-compiled.specifics* part (see below), use PKGNAMEPREFIX and PKGNAMESUFFIX, respectively. Do not make them part of PORTNAME.

5.2.4. Package Naming Conventions

These are the conventions to follow when naming packages. This is to make the package directory easy to scan, as there are already thousands of packages and users are going to turn away if they hurt their eyes!

Package names take the form of *language_region-name-compiled.specifics-version.numbers* .

The package name is defined as ${PKGNAMEPREFIX}${PORTNAME}${PKGNAMESUFFIX}-${PORTVERSION} . Make sure to set the variables to conform to that format.

language_region-

> FreeBSD strives to support the native language of its users. The *language-* part is a two letter abbreviation of the natural language defined by ISO-639 when the port is specific to a certain language. Examples are ja for Japanese, ru for Russian, vi for Vietnamese, zh for Chinese, ko for Korean and de for German.
>
> If the port is specific to a certain region within the language area, add the two letter country code as well. Examples are en_US for US English and fr_CH for Swiss French.
>
> The *language-* part is set in PKGNAMEPREFIX.

name

> Make sure that the port's name and version are clearly separated and placed into PORTNAME and PORTVERSION . The only reason for PORTNAME to contain a version part is if the upstream distribution is really named that way, as in the textproc/libxml2 or japanese/kinput2-freewnn ports. Otherwise, PORTNAME cannot contain any version-specific information. It is quite normal for several ports to have the same PORTNAME, as the www/apache* ports do; in that case, different versions (and different index entries) are distinguished by PKGNAMEPREFIX and PKGNAMESUFFIX values.
>
> There is a tradition of naming Perl 5 modules by prepending p5- and converting the double-colon separator to a hyphen. For example, the Data::Dumper module becomes p5-Data-Dumper .

-compiled.specifics

> If the port can be built with different hardcoded defaults (usually part of the directory name in a family of ports), the *-compiled.specifics* part states the compiled-in defaults. The hyphen is optional. Examples are paper size and font units.
>
> The *-compiled.specifics* part is set in PKGNAMESUFFIX.

-version.numbers

> The version string follows a dash (-) and is a period-separated list of integers and single lowercase alphabetics. In particular, it is not permissible to have another dash inside the version string. The only exception is the string pl (meaning "patchlevel"), which can be used *only* when there are no major and minor version numbers in the software. If the software version has strings like "alpha", "beta", "rc", or "pre", take the first letter and put it immediately after a period. If the version string continues after those names, the numbers follow the single alphabet without an extra period between them (for example, 1.0b2).
>
> The idea is to make it easier to sort ports by looking at the version string. In particular, make sure version number components are always delimited by a period, and if the date is part of the string, use the 0.0.*yyyy*.*mm*.*dd* format, not *dd*.*mm*.*yyyy* or the non-Y2K compliant *yy*.*mm*.*dd* format. It is important to prefix the version with 0.0. in case a release with an actual version number is made, which would be numerically less than *yyyy*.

Important

Package name must be unique among all of the ports tree, check that there is not already a port with the same PORTNAME and if there is add one of PKGNAMEPREFIX or PKGNAMESUFFIX.

Here are some (real) examples on how to convert the name as called by the software authors to a suitable package name:

Table 5.1. Package Naming Examples

Distribution Name	PKGNAMEPREFIX	PORTNAME	PKGNAMESUFFIX	PORTVERSION	Reason
mule-2.2.2	(empty)	mule	(empty)	2.2.2	No changes required
mule-1.0.1	(empty)	mule	1	1.0.1	mule already exists
EmiClock-1.0.2	(empty)	emiclock	(empty)	1.0.2	No uppercase names for single programs
rdist-1.3alpha	(empty)	rdist	(empty)	1.3.a	No strings like alpha allowed
es-0.9-beta1	(empty)	es	(empty)	0.9.b1	No strings like beta allowed
mailman-2.0rc3	(empty)	mailman	(empty)	2.0.r3	No strings like rc allowed
v3.3beta021.src	(empty)	tiff	(empty)	3.3	What the heck was that anyway?
tvtwm	(empty)	tvtwm	(empty)	pl11	Version string always required
piewm	(empty)	piewm	(empty)	1.0	Version string always required
xvgr-2.10pl1	(empty)	xvgr	(empty)	2.10.1	pl allowed only when no major/minor version numbers
gawk-2.15.6	ja-	gawk	(empty)	2.15.6	Japanese language version
psutils-1.13	(empty)	psutils	-letter	1.13	Paper size hardcoded at package build time
pkfonts	(empty)	pkfonts	300	1.0	Package for 300dpi fonts

If there is absolutely no trace of version information in the original source and it is unlikely that the original author will ever release another version, just set the version string to 1.0 (like the piewm example above). Otherwise, ask the original author or use the date string the source file was released on (0.0.*yyyy*.*mm*.*dd*) as the version.

5.3. Categorization

5.3.1. CATEGORIES

When a package is created, it is put under /usr/ports/packages/All and links are made from one or more sub-directories of /usr/ports/packages . The names of these subdirectories are specified by the variable CATEGORIES. It is intended to make life easier for the user when he is wading through the pile of packages on the FTP site or the CDROM. Please take a look at the current list of categories and pick the ones that are suitable for the port.

This list also determines where in the ports tree the port is imported. If there is more than one category here, the port files must be put in the subdirectory with the name of the first category. See below for more discussion about how to pick the right categories.

5.3.2. Current List of Categories

Here is the current list of port categories. Those marked with an asterisk (*) are *virtual* categories—those that do not have a corresponding subdirectory in the ports tree. They are only used as secondary categories, and only for search purposes.

> Note
>
> For non-virtual categories, there is a one-line description in COMMENT in that subdirectory's Makefile.

Category	Description	Notes
accessibility	Ports to help disabled users.	
afterstep*	Ports to support the AfterStep window manager.	
arabic	Arabic language support.	
archivers	Archiving tools.	
astro	Astronomical ports.	
audio	Sound support.	
benchmarks	Benchmarking utilities.	
biology	Biology-related software.	
cad	Computer aided design tools.	
chinese	Chinese language support.	
comms	Communication software.	Mostly software to talk to the serial port.
converters	Character code converters.	
databases	Databases.	
deskutils	Things that used to be on the desktop before computers were invented.	
devel	Development utilities.	Do not put libraries here just because they are libraries. They should *not* be in this category unless they truly do not belong anywhere else.
dns	DNS-related software.	

Category	Description	Notes
docs*	Meta-ports for FreeBSD documentation.	
editors	General editors.	Specialized editors go in the section for those tools. For example, a mathematical-formula editor will go in math, and have editors as a second category.
elisp*	Emacs-lisp ports.	
emulators	Emulators for other operating systems.	Terminal emulators do *not* belong here. X-based ones go to x11 and text-based ones to either comms or misc, depending on the exact functionality.
finance	Monetary, financial and related applications.	
french	French language support.	
ftp	FTP client and server utilities.	If the port speaks both FTP and HTTP, put it in ftp with a secondary category of www.
games	Games.	
geography*	Geography-related software.	
german	German language support.	
gnome*	Ports from the GNOME Project.	
gnustep*	Software related to the GNUstep desktop environment.	
graphics	Graphics utilities.	
hamradio*	Software for amateur radio.	
haskell*	Software related to the Haskell language.	
hebrew	Hebrew language support.	
hungarian	Hungarian language support.	
ipv6*	IPv6 related software.	
irc	Internet Relay Chat utilities.	
japanese	Japanese language support.	
java	Software related to the Java™ language.	The java category must not be the only one for a port. Save for ports directly related to the Java language, porters are also encouraged not to use java as the main category of a port.
kde*	Ports from the KDE Project.	
kld*	Kernel loadable modules.	
korean	Korean language support.	
lang	Programming languages.	

Category	Description	Notes
linux*	Linux applications and support utilities.	
lisp*	Software related to the Lisp language.	
mail	Mail software.	
math	Numerical computation software and other utilities for mathematics.	
mbone*	MBone applications.	
misc	Miscellaneous utilities	Things that do not belong anywhere else. If at all possible, try to find a better category for the port than misc, as ports tend to be overlooked in here.
multimedia	Multimedia software.	
net	Miscellaneous networking software.	
net-im	Instant messaging software.	
net-mgmt	Networking management software.	
net-p2p	Peer to peer network applications.	
news	USENET news software.	
palm	Software support for the Palm™ series.	
parallel*	Applications dealing with parallelism in computing.	
pear*	Ports related to the Pear PHP framework.	
perl5*	Ports that require Perl version 5 to run.	
plan9*	Various programs from Plan9.	
polish	Polish language support.	
ports-mgmt	Ports for managing, installing and developing FreeBSD ports and packages.	
portuguese	Portuguese language support.	
print	Printing software.	Desktop publishing tools (previewers, etc.) belong here too.
python*	Software related to the Python language.	
ruby*	Software related to the Ruby language.	
rubygems*	Ports of RubyGems packages.	
russian	Russian language support.	
scheme*	Software related to the Scheme language.	

Category	Description	Notes
science	Scientific ports that do not fit into other categories such as astro, biology and math.	
security	Security utilities.	
shells	Command line shells.	
spanish*	Spanish language support.	
sysutils	System utilities.	
tcl*	Ports that use Tcl to run.	
textproc	Text processing utilities.	It does not include desktop publishing tools, which go to print.
tk*	Ports that use Tk to run.	
ukrainian	Ukrainian language support.	
vietnamese	Vietnamese language support.	
windowmaker*	Ports to support the WindowMaker window manager.	
www	Software related to the World Wide Web.	HTML language support belongs here too.
x11	The X Window System and friends.	This category is only for software that directly supports the window system. Do not put regular X applications here. Most of them go into other x11-* categories (see below).
x11-clocks	X11 clocks.	
x11-drivers	X11 drivers.	
x11-fm	X11 file managers.	
x11-fonts	X11 fonts and font utilities.	
x11-servers	X11 servers.	
x11-themes	X11 themes.	
x11-toolkits	X11 toolkits.	
x11-wm	X11 window managers.	
xfce*	Ports related to the Xfce desktop environment.	
zope*	Zope support.	

5.3.3. Choosing the Right Category

As many of the categories overlap, choosing which of the categories will be the primary category of the port can be tedious. There are several rules that govern this issue. Here is the list of priorities, in decreasing order of precedence:

- The first category must be a physical category (see above). This is necessary to make the packaging work. Virtual categories and physical categories may be intermixed after that.

- Language specific categories always come first. For example, if the port installs Japanese X11 fonts, then the CATEGORIES line would read japanese x11-fonts.

- Specific categories are listed before less-specific ones. For instance, an HTML editor is listed as www editors, not the other way around. Also, do not list net when the port belongs to any of irc, mail, news, security, or www, as net is included implicitly.

- x11 is used as a secondary category only when the primary category is a natural language. In particular, do not put x11 in the category line for X applications.

- Emacs modes are placed in the same ports category as the application supported by the mode, not in editors. For example, an Emacs mode to edit source files of some programming language goes into lang.

- Ports installing loadable kernel modules also have the virtual category kld in their CATEGORIES line. This is one of the things handled automatically by adding USES=kmod.

- misc does not appear with any other non-virtual category. If there is misc with something else in CATEGORIES, that means misc can safely be deleted and the port placed only in the other subdirectory.

- If the port truly does not belong anywhere else, put it in misc.

If the category is not clearly defined, please put a comment to that effect in the port submission in the bug database so we can discuss it before we import it. As a committer, send a note to the FreeBSD ports mailing list so we can discuss it first. Too often, new ports are imported to the wrong category only to be moved right away. This causes unnecessary and undesirable bloat in the master source repository.

5.3.4. Proposing a New Category

As the Ports Collection has grown over time, various new categories have been introduced. New categories can either be *virtual* categories—those that do not have a corresponding subdirectory in the ports tree— or *physical* categories—those that do. This section discusses the issues involved in creating a new physical category. Read it thouroughly before proposing a new one.

Our existing practice has been to avoid creating a new physical category unless either a large number of ports would logically belong to it, or the ports that would belong to it are a logically distinct group that is of limited general interest (for instance, categories related to spoken human languages), or preferably both.

The rationale for this is that such a change creates a fair amount of work for both the committers and also for all users who track changes to the Ports Collection. In addition, proposed category changes just naturally seem to attract controversy. (Perhaps this is because there is no clear consensus on when a category is "too big", nor whether categories should lend themselves to browsing (and thus what number of categories would be an ideal number), and so forth.)

Here is the procedure:

1. Propose the new category on FreeBSD ports mailing list. Include a detailed rationale for the new category, including why the existing categories are not sufficient, and the list of existing ports proposed to move. (If there are new ports pending in Bugzilla that would fit this category, list them too.) If you are the maintainer and/or submitter, respectively, mention that as it may help the case.

2. Participate in the discussion.

3. If it seems that there is support for the idea, file a PR which includes both the rationale and the list of existing ports that need to be moved. Ideally, this PR would also include these patches:

   - Makefiles for the new ports once they are repocopied

   - Makefile for the new category

   - Makefile for the old ports' categories

- `Makefiles` for ports that depend on the old ports

- (for extra credit, include the other files that have to change, as per the procedure in the Committer's Guide.)

4. Since it affects the ports infrastructure and involves moving and patching many ports but also possibly running regression tests on the build cluster, assign the PR to the Ports Management Team `<portmgr@FreeBSD.org>`.

5. If that PR is approved, a committer will need to follow the rest of the procedure that is outlined in the Committer's Guide.

Proposing a new virtual category is similar to the above but much less involved, since no ports will actually have to move. In this case, the only patches to include in the PR would be those to add the new category to `CATEGORIES` of the affected ports.

5.3.5. Proposing Reorganizing All the Categories

Occasionally someone proposes reorganizing the categories with either a 2-level structure, or some other kind of keyword structure. To date, nothing has come of any of these proposals because, while they are very easy to make, the effort involved to retrofit the entire existing ports collection with any kind of reorganization is daunting to say the very least. Please read the history of these proposals in the mailing list archives before posting this idea. Furthermore, be prepared to be challenged to offer a working prototype.

5.4. The Distribution Files

The second part of the `Makefile` describes the files that must be downloaded to build the port, and where they can be downloaded.

5.4.1. DISTVERSION/DISTNAME

`DISTNAME` is the name of the port as called by the authors of the software. `DISTNAME` defaults to `${PORTNAME}-${DISTVERSIONPREFIX}${DISTVERSION}${DISTVERSIONSUFFIX}`, and `DISTVERSION` defaults to `${PORTVERSION}` so override it only if necessary. `DISTNAME` is only used in two places. First, the distribution file list (`DISTFILES`) defaults to `${DISTNAME}${EXTRACT_SUFX}`. Second, the distribution file is expected to extract into a subdirectory named `WRKSRC`, which defaults to `work/${DISTNAME}`.

Some vendor's distribution names which do not fit into the `${PORTNAME}-${PORTVERSION}` -scheme can be handled automatically by setting `DISTVERSION`. `PORTVERSION` will be derived from it automatically.

> ### Note
>
> Only one of `PORTVERSION` and `DISTVERSION` can be set at a time. If `DISTVERSION` does not derive a correct `PORTVERSION`, do not use `DISTVERSION`, set `PORTVERSION` to the right value and set `DISTNAME` with `PORTNAME` with either some computation of `PORTVERSION` or the verbatim upstream version.

Table 5.2. Examples of `DISTVERSION` and the Derived `PORTVERSION`

DISTVERSION	PORTVERSION
0.7.1d	0.7.1.d
10Alpha3	10.a3
3Beta7-pre2	3.b7.p2

DISTVERSION	PORTVERSION
8:f_17	8f.17

> **Note**
>
> PKGNAMEPREFIX and PKGNAMESUFFIX do not affect DISTNAME. Also note that if WRKSRC is equal to ${WRKDIR}/${DISTNAME} while the original source archive is named something other than ${PORTNAME}-${PORTVERSION}${EXTRACT_SUFX}, leave DISTNAME alone—defining only DIST-FILES is easier than both DISTNAME and WRKSRC (and possibly EXTRACT_SUFX).

5.4.2. MASTER_SITES

Record the directory part of the FTP/HTTP-URL pointing at the original tarball in MASTER_SITES . Do not forget the trailing slash (/)!

The make macros will try to use this specification for grabbing the distribution file with FETCH if they cannot find it already on the system.

It is recommended that multiple sites are included on this list, preferably from different continents. This will safe-guard against wide-area network problems. We are even planning to add support for automatically determining the closest master site and fetching from there; having multiple sites will go a long way towards helping this effort.

> **Important**
>
> MASTER_SITES must not be blank. It must point to the actual site hosting the distribution files. It cannot point to web archives, or the FreeBSD distribution files cache sites. The only exception to this rule is ports that do not have any distribution files. For example, meta-ports do not have any distribution files, so MASTER_SITES does not need to be set.

5.4.2.1. Using MASTER_SITE_ * Variables

Shortcut abbreviations are available for popular archives like SourceForge (SOURCEFORGE), GNU (GNU), or Perl CPAN (PERL_CPAN). MASTER_SITES can use them directly:

```
MASTER_SITES= GNU/make
```

The older expanded format still works, but all ports have been converted to the compact format. The expanded format looks like this:

```
MASTER_SITES=  ${MASTER_SITE_GNU}
MASTER_SITE_SUBDIR= make
```

These values and variables are defined in Mk/bsd.sites.mk. New entries are added often, so make sure to check the latest version of this file before submitting a port.

> **Tip**
>
> For any MASTER_SITE_ *FOO* variable, the shorthand *FOO* can be used. For example, use:
>
> ```
> MASTER_SITES= FOO
> ```
>
> If MASTER_SITE_SUBDIR is needed, use this:

```
MASTER_SITES= FOO/bar
```

Note

Some `MASTER_SITE_ *` names are quite long, and for ease of use, shortcuts have been defined:

Table 5.3. Shortcuts for `MASTER_SITE_ *` Macros

Macro	Shortcut
PERL_CPAN	CPAN
GITHUB	GH
GITHUB_CLOUD	GHC
LIBREOFFICE_DEV	LODEV
NETLIB	NL
RUBYGEMS	RG
SOURCEFORGE	SF
SOURCEFORGE_JP	SFJP

5.4.2.2. Magic MASTER_SITES Macros

Several "magic" macros exist for popular sites with a predictable directory structure. For these, just use the abbreviation and the system will choose a subdirectory automatically. For a port named `Stardict`, of version `1.2.3`, and hosted on SourceForge, adding this line:

```
MASTER_SITES= SF
```

infers a subdirectory named `/project/stardict/stardict/1.2.3` . If the inferred directory is incorrect, it can be overridden:

```
MASTER_SITES= SF/stardict/WyabdcRealPeopleTTS/${PORTVERSION}
```

This can also be written as

```
MASTER_SITES= SF
MASTER_SITE_SUBDIR= stardict/WyabdcRealPeopleTTS/${PORTVERSION}
```

Table 5.4. Magic `MASTER_SITES` Macros

Macro	Assumed subdirectory
APACHE_COMMONS_BINARIES	${PORTNAME:S,commons-,,}
APACHE_COMMONS_SOURCE	${PORTNAME:S,commons-,,}
APACHE_JAKARTA	${PORTNAME:S,-,/,}/source
BERLIOS	${PORTNAME:tl}.berlios
CHEESESHOP	source/${DISTNAME:C/(.).*/\1/}/ ${DISTNAME:C/(.*)-[0-9].*/\1/}
CPAN	${PORTNAME:C/-.*//}
DEBIAN	pool/main/${PORTNAME:C/^((lib)?.).*$/\1/}/ ${PORTNAME}
FARSIGHT	${PORTNAME}

Macro	Assumed subdirectory
FESTIVAL	${PORTREVISION}
GCC	releases/${DISTNAME}
GENTOO	distfiles
GIMP	${PORTNAME}/${PORTVERSION:R}/
GH	${GH_ACCOUNT}/${GH_PROJECT}/tar.gz/ ${GH_TAGNAME}?dummy=/
GHC	${GH_ACCOUNT}/${GH_PROJECT}/
GNOME	sources/${PORTNAME}/${PORTVERSION:C/^([0-9]+ \.[0-9]+).*/\1/}
GNU	${PORTNAME}
GNUPG	${PORTNAME}
GNU_ALPHA	${PORTNAME}
HORDE	${PORTNAME}
LODEV	${PORTNAME}
MATE	${PORTVERSION:C/^([0-9]+\.[0-9]+).*/\1/}
MOZDEV	${PORTNAME:tl}
NL	${PORTNAME}
QT	archive/qt/${PORTVERSION:R}
SAMBA	${PORTNAME}
SAVANNAH	${PORTNAME:tl}
SF	${PORTNAME:tl}/${PORTNAME:tl}/${PORTVERSION}

5.4.3. USE_GITHUB

If the distribution file comes from a specific commit or tag on GitHub for which there is no officially released file, there is an easy way to set the right DISTNAME and MASTER_SITES automatically. These variables are available:

Table 5.5. USE_GITHUB Description

Variable	Description	Default
GH_ACCOUNT	Account name of the GitHub user hosting the project	${PORTNAME}
GH_PROJECT	Name of the project on GitHub	${PORTNAME}
GH_TAGNAME	Name of the tag to download (2.0.1, hash, ...) Using the name of a branch here is incorrect. It is also possible to use the hash of a commit id to do a snapshot.	${DISTVERSIONPRE-FIX}${DISTVERSION}${DISTVERSIONSUF-FIX}
GH_SUBDIR	When the software needs an additional distribution file to be extracted within ${WRKSRC}, this variable can be used. See the examples in Section 5.4.3.1, "Fetching Multiple Files from GitHub" for more information.	(none)
GH_TUPLE	GH_TUPLE allows putting GH_ACCOUNT, GH_PROJECT, GH_TAGNAME, and	

Variable	Description	Default
	GH_SUBDIR into a single variable. The format is *account*:*project*:*tagname*:*group*/*subdir*. The /*subdir* part is optional. It is helpful when there is more than one GitHub project from which to fetch.	

> ⚠️ **Important**
>
> Do not use GH_TUPLE for the default distribution file, as it has no default.

Example 5.1. Simple Use of USE_GITHUB

While trying to make a port for version 1.2.7 of pkg from the FreeBSD user on github, at https://github.com/freebsd/pkg, The Makefile would end up looking like this (slightly stripped for the example):

```
PORTNAME= pkg
PORTVERSION= 1.2.7

USE_GITHUB= yes
GH_ACCOUNT= freebsd
```

It will automatically have MASTER_SITES set to GH GHC and WRKSRC to ${WRKDIR}/pkg-1.2.7 .

Example 5.2. More Complete Use of USE_GITHUB

While trying to make a port for the bleeding edge version of pkg from the FreeBSD user on github, at https://github.com/freebsd/pkg, the Makefile ends up looking like this (slightly stripped for the example):

```
PORTNAME= pkg-devel
PORTVERSION= 1.3.0.a.20140411

USE_GITHUB= yes
GH_ACCOUNT= freebsd
GH_PROJECT= pkg
GH_TAGNAME= 6dbb17b
```

It will automatically have MASTER_SITES set to GH GHC and WRKSRC to ${WRKDIR}/pkg-6dbb17b .

Example 5.3. Use of USE_GITHUB with DISTVERSIONPREFIX

From time to time, GH_TAGNAME is a slight variation from DISTVERSION . For example, if the version is 1.0.2, the tag is v1.0.2. In those cases, it is possible to use DISTVERSIONPREFIX or DISTVERSIONSUFFIX:

```
PORTNAME= foo
```

```
PORTVERSION= 1.0.2
DISTVERSIONPREFIX= v

USE_GITHUB= yes
```

It will automatically set `GH_TAGNAME` to `v1.0.2`, while `WRKSRC` will be kept to `${WRKDIR}/foo-1.0.2` .

5.4.3.1. Fetching Multiple Files from GitHub

The `USE_GITHUB` framework also supports fetching multiple distribution files from different places in GitHub. It works in a way very similar to Section 5.4.8, "Multiple Distribution or Patches Files from Multiple Locations".

Multiple values are added to `GH_ACCOUNT`, `GH_PROJECT` , and `GH_TAGNAME`. Each different value is assigned a tag. The main value can either have no tag, or the `:DEFAULT` tag. A value can be omitted if it is the same as the default as listed in Table 5.5, "`USE_GITHUB` Description".

`GH_TUPLE` can also be used when there are a lot of distribution files. It helps keep the account, project, tagname, and group information at the same place.

For each tag, a `${WRKSRC_tag}` helper variable is created, containing the directory into which the file has been extracted. The `${WRKSRC_tag}` variables can be used to move directories around during `post-extract` , or add to `CONFIGURE_ARGS`, or whatever is needed so that the software builds correctly.

> Note
>
> As this is only syntastic sugar above `DISTFILES` and `MASTER_SITES` , the tag names must adhere to the restrictions on group names outlined in Section 5.4.8, "Multiple Distribution or Patches Files from Multiple Locations"

Example 5.4. Use of USE_GITHUB with Multiple Distribution Files

From time to time, there is a need to fetch more than one distribution file. For example, when the upstream git repository uses submodules. This can be done easily using tags in the `GH_*` variables:

```
PORTNAME= foo
PORTVERSION= 1.0.2

USE_GITHUB= yes
GH_ACCOUNT= bar:icons,contrib
GH_PROJECT= foo-icons:icons foo-contrib:contrib
GH_TAGNAME= 1.0:icons fa579bc:contrib
GH_SUBDIR= ext/icons:icons

CONFIGURE_ARGS= --with-contrib=${WRKSRC_contrib}
```

This will fetch three distribution files from github. The default one comes from `foo/foo` and is version `1.0.2`. The second one, tagged `icons`, comes from `bar/foo-icons` and is in version `1.0`. The third one comes from `bar/foo-contrib` and uses the Git commit `fa579bc`. The distribution files are named `foo-foo-1.0.2_GH0.tar.gz` , `bar-foo-icons-1.0_GH0.tar.gz`, and `bar-foo-contrib-fa579bc_GH0.tar.gz` .

All the distribution files are extracted in `${WRKDIR}` in their respective subdirectories. The default file is still extracted in `${WRKSRC}` , in this case, `${WRKDIR}/foo-1.0.2` . Each additional distribution file is extracted in `${WRKSRC_tag}`. Here, for the `icons` tag, it is called `${WRKSRC_icons}` and it contains `${WRKDIR}/`

foo-icons-1.0 . The file with the contrib tag is called ${WRKSRC_contrib} and contains ${WRKDIR}/foo-contrib-fa579bc .

The software's build system expects to find the icons in a ext/icons subdirectory in its sources, so GH_SUB-DIR is used. GH_SUBDIR makes sure that ext exists, but that ext/icons does not already exist. Then it does this:

```
post-extract:
    @${MV} ${WRKSRC_icons} ${WRKSRC}/ext/icons
```

Example 5.5. Use of USE_GITHUB with Multiple Distribution Files Using GH_TUPLE

This is functionally equivalent to Example 5.4, "Use of USE_GITHUB with Multiple Distribution Files", but using GH_TUPLE:

```
PORTNAME= foo
PORTVERSION= 1.0.2

USE_GITHUB= yes
GH_TUPLE= bar:foo-icons:1.0:icons/ext/icons \
  bar:foo-contrib:fa579bc:contrib

CONFIGURE_ARGS= --with-contrib=${WRKSRC_contrib}
```

Grouping was used in the previous example with bar:icons,contrib. Some redundant information is present with GH_TUPLE because grouping is not possible.

Example 5.6. How to Use USE_GITHUB with Git Submodules?

Ports with GitHub as an upstream repository sometimes use submodules. See git-submodule(1) for more information.

The problem with submodules is that each is a separate repository. As such, they each must be fetched separately.

Using finance/moneymanagerex as an example, its GitHub repository is https://github.com/moneyman-agerex/moneymanagerex. It has a .gitmodules file at the root. This file describes all the submodules used in this repository, and lists additional repositories needed. This file will tell what additional repositories are needed:

```
[submodule "lib/wxsqlite3"]
 path = lib/wxsqlite3
 url = https://github.com/utelle/wxsqlite3.git
[submodule "3rd/mongoose"]
 path = 3rd/mongoose
 url = https://github.com/cesanta/mongoose.git
[submodule "3rd/LuaGlue"]
 path = 3rd/LuaGlue
 url = https://github.com/moneymanagerex/LuaGlue.git
[submodule "3rd/cgitemplate"]
 path = 3rd/cgitemplate
 url = https://github.com/moneymanagerex/html-template.git
```

```
[...-]
```

The only information missing from that file is the commit hash or tag to use as a version. This information is found after cloning the repository:

```
% git clone --recurse-submodules https://github.com/moneymanagerex/moneymanagerex.↵
git
Cloning into 'moneymanagerex'...
remote: Counting objects: 32387, done.
[...-]
Submodule '3rd/LuaGlue' (https://github.com/moneymanagerex/LuaGlue.git) ↵
registered for path '3rd/LuaGlue'
Submodule '3rd/cgitemplate' (https://github.com/moneymanagerex/html-template.git) ↵
registered for path '3rd/cgitemplate'
Submodule '3rd/mongoose' (https://github.com/cesanta/mongoose.git) registered for ↵
path '3rd/mongoose'
Submodule 'lib/wxsqlite3' (https://github.com/utelle/wxsqlite3.git) registered ↵
for path 'lib/wxsqlite3'
[...-]
Cloning into '/home/mat/work/freebsd/ports/finance/moneymanagerex/
moneymanagerex/3rd/LuaGlue'...
Cloning into '/home/mat/work/freebsd/ports/finance/moneymanagerex/
moneymanagerex/3rd/cgitemplate'...
Cloning into '/home/mat/work/freebsd/ports/finance/moneymanagerex/
moneymanagerex/3rd/mongoose'...
Cloning into '/home/mat/work/freebsd/ports/finance/moneymanagerex/moneymanagerex/
lib/wxsqlite3'...
[...-]
Submodule path '3rd/LuaGlue': checked out
 'c51d11a247ee4d1e9817dfa2a8da8d9e2f97ae3b'
Submodule path '3rd/cgitemplate': checked out
 'cd434eeeb35904ebcd3d718ba29c281a649b192c'
Submodule path '3rd/mongoose': checked out
 '2140e5992ab9a3a9a34ce9a281abf57f00f95cda'
Submodule path 'lib/wxsqlite3': checked out
 'fb66eb230d8aed21dec273b38c7c054dcb7d6b51'
[...-]
% cd moneymanagerex
% git submodule status
 c51d11a247ee4d1e9817dfa2a8da8d9e2f97ae3b 3rd/LuaGlue (heads/master)
 cd434eeeb35904ebcd3d718ba29c281a649b192c 3rd/cgitemplate (cd434ee)
 2140e5992ab9a3a9a34ce9a281abf57f00f95cda 3rd/mongoose (6.2-138-g2140e59)
 fb66eb230d8aed21dec273b38c7c054dcb7d6b51 lib/wxsqlite3 (v3.4.0)
[...-]
```

It can also be found on GitHub. Each subdirectory that is a submodule is shown as *directory* @ *hash*, for example, mongoose @ 2140e59.

Note

While getting the information from GitHub seems more straightforward, the information found using git submodule status will provide more meaningful information. For example, here, lib/wxsqlite3 's commit hash fb66eb2 correspond to v3.4.0. Both can be used interchangeably, but when a tag is available, use it.

Now that all the required information has been gathered, the Makefile can be written (only GitHub-related lines are shown):

```
PORTNAME= moneymanagerex
PORTVERSION= 1.3.0
DISTVERSIONPREFIX= v
```

```
USE_GITHUB= yes
GH_TUPLE= utelle:wxsqlite3:v3.4.0:wxsqlite3/lib/wxsqlite3 \
   moneymanagerex:LuaGlue:c51d11a:lua_glue/3rd/LuaGlue \
   moneymanagerex:html-template:cd434ee:html_template/3rd/cgitemplate \
   cesanta:mongoose:2140e59:mongoose/3rd/mongoose \
   [...-]
```

5.4.4. EXTRACT_SUFX

If there is one distribution file, and it uses an odd suffix to indicate the compression mechanism, set EXTRACT_SUFX.

For example, if the distribution file was named `foo.tar.gzip` instead of the more normal `foo.tar.gz`, write:

```
DISTNAME= foo
EXTRACT_SUFX= .tar.gzip
```

The USES=tar[:*xxx*], USES=lha or USES=zip automatically set EXTRACT_SUFX to the most common archives extensions as necessary, see Chapter 15, *Using USES Macros* for more details. If neither of these are set then EXTRACT_SUFX defaults to `.tar.gz`.

> **Note**
>
> As EXTRACT_SUFX is only used in DISTFILES, only set one of them..

5.4.5. DISTFILES

Sometimes the names of the files to be downloaded have no resemblance to the name of the port. For example, it might be called `source.tar.gz` or similar. In other cases the application's source code might be in several different archives, all of which must be downloaded.

If this is the case, set DISTFILES to be a space separated list of all the files that must be downloaded.

```
DISTFILES= source1.tar.gz source2.tar.gz
```

If not explicitly set, DISTFILES defaults to ${DISTNAME}${EXTRACT_SUFX}.

5.4.6. EXTRACT_ONLY

If only some of the DISTFILES must be extracted—for example, one of them is the source code, while another is an uncompressed document—list the filenames that must be extracted in EXTRACT_ONLY.

```
DISTFILES= source.tar.gz manual.html
EXTRACT_ONLY= source.tar.gz
```

When none of the DISTFILES need to be uncompressed, set EXTRACT_ONLY to the empty string.

```
EXTRACT_ONLY=
```

5.4.7. PATCHFILES

If the port requires some additional patches that are available by FTP or HTTP, set PATCHFILES to the names of the files and PATCH_SITES to the URL of the directory that contains them (the format is the same as MASTER_SITES).

If the patch is not relative to the top of the source tree (that is, WRKSRC) because it contains some extra pathnames, set PATCH_DIST_STRIP accordingly. For instance, if all the pathnames in the patch have an extra `foozolix-1.0/` in front of the filenames, then set PATCH_DIST_STRIP=-p1.

Do not worry if the patches are compressed; they will be decompressed automatically if the filenames end with `.Z`, `.gz`, `.bz2` or `.xz`.

If the patch is distributed with some other files, such as documentation, in a `gzip`ped tarball, using `PATCHFILES` is not possible. If that is the case, add the name and the location of the patch tarball to `DISTFILES` and `MASTER_SITES`. Then, use `EXTRA_PATCHES` to point to those files and `bsd.port.mk` will automatically apply them. In particular, do *not* copy patch files into `${PATCHDIR}`. That directory may not be writable.

Tip

If there are multiple patches and they need mixed values for the strip parameter, it can be added alongside the patch name in `PATCHFILES`, e.g:

```
PATCHFILES= patch1 patch2:-p1
```

This does not conflict with the master site grouping feature, adding a group also works:

```
PATCHFILES= patch2:-p1:source2
```

Note

The tarball will have been extracted alongside the regular source by then, so there is no need to explicitly extract it if it is a regular `gzip`ped or `compress`ed tarball. Take extra care not to overwrite something that already exists in that directory if extracting it manually. Also, do not forget to add a command to remove the copied patch in the `pre-clean` target.

5.4.8. Multiple Distribution or Patches Files from Multiple Locations

(Consider this to be a somewhat "advanced topic"; those new to this document may wish to skip this section at first).

This section has information on the fetching mechanism known as both `MASTER_SITES:n` and `MASTER_SITES_NN`. We will refer to this mechanism as `MASTER_SITES:n`.

A little background first. OpenBSD has a neat feature inside `DISTFILES` and `PATCHFILES` which allows files and patches to be postfixed with `:n` identifiers. Here, n can be any word containing `[0-9a-zA-Z_]` and denote a group designation. For example:

```
DISTFILES= alpha:0 beta:1
```

In OpenBSD, distribution file `alpha` will be associated with variable `MASTER_SITES0` instead of our common `MASTER_SITES` and `beta` with `MASTER_SITES1`.

This is a very interesting feature which can decrease that endless search for the correct download site.

Just picture 2 files in `DISTFILES` and 20 sites in `MASTER_SITES`, the sites slow as hell where `beta` is carried by all sites in `MASTER_SITES`, and `alpha` can only be found in the 20th site. It would be such a waste to check all of them if the maintainer knew this beforehand, would it not? Not a good start for that lovely weekend!

Now that you have the idea, just imagine more `DISTFILES` and more `MASTER_SITES`. Surely our "distfiles survey meister" would appreciate the relief to network strain that this would bring.

In the next sections, information will follow on the FreeBSD implementation of this idea. We improved a bit on OpenBSD's concept.

Important

The group names cannot have dashes in them (-), in fact, they cannot have any characters out of the [a-zA-Z0-9_] range. This is because, while make(1) is ok with variable names containing dashes, sh(1) is not.

5.4.8.1. Simplified Information

This section explains how to quickly prepare fine grained fetching of multiple distribution files and patches from different sites and subdirectories. We describe here a case of simplified MASTER_SITES:n usage. This will be sufficient for most scenarios. More detailed information are available in Section 5.4.8.2, "Detailed Information".

Some applications consist of multiple distribution files that must be downloaded from a number of different sites. For example, Ghostscript consists of the core of the program, and then a large number of driver files that are used depending on the user's printer. Some of these driver files are supplied with the core, but many others must be downloaded from a variety of different sites.

To support this, each entry in DISTFILES may be followed by a colon and a "tag name". Each site listed in MASTER_SITES is then followed by a colon, and the tag that indicates which distribution files are downloaded from this site.

For example, consider an application with the source split in two parts, source1.tar.gz and source2.tar.gz , which must be downloaded from two different sites. The port's Makefile would include lines like Example 5.7, "Simplified Use of MASTER_SITES:n with One File Per Site".

Example 5.7. Simplified Use of MASTER_SITES:n with One File Per Site

```
MASTER_SITES= ftp://ftp1.example.com/:source1 \
   http://www.example.com/:source2
DISTFILES= source1.tar.gz:source1 \
   source2.tar.gz:source2
```

Multiple distribution files can have the same tag. Continuing the previous example, suppose that there was a third distfile, source3.tar.gz , that is downloaded from ftp.example2.com. The Makefile would then be written like Example 5.8, "Simplified Use of MASTER_SITES:n with More Than One File Per Site".

Example 5.8. Simplified Use of MASTER_SITES:n with More Than One File Per Site

```
MASTER_SITES= ftp://ftp.example.com/:source1 \
   http://www.example.com/:source2
DISTFILES= source1.tar.gz:source1 \
   source2.tar.gz:source2 \
   source3.tar.gz:source2
```

5.4.8.2. Detailed Information

Okay, so the previous example did not reflect the new port's needs? In this section we will explain in detail how the fine grained fetching mechanism MASTER_SITES:n works and how it can be used.

1. Elements can be postfixed with :*n* where *n* is [^:,]+, that is, *n* could conceptually be any alphanumeric string but we will limit it to [a-zA-Z_][0-9a-zA-Z_]+ for now.

   Moreover, string matching is case sensitive; that is, n is different from N.

   However, these words cannot be used for postfixing purposes since they yield special meaning: default, all and ALL (they are used internally in item ii). Furthermore, DEFAULT is a special purpose word (check item 3).

2. Elements postfixed with :n belong to the group n, :m belong to group m and so forth.

3. Elements without a postfix are groupless, they all belong to the special group DEFAULT. Any elements postfixed with DEFAULT, is just being redundant unless an element belongs to both DEFAULT and other groups at the same time (check item 5).

   These examples are equivalent but the first one is preferred:

   ```
   MASTER_SITES= alpha
   ```

   ```
   MASTER_SITES= alpha:DEFAULT
   ```

4. Groups are not exclusive, an element may belong to several different groups at the same time and a group can either have either several different elements or none at all.

5. When an element belongs to several groups at the same time, use the comma operator (,).

   Instead of repeating it several times, each time with a different postfix, we can list several groups at once in a single postfix. For instance, :m,n,o marks an element that belongs to group m, n and o.

   All these examples are equivalent but the last one is preferred:

   ```
   MASTER_SITES= alpha alpha:SOME_SITE
   ```

   ```
   MASTER_SITES= alpha:DEFAULT alpha:SOME_SITE
   ```

   ```
   MASTER_SITES= alpha:SOME_SITE,DEFAULT
   ```

   ```
   MASTER_SITES= alpha:DEFAULT,SOME_SITE
   ```

6. All sites within a given group are sorted according to MASTER_SORT_AWK . All groups within MASTER_SITES and PATCH_SITES are sorted as well.

7. Group semantics can be used in any of the variables MASTER_SITES , PATCH_SITES , MASTER_SITE_SUBDIR, PATCH_SITE_SUBDIR, DISTFILES, and PATCHFILES according to this syntax:

   a. All MASTER_SITES , PATCH_SITES , MASTER_SITE_SUBDIR and PATCH_SITE_SUBDIR elements must be terminated with the forward slash / character. If any elements belong to any groups, the group postfix :*n* must come right after the terminator /. The MASTER_SITES:n mechanism relies on the existence of the terminator / to avoid confusing elements where a :n is a valid part of the element with occurrences where :n denotes group n. For compatibility purposes, since the / terminator was not required before in both MASTER_SITE_SUBDIR and PATCH_SITE_SUBDIR elements, if the postfix immediate preceding character is not a / then :n will be considered a valid part of the element instead of a group postfix even if an element is postfixed with :n. See both Example 5.9, "Detailed Use of MASTER_SITES:n in MASTER_SITE_SUBDIR" and Example 5.10, "Detailed Use of MASTER_SITES:n with Comma Operator, Multiple Files, Multiple Sites and Multiple Subdirectories".

   > ## Example 5.9. Detailed Use of MASTER_SITES:n in MASTER_SITE_SUBDIR
   >
   > ```
   > MASTER_SITE_SUBDIR= old:n new/:NEW
   > ```
   >
   > • Directories within group DEFAULT -> old:n

- Directories within group NEW -> new

Example 5.10. Detailed Use of MASTER_SITES:n with Comma Operator, Multiple Files, Multiple Sites and Multiple Subdirectories

```
MASTER_SITES= http://site1/%SUBDIR%/ http://site2/:DEFAULT \
  http://site3/:group3 http://site4/:group4 \
  http://site5/:group5 http://site6/:group6 \
  http://site7/:DEFAULT,group6 \
  http://site8/%SUBDIR%/:group6,group7 \
  http://site9/:group8
DISTFILES= file1 file2:DEFAULT file3:group3 \
  file4:group4,group5,group6 file5:grouping \
  file6:group7
MASTER_SITE_SUBDIR= directory-trial:1 directory-n/:groupn \
  directory-one/:group6,DEFAULT \
  directory
```

The previous example results in this fine grained fetching. Sites are listed in the exact order they will be used.

- file1 will be fetched from

  - MASTER_SITE_OVERRIDE

  - http://site1/directory-trial:1/

  - http://site1/directory-one/

  - http://site1/directory/

  - http://site2/

  - http://site7/

  - MASTER_SITE_BACKUP

- file2 will be fetched exactly as file1 since they both belong to the same group

  - MASTER_SITE_OVERRIDE

  - http://site1/directory-trial:1/

  - http://site1/directory-one/

  - http://site1/directory/

  - http://site2/

  - http://site7/

  - MASTER_SITE_BACKUP

- file3 will be fetched from

  - MASTER_SITE_OVERRIDE

- http://site3/

  - MASTER_SITE_BACKUP

- file4 will be fetched from

  - MASTER_SITE_OVERRIDE

  - http://site4/

  - http://site5/

  - http://site6/

  - http://site7/

  - http://site8/directory-one/

  - MASTER_SITE_BACKUP

- file5 will be fetched from

  - MASTER_SITE_OVERRIDE

  - MASTER_SITE_BACKUP

- file6 will be fetched from

  - MASTER_SITE_OVERRIDE

  - http://site8/

  - MASTER_SITE_BACKUP

8. How do I group one of the special macros from bsd.sites.mk, for example, SourceForge (SF)?

   This has been simplified as much as possible. See Example 5.11, "Detailed Use of MASTER_SITES:n with Source-
   Forge (SF)".

Example 5.11. Detailed Use of MASTER_SITES:n with SourceForge (SF)

```
MASTER_SITES= http://site1/ SF/something/1.0:sourceforge,TEST
DISTFILES= something.tar.gz:sourceforge
```

something.tar.gz will be fetched from all sites within SourceForge.

---

9. How do I use this with PATCH*?

   All examples were done with MASTER* but they work exactly the same for PATCH* ones as can be seen in Example 5.12, "Simplified Use of MASTER_SITES:n with PATCH_SITES".

Example 5.12. Simplified Use of **MASTER_SITES:n** with **PATCH_SITES**

```
PATCH_SITES= http://site1/ http://site2/:test
PATCHFILES= patch1:test
```

5.4.8.3. What Does Change for Ports? What Does Not?

i. All current ports remain the same. The MASTER_SITES:n feature code is only activated if there are elements postfixed with :n like elements according to the aforementioned syntax rules, especially as shown in item 7.

ii. The port targets remain the same: checksum, makesum, patch, configure, build, etc. With the obvious exceptions of do-fetch, fetch-list, master-sites and patch-sites.

    * do-fetch : deploys the new grouping postfixed DISTFILES and PATCHFILES with their matching group elements within both MASTER_SITES and PATCH_SITES which use matching group elements within both MASTER_SITE_SUBDIR and PATCH_SITE_SUBDIR. Check Example 5.10, "Detailed Use of MASTER_SITES:n with Comma Operator, Multiple Files, Multiple Sites and Multiple Subdirectories".

    * fetch-list : works like old fetch-list with the exception that it groups just like do-fetch.

    * master-sites and patch-sites : (incompatible with older versions) only return the elements of group DEFAULT; in fact, they execute targets master-sites-default and patch-sites-default respectively.

      Furthermore, using target either master-sites-all or patch-sites-all is preferred to directly checking either MASTER_SITES or PATCH_SITES . Also, directly checking is not guaranteed to work in any future versions. Check item B for more information on these new port targets.

iii. New port targets

    A. There are master-sites- n and patch-sites- n targets which will list the elements of the respective group n within MASTER_SITES and PATCH_SITES respectively. For instance, both master-sites-DEFAULT and patch-sites-DEFAULT will return the elements of group DEFAULT, master-sites-test and patch-sites-test of group test, and thereon.

    B. There are new targets master-sites-all and patch-sites-all which do the work of the old master-sites and patch-sites ones. They return the elements of all groups as if they all belonged to the same group with the caveat that it lists as many MASTER_SITE_BACKUP and MASTER_SITE_OVERRIDE as there are groups defined within either DISTFILES or PATCHFILES; respectively for master-sites-all and patch-sites-all .

5.4.9. DIST_SUBDIR

Do not let the port clutter /usr/ports/distfiles . If the port requires a lot of files to be fetched, or contains a file that has a name that might conflict with other ports (for example, Makefile), set DIST_SUBDIR to the name of the port (${PORTNAME} or ${PKGNAMEPREFIX}${PORTNAME} are fine). This will change DISTDIR from the default /usr/ports/distfiles to /usr/ports/distfiles/${DIST_SUBDIR} , and in effect puts everything that is required for the port into that subdirectory.

It will also look at the subdirectory with the same name on the backup master site at ftp.FreeBSD.org. (Setting DISTDIR explicitly in Makefile will not accomplish this, so please use DIST_SUBDIR.)

Note

This does not affect `MASTER_SITES` defined in the `Makefile`.

5.4.10. ALWAYS_KEEP_DISTFILES

If the port uses binary distfiles and has a license that requires that the source code is provided with packages distributed in binary form, like GPL, `ALWAYS_KEEP_DISTFILES` will instruct the FreeBSD build cluster to keep a copy of the files specified in `DISTFILES`. Users of these ports will generally not need these files, so it is a good idea to only add the source distfiles to `DISTFILES` when `PACKAGE_BUILDING` is defined.

Example 5.13. Use of ALWAYS_KEEP_DISTFILES

```
.if defined(PACKAGE_BUILDING)
DISTFILES+=  foo.tar.gz
ALWAYS_KEEP_DISTFILES= yes
.endif
```

When adding extra files to `DISTFILES`, make sure to also add them to `distinfo`. Also, the additional files will normally be extracted into `WRKDIR` as well, which for some ports may lead to undesirable side effects and require special handling.

5.5. MAINTAINER

Set your mail-address here. Please. *:-)*

Only a single address without the comment part is allowed as a `MAINTAINER` value. The format used is `user@host-name.domain`. Please do not include any descriptive text such as a real name in this entry. That merely confuses the Ports infrastructure and most tools using it.

The maintainer is responsible for keeping the port up to date and making sure that it works correctly. For a detailed description of the responsibilities of a port maintainer, refer to The challenge for port maintainers.

Note

A maintainer volunteers to keep a port in good working order. Maintainers have the primary responsibility for their ports, but not exclusive ownership. Ports exist for the benefit of the community and, in reality, belong to the community. What this means is that people other than the maintainer can make changes to a port. Large changes to the Ports Collection might require changes to many ports. The FreeBSD Ports Management Team or members of other teams might modify ports to fix dependency issues or other problems, like a version bump for a shared library update.

Some types of fixes have "blanket approval" from the Ports Management Team <portm-gr@FreeBSD.org>, allowing any committer to fix those categories of problems on any port. These fixes do not need approval from the maintainer. Blanket approval does not apply to ports that are maintained by teams like <autotools@FreeBSD.org>, <x11@FreeBSD.org>, <gnome@FreeBSD.org>, or <kde@FreeBSD.org>. These teams use external repositories and

> can have work that would conflict with changes that would normally fall under blanket approval.
>
> Blanket approval for most ports applies to these types of fixes:
>
> - Most infrastructure changes to a port (that is, modernizing, but not changing the functionality). For example, converting to staging, USE_GMAKE to USES=gmake, the new LIB_DEPENDS format...
>
> - Trivial and *tested* build and runtime fixes.

Other changes to the port will be sent to the maintainer for review and approval before being committed. If the maintainer does not respond to an update request after two weeks (excluding major public holidays), then that is considered a maintainer timeout, and the update may be made without explicit maintainer approval. If the maintainer does not respond within three months, or if there have been three consecutive timeouts, then that maintainer is considered absent without leave, and can be replaced as the maintainer of the particular port in question. Exceptions to this are anything maintained by the Ports Management Team <portmgr@FreeBSD.org>, or the Security Officer Team <security-officer@FreeBSD.org>. No unauthorized commits may ever be made to ports maintained by those groups.

We reserve the right to modify the maintainer's submission to better match existing policies and style of the Ports Collection without explicit blessing from the submitter or the maintainer. Also, large infrastructural changes can result in a port being modified without the maintainer's consent. These kinds of changes will never affect the port's functionality.

The Ports Management Team <portmgr@FreeBSD.org> reserves the right to revoke or override anyone's maintainership for any reason, and the Security Officer Team <security-officer@FreeBSD.org> reserves the right to revoke or override maintainership for security reasons.

5.6. COMMENT

The comment is a one-line description of a port shown by `pkg info`. Please follow these rules when composing it:

1. The COMMENT string should be 70 characters or less.

2. Do *not* include the package name or version number of software.

3. The comment must begin with a capital and end without a period.

4. Do not start with an indefinite article (that is, A or An).

5. Capitalize names such as Apache, JavaScript, or Perl.

6. Use a serial comma for lists of words: "green, red, and blue."

7. Check for spelling errors.

Here is an example:

```
COMMENT= Cat chasing a mouse all over the screen
```

The COMMENT variable immediately follows the MAINTAINER variable in the `Makefile`.

5.7. PORTSCOUT

Portscout is an automated distfile check utility for the FreeBSD Ports Collection, described in detail in Section 14.5, "Portscout: the FreeBSD Ports Distfile Scanner".

PORTSCOUT defines special conditions within which the Portscout distfile scanner is restricted.

Situations where PORTSCOUT is set include:

- When distfiles have to be ignored, whether for specific versions, or specific minor revisions. For example, to exclude version *8.2* from distfile version checks because it is known to be broken, add:

```
PORTSCOUT= ignore:8.2
```

- When specific versions or specific major and minor revisions of a distfile must be checked. For example, if only version *0.6.4* must be monitored because newer versions have compatibility issues with FreeBSD, add:

```
PORTSCOUT= limit:^0\.6\.4
```

- When URLs listing the available versions differ from the download URLs. For example, to limit distfile version checks to the download page for the databases/pgtune port, add:

```
PORTSCOUT= site:http://pgfoundry.org/frs/?group_id=1000416
```

5.8. Dependencies

Many ports depend on other ports. This is a very convenient feature of most Unix-like operating systems, including FreeBSD. Multiple ports can share a common dependency, rather than bundling that dependency with every port or package that needs it. There are seven variables that can be used to ensure that all the required bits will be on the user's machine. There are also some pre-supported dependency variables for common cases, plus a few more to control the behavior of dependencies.

5.8.1. LIB_DEPENDS

This variable specifies the shared libraries this port depends on. It is a list of *lib:dir* tuples where *lib* is the name of the shared library, *dir* is the directory in which to find it in case it is not available. For example,

```
LIB_DEPENDS=   libjpeg.so:graphics/jpeg
```

will check for a shared jpeg library with any version, and descend into the graphics/jpeg subdirectory of the ports tree to build and install it if it is not found.

The dependency is checked twice, once from within the build target and then from within the install target. Also, the name of the dependency is put into the package so that pkg install (see pkg-install(8)) will automatically install it if it is not on the user's system.

5.8.2. RUN_DEPENDS

This variable specifies executables or files this port depends on during run-time. It is a list of *path:dir[:target]* tuples where *path* is the name of the executable or file, *dir* is the directory in which to find it in case it is not available, and *target* is the target to call in that directory. If *path* starts with a slash (/), it is treated as a file and its existence is tested with test -e; otherwise, it is assumed to be an executable, and which -s is used to determine if the program exists in the search path.

For example,

```
RUN_DEPENDS= ${LOCALBASE}/news/bin/innd:news/inn \
  xmlcatmgr:textproc/xmlcatmgr
```

will check if the file or directory /usr/local/news/bin/innd exists, and build and install it from the news/inn subdirectory of the ports tree if it is not found. It will also see if an executable called xmlcatmgr is in the search path, and descend into textproc/xmlcatmgr to build and install it if it is not found.

Note

In this case, innd is actually an executable; if an executable is in a place that is not expected to be in the search path, use the full pathname.

Note

The official search PATH used on the ports build cluster is

```
/sbin:/bin:/usr/sbin:/usr/bin:/usr/local/sbin:/usr/local/bin
```

The dependency is checked from within the install target. Also, the name of the dependency is put into the package so that pkg install (see pkg-install(8)) will automatically install it if it is not on the user's system. The *target* part can be omitted if it is the same as DEPENDS_TARGET.

A quite common situation is when RUN_DEPENDS is literally the same as BUILD_DEPENDS, especially if ported software is written in a scripted language or if it requires the same build and run-time environment. In this case, it is both tempting and intuitive to directly assign one to the other:

```
RUN_DEPENDS= ${BUILD_DEPENDS}
```

However, such assignment can pollute run-time dependencies with entries not defined in the port's original BUILD_DEPENDS. This happens because of make(1)'s lazy evaluation of variable assignment. Consider a Makefile with USE_*, which are processed by ports/Mk/bsd.*.mk to augment initial build dependencies. For example, USES= gmake adds devel/gmake to BUILD_DEPENDS. To prevent such additional dependencies from polluting RUN_DEPENDS, create another variable with the current content of BUILD_DEPENDS and assign it to both BUILD_DE-PENDS and RUN_DEPENDS:

```
MY_DEPENDS= some:devel/some \
  other:lang/other
BUILD_DEPENDS= ${MY_DEPENDS}
RUN_DEPENDS= ${MY_DEPENDS}
```

Important

Do not use := to assign BUILD_DEPENDS to RUN_DEPENDS or vice-versa. All variables are expand-ed immediately, which is exactly the wrong thing to do and almost always a failure.

5.8.3. BUILD_DEPENDS

This variable specifies executables or files this port requires to build. Like RUN_DEPENDS, it is a list of *path:dir*[:*tar-get*] tuples. For example,

```
BUILD_DEPENDS= unzip:archivers/unzip
```

will check for an executable called unzip, and descend into the archivers/unzip subdirectory of the ports tree to build and install it if it is not found.

Note

"build" here means everything from extraction to compilation. The dependency is checked from within the `extract` target. The *target* part can be omitted if it is the same as DE-PENDS_TARGET

5.8.4. FETCH_DEPENDS

This variable specifies executables or files this port requires to fetch. Like the previous two, it is a list of *path:dir[:target]* tuples. For example,

```
FETCH_DEPENDS= ncftp2:net/ncftp2
```

will check for an executable called `ncftp2`, and descend into the `net/ncftp2` subdirectory of the ports tree to build and install it if it is not found.

The dependency is checked from within the `fetch` target. The *target* part can be omitted if it is the same as DEPENDS_TARGET.

5.8.5. EXTRACT_DEPENDS

This variable specifies executables or files this port requires for extraction. Like the previous, it is a list of *path:dir[:target]* tuples. For example,

```
EXTRACT_DEPENDS= unzip:archivers/unzip
```

will check for an executable called `unzip`, and descend into the `archivers/unzip` subdirectory of the ports tree to build and install it if it is not found.

The dependency is checked from within the `extract` target. The *target* part can be omitted if it is the same as DEPENDS_TARGET.

Note

Use this variable only if the extraction does not already work (the default assumes `tar`) and cannot be made to work using USES=tar , USES=lha or USES=zip described in Chapter 15, *Using USES Macros*.

5.8.6. PATCH_DEPENDS

This variable specifies executables or files this port requires to patch. Like the previous, it is a list of *path:dir[:target]* tuples. For example,

```
PATCH_DEPENDS= ${NONEXISTENT}:java/jfc:extract
```

will descend into the `java/jfc` subdirectory of the ports tree to extract it.

The dependency is checked from within the `patch` target. The *target* part can be omitted if it is the same as DEPENDS_TARGET.

5.8.7. USES

Parameters can be added to define different features and dependencies used by the port. They are specified by adding this line to the `Makefile`:

```
USES= feature[:arguments]
```

For the complete list of values, please see Chapter 15, *Using USES Macros*.

 Warning

USES cannot be assigned after inclusion of `bsd.port.pre.mk`.

5.8.8. USE_*

Several variables exist to define common dependencies shared by many ports. Their use is optional, but helps to reduce the verbosity of the port `Makefiles`. Each of them is styled as `USE_*`. These variables may be used only in the port `Makefiles` and `ports/Mk/bsd.*.mk` . They are not meant for user-settable options — use `PORT_OPTIONS` for that purpose.

 Note

It is *always* incorrect to set any `USE_*` in `/etc/make.conf` . For instance, setting

```
USE_GCC=X.Y
```

(where X.Y is version number) would add a dependency on gccXY for every port, including `lang/gccXY` itself!

Table 5.6. USE_*

Variable	Means
USE_GCC	The port requires GCC (gcc or g++) to build. Some ports need any GCC version, some require modern, recent versions. It is typically set to **any** (in this case, GCC from base would be used on versions of FreeBSD that still have it, or `lang/gcc` port would be installed when default C/ C++ compiler is Clang); or **yes** (means always use stable, modern GCC from `lang/gcc` port). The exact version can also be specified, with a value such as 4.7. The minimal required version can be specified as 4.6+. The GCC from the base system is used when it satisfies the requested version, otherwise an appropriate compiler is built from the port, and `CC` and `CXX` are adjusted accordingly.

Variables related to gmake and `configure` are described in Section 6.5, "Building Mechanisms", while autoconf, automake and libtool are described in Section 6.6, "Using GNU Autotools". Perl related variables are described in Section 6.8, "Using Perl". X11 variables are listed in Section 6.9, "Using X11". Section 6.10, "Using GNOME" deals with GNOME and Section 6.13, "Using KDE" with KDE related variables. Section 6.14, "Using Java" documents Java variables, while Section 6.15, "Web Applications, Apache and PHP" contains information on Apache, PHP and PEAR modules. Python is discussed in Section 6.16, "Using Python", while Ruby in Section 6.19, "Using Ruby". Section 6.20, "Using SDL" provides variables used for SDL applications and finally, Section 6.24, "Using Xfce" contains information on Xfce.

5.8.9. Minimal Version of a Dependency

A minimal version of a dependency can be specified in any *_DEPENDS except LIB_DEPENDS using this syntax:

```
p5-Spiffy>=0.26:devel/p5-Spiffy
```

The first field contains a dependent package name, which must match the entry in the package database, a comparison sign, and a package version. The dependency is satisfied if p5-Spiffy-0.26 or newer is installed on the machine.

5.8.10. Notes on Dependencies

As mentioned above, the default target to call when a dependency is required is DEPENDS_TARGET. It defaults to install. This is a user variable; it is never defined in a port's Makefile. If the port needs a special way to handle a dependency, use the :target part of *_DEPENDS instead of redefining DEPENDS_TARGET.

When running make clean, the port dependencies are automatically cleaned too. If this is not desirable, define NOCLEANDEPENDS in the environment. This may be particularly desirable if the port has something that takes a long time to rebuild in its dependency list, such as KDE, GNOME or Mozilla.

To depend on another port unconditionally, use the variable ${NONEXISTENT} as the first field of BUILD_DEPENDS or RUN_DEPENDS. Use this only when the source of the other port is needed. Compilation time can be saved by specifying the target too. For instance

```
BUILD_DEPENDS= ${NONEXISTENT}:graphics/jpeg:extract
```

will always descend to the jpeg port and extract it.

5.8.11. Circular Dependencies Are Fatal

Important

Do not introduce any circular dependencies into the ports tree!

The ports building technology does not tolerate circular dependencies. If one is introduced, someone, somewhere in the world, will have their FreeBSD installation broken almost immediately, with many others quickly to follow. These can really be hard to detect. If in doubt, before making that change, make sure to run: cd /usr/ports; make index. That process can be quite slow on older machines, but it may be able to save a large number of people, including yourself, a lot of grief in the process.

5.8.12. Problems Caused by Automatic Dependencies

Dependencies must be declared either explicitly or by using the OPTIONS framework. Using other methods like automatic detection complicates indexing, which causes problems for port and package management.

Example 5.14. Wrong Declaration of an Optional Dependency

```
.include <bsd.port.pre.mk>

.if exists(${LOCALBASE}/bin/foo)
LIB_DEPENDS= libbar.so:foo/bar
.endif
```

The problem with trying to automatically add dependencies is that files and settings outside an individual port can change at any time. For example: an index is built, then a batch of ports are installed. But one of the ports installs the tested file. The index is now incorrect, because an installed port unexpectedly has a new dependency. The index may still be wrong even after rebuilding if other ports also determine their need for dependencies based on the existence of other files.

Example 5.15. Correct Declaration of an Optional Dependency

```
OPTIONS_DEFINE= BAR
BAR_DESC= Calling cellphones via bar

BAR_LIB_DEPENDS= libbar.so:foo/bar
```

Testing option variables is the correct method. It will not cause inconsistencies in the index of a batch of ports, provided the options were defined prior to the index build. Simple scripts can then be used to automate the building, installation, and updating of these ports and their packages.

5.8.13. USE_* and WANT_*

USE_* are set by the port maintainer to define software on which this port depends. A port that needs Firefox would set

```
USE_FIREFOX= yes
```

Some USE_* can accept version numbers or other parameters. For example, a port that requires Apache 2.2 would set

```
USE_APACHE= 22
```

For more control over dependencies in some cases, WANT_* are available to more precisely specify what is needed. For example, consider the mail/squirrelmail port. This port needs some PHP modules, which are listed in USE_PHP :

```
USE_PHP= session mhash gettext mbstring pcre openssl xml
```

Those modules may be available in CLI or web versions, so the web version is selected with WANT_*:

```
WANT_PHP_WEB= yes
```

Available USE_* and WANT_* are defined in the files in /usr/ports/Mk .

5.9. Slave Ports and MASTERDIR

If the port needs to build slightly different versions of packages by having a variable (for instance, resolution, or paper size) take different values, create one subdirectory per package to make it easier for users to see what to do, but try to share as many files as possible between ports. Typically, by using variables cleverly, only a very short Makefile is needed in all but one of the directories. In the sole Makefile, use MASTERDIR to specify the directory where the rest of the files are. Also, use a variable as part of PKGNAMESUFFIX so the packages will have different names.

This will be best demonstrated by an example. This is part of japanese/xdvi300/Makefile;

```
PORTNAME= xdvi
PORTVERSION= 17
PKGNAMEPREFIX= ja-
PKGNAMESUFFIX= ${RESOLUTION}

# default
```

```
RESOLUTION?= 300
.if ${RESOLUTION} != 118 && ${RESOLUTION} != 240 && \
    ${RESOLUTION} != 300 && ${RESOLUTION} != 400
pre-everything::
 @${ECHO_MSG} "Error: invalid value for RESOLUTION: \"${RESOLUTION}\""
 @${ECHO_MSG} "Possible values are: 118, 240, 300 (default) and 400."
 @${FALSE}
.endif
```

japanese/xdvi300 also has all the regular patches, package files, etc. Running make there, it will take the default value for the resolution (300) and build the port normally.

As for other resolutions, this is the *entire* xdvi118/Makefile:

```
RESOLUTION= 118
MASTERDIR= ${.CURDIR}/../xdvi300

.include "${MASTERDIR}/Makefile"
```

(xdvi240/Makefile and xdvi400/Makefile are similar). MASTERDIR definition tells bsd.port.mk that the regular set of subdirectories like FILESDIR and SCRIPTDIR are to be found under xdvi300. The RESOLUTION=118 line will override the RESOLUTION=300 line in xdvi300/Makefile and the port will be built with resolution set to 118.

5.10. Man Pages

If the port anchors its man tree somewhere other than PREFIX, use MANDIRS to specify those directories. Note that the files corresponding to manual pages must be placed in pkg-plist along with the rest of the files. The purpose of MANDIRS is to enable automatic compression of manual pages, therefore the file names are suffixed with .gz.

5.11. Info Files

If the package needs to install GNU info files, list them in INFO (without the trailing .info), one entry per document. These files are assumed to be installed to PREFIX/INFO_PATH. Change INFO_PATH if the package uses a different location. However, this is not recommended. These entries contain just the path relative to PREFIX/INFO_PATH. For example, lang/gcc34 installs info files to PREFIX/INFO_PATH/gcc34, and INFO will be something like this:

```
INFO= gcc34/cpp gcc34/cppinternals gcc34/g77 ...
```

Appropriate installation/de-installation code will be automatically added to the temporary pkg-plist before package registration.

5.12. Makefile Options

Many applications can be built with optional or differing configurations. Examples include choice of natural (human) language, GUI versus command-line, or type of database to support. Users may need a different configuration than the default, so the ports system provides hooks the port author can use to control which variant will be built. Supporting these options properly will make users happy, and effectively provide two or more ports for the price of one.

5.12.1. OPTIONS

5.12.1.1. Background

OPTIONS_* give the user installing the port a dialog showing the available options, and then saves those options to ${PORT_DBDIR}/${OPTIONS_NAME}/options. The next time the port is built, the options are reused. PORT_DBDIR defaults to /var/db/ports . OPTIONS_NAME is to the port origin with an underscore as the space separator, for example, for dns/bind99 it will be dns_bind99 .

When the user runs `make config` (or runs `make build` for the first time), the framework checks for `${PORT_DB-DIR}/${OPTIONS_NAME}/options`. If that file does not exist, the values of `OPTIONS_*` are used, and a dialog box is displayed where the options can be enabled or disabled. Then `options` is saved and the configured variables are used when building the port.

If a new version of the port adds new `OPTIONS`, the dialog will be presented to the user with the saved values of old `OPTIONS` prefilled.

`make showconfig` shows the saved configuration. Use `make rmconfig` to remove the saved configuration.

5.12.1.2. Syntax

`OPTIONS_DEFINE` contains a list of `OPTIONS` to be used. These are independent of each other and are not grouped:

```
OPTIONS_DEFINE= OPT1 OPT2
```

Once defined, `OPTIONS` are described (optional, but strongly recommended):

```
OPT1_DESC= Describe OPT1
OPT2_DESC= Describe OPT2
OPT3_DESC= Describe OPT3
OPT4_DESC= Describe OPT4
OPT5_DESC= Describe OPT5
OPT6_DESC= Describe OPT6
```

`ports/Mk/bsd.options.desc.mk` has descriptions for many common `OPTIONS`. While often useful, override them if the description is insufficient for the port.

Tip

When describing options, view it from the perspective of the user: "What functionality does it change?" and "Why would I want to enable this?" Do not just repeat the name. For example, describing the NLS option as "include NLS support" does not help the user, who can already see the option name but may not know what it means. Describing it as "Native Language Support via gettext utilities" is much more helpful.

Important

Option names are always in all uppercase. They cannot use mixed case or lowercase.

`OPTIONS` can be grouped as radio choices, where only one choice from each group is allowed:

```
OPTIONS_SINGLE=  SG1
OPTIONS_SINGLE_SG1= OPT3 OPT4
```

Warning

There *must* be one of each `OPTIONS_SINGLE` group selected at all times for the options to be valid. One option of each group *must* be added to `OPTIONS_DEFAULT`.

`OPTIONS` can be grouped as radio choices, where none or only one choice from each group is allowed:

```
OPTIONS_RADIO=  RG1
OPTIONS_RADIO_RG1= OPT7 OPT8
```

OPTIONS can also be grouped as "multiple-choice" lists, where *at least one* option must be enabled:

```
OPTIONS_MULTI=  MG1
OPTIONS_MULTI_MG1= OPT5 OPT6
```

OPTIONS can also be grouped as "multiple-choice" lists, where none or any option can be enabled:

```
OPTIONS_GROUP=  GG1
OPTIONS_GROUP_GG1= OPT9 OPT10
```

OPTIONS are unset by default, unless they are listed in OPTIONS_DEFAULT:

```
OPTIONS_DEFAULT= OPT1 OPT3 OPT6
```

OPTIONS definitions must appear before the inclusion of bsd.port.options.mk. PORT_OPTIONS values can only be tested after the inclusion of bsd.port.options.mk. Inclusion of bsd.port.pre.mk can be used instead, too, and is still widely used in ports written before the introduction of bsd.port.options.mk. But be aware that some variables will not work as expected after the inclusion of bsd.port.pre.mk, typically some USE_* flags.

Example 5.16. Simple Use of OPTIONS

```
OPTIONS_DEFINE= FOO BAR
FOO_DESC= Option foo support
BAR_DESC= Feature bar support

OPTIONS_DEFAULT=FOO

# Will add --with-foo / --without-foo
FOO_CONFIGURE_WITH= foo
BAR_RUN_DEPENDS= bar:bar/bar

.include <bsd.port.mk>
```

Example 5.17. Check for Unset Port OPTIONS

```
.if ! ${PORT_OPTIONS:MEXAMPLES}
CONFIGURE_ARGS+=--without-examples
.endif
```

The form shown above is discouraged. The preferred method is using a configure knob to really enable and disable the feature to match the option:

```
# Will add --with-examples / --without-examples
EXAMPLES_CONFIGURE_WITH= examples
```

Example 5.18. Practical Use of OPTIONS

```
OPTIONS_DEFINE=  EXAMPLES
```

```
OPTIONS_SINGLE=  BACKEND
OPTIONS_SINGLE_BACKEND= MYSQL PGSQL BDB

OPTIONS_MULTI=  AUTH
OPTIONS_MULTI_AUTH= LDAP PAM SSL

EXAMPLES_DESC=  Install extra examples
MYSQL_DESC=  Use MySQL as backend
PGSQL_DESC=  Use PostgreSQL as backend
BDB_DESC=  Use Berkeley DB as backend
LDAP_DESC=  Build with LDAP authentication support
PAM_DESC=  Build with PAM support
SSL_DESC=  Build with OpenSSL support

OPTIONS_DEFAULT= PGSQL LDAP SSL

# Will add USE_PGSQL=yes
PGSQL_USE= pgsql=yes
# Will add --enable-postgres / --disable-postgres
PGSQL_CONFIGURE_ENABLE= postgres

ICU_LIB_DEPENDS= libicuuc.so:devel/icu

# Will add --with-examples / --without-examples
EXAMPLES_CONFIGURE_WITH= examples

# Check other OPTIONS

.include <bsd.port.mk>
```

5.12.1.3. Default Options

These options are always on by default.

- DOCS — build and install documentation.

- NLS — Native Language Support.

- EXAMPLES — build and install examples.

- IPV6 — IPv6 protocol support.

Note

There is no need to add these to OPTIONS_DEFAULT. To have them active, and show up in the options selection dialog, however, they must be added to OPTIONS_DEFINE.

5.12.2. Feature Auto-Activation

When using a GNU configure script, keep an eye on which optional features are activated by auto-detection. Explicitly disable optional features that are not needed by adding --without-xxx or --disable-xxx in CONFIGURE_ARGS.

Example 5.19. Wrong Handling of an Option

```
.if ${PORT_OPTIONS:MFOO}
```

```
LIB_DEPENDS+=  libfoo.so:devel/foo
CONFIGURE_ARGS+= --enable-foo
.endif
```

In the example above, imagine a library libfoo is installed on the system. The user does not want this application to use libfoo, so he toggled the option off in the make config dialog. But the application's configure script detects the library present in the system and includes its support in the resulting executable. Now when the user decides to remove libfoo from the system, the ports system does not protest (no dependency on libfoo was recorded) but the application breaks.

Example 5.20. Correct Handling of an Option

```
FOO_LIB_DEPENDS=  libfoo.so:devel/foo
# Will add --enable-foo / --disable-foo
FOO_CONFIGURE_ENABLE= foo
```

Note

Under some circumstances, the shorthand conditional syntax can cause problems with complex constructs. The errors are usually Malformed conditional, an alternative syntax can be used.

```
.if !empty(VARIABLE:MVALUE)
```

as an alternative to

```
.if ${VARIABLE:MVALUE}
```

5.12.3. Options Helpers

There are some macros to help simplify conditional values which differ based on the options set.

5.12.3.1. OPTIONS_SUB

If OPTIONS_SUB is set to yes then each of the options added to OPTIONS_DEFINE will be added to PLIST_SUB and SUB_LIST, for example:

```
OPTIONS_DEFINE= OPT1
OPTIONS_SUB= yes
```

is equivalent to:

```
OPTIONS_DEFINE= OPT1

.include <bsd.port.options.mk>

.if ${PORT_OPTIONS:MOPT1}
PLIST_SUB+= OPT1="" NO_OPT1="@comment "
SUB_LIST+= OPT1="" NO_OPT1="@comment "
.else
PLIST_SUB+= OPT1="@comment " NO_OPT1=""
SUB_LIST+= OPT1="@comment " NO_OPT1=""
.endif
```

Note

The value of `OPTIONS_SUB` is ignored. Setting it to any value will add `PLIST_SUB` and `SUB_LIST` entries for *all* options.

5.12.3.2. *OPT*_USE and *OPT*_USE_OFF

When option *OPT* is selected, for each *key=value* pair in *OPT*_USE, *value* is appended to the corresponding USE_*KEY*. If *value* has spaces in it, replace them with commas and they will be changed back to spaces during processing. *OPT*_USE_OFF works the same way, but when OPT is *not* selected. For example:

```
OPTIONS_DEFINE= OPT1
OPT1_USE= mysql=yes xorg=x11,xextproto,xext,xrandr
OPT1_USE_OFF= openssl=yes
```

is equivalent to:

```
OPTIONS_DEFINE= OPT1

.include <bsd.port.options.mk>

.if ${PORT_OPTIONS:MOPT1}
USE_MYSQL= yes
USE_XORG= x11 xextproto xext xrandr
.else
USE_OPENSSL= yes
.endif
```

5.12.3.3. *OPT*_CONFIGURE_ENABLE

When option *OPT* is selected, for each *entry* in *OPT*_CONFIGURE_ENABLE then `--enable-`*entry* is appended to CONFIGURE_ARGS. When option *OPT* is *not* selected, `--disable-`*entry* is appended to CONFIGURE_ARGS. An optional argument can be specified with an = symbol. This argument is only appended to the `--enable-`*entry* configure option. For example:

```
OPTIONS_DEFINE= OPT1 OPT2
OPT1_CONFIGURE_ENABLE= test1 test2
OPT2_CONFIGURE_ENABLE= test2=exhaustive
```

is equivalent to:

```
OPTIONS_DEFINE= OPT1

.include <bsd.port.options.mk>

.if ${PORT_OPTIONS:MOPT1}
CONFIGURE_ARGS+= --enable-test1 --enable-test2
.else
CONFIGURE_ARGS+= --disable-test1 --disable-test2
.endif

.if ${PORT_OPTIONS:MOPT2}
CONFIGURE_ARGS+= --enable-test2=exhaustive
.else
CONFIGURE_ARGS+= --disable-test2
.endif
```

5.12.3.4. *OPT*_CONFIGURE_WITH

When option *OPT* is selected, for each *entry* in *OPT*_CONFIGURE_WITH then `--with-`*entry* is appended to CONFIGURE_ARGS. When option *OPT* is *not* selected, `--without-`*entry* is appended to CONFIGURE_ARGS. An optional argument can be specified with an = symbol. This argument is only appended to the `--with-`*entry* configure option. For example:

```
OPTIONS_DEFINE= OPT1 OPT2
OPT1_CONFIGURE_WITH= test1
OPT2_CONFIGURE_WITH= test2=exhaustive
```

is equivalent to:

```
OPTIONS_DEFINE= OPT1 OPT2

.include <bsd.port.options.mk>

.if ${PORT_OPTIONS:MOPT1}
CONFIGURE_ARGS+= --with-test1
.else
CONFIGURE_ARGS+= --without-test1
.endif

.if ${PORT_OPTIONS:MOPT2}
CONFIGURE_ARGS+= --with-test2=exhaustive
.else
CONFIGURE_ARGS+= --without-test2
.endif
```

5.12.3.5. *OPT*_CONFIGURE_ON and *OPT*_CONFIGURE_OFF

When option *OPT* is selected, the value of *OPT*_CONFIGURE_ON, if defined, is appended to `CONFIGURE_ARGS`. *OPT*_CONFIGURE_OFF works the same way, but when OPT is *not* selected. For example:

```
OPTIONS_DEFINE= OPT1
OPT1_CONFIGURE_ON= --add-test
OPT1_CONFIGURE_OFF= --no-test
```

is equivalent to:

```
OPTIONS_DEFINE= OPT1

.include <bsd.port.options.mk>

.if ${PORT_OPTIONS:MOPT1}
CONFIGURE_ARGS+= --add-test
.else
CONFIGURE_ARGS+= --no-test
.endif
```

5.12.3.6. *OPT*_CMAKE_ON and *OPT*_CMAKE_OFF

When option *OPT* is selected, the value of *OPT*_CMAKE_ON, if defined, is appended to `CMAKE_ARGS`. *OPT*_CMAKE_OFF works the same way, but when OPT is *not* selected. For example:

```
OPTIONS_DEFINE= OPT1
OPT1_CMAKE_ON= -DTEST:BOOL=true -DDEBUG:BOOL=true
OPT1_CMAKE_OFF= -DOPTIMIZE:BOOL=true
```

is equivalent to:

```
OPTIONS_DEFINE= OPT1

.include <bsd.port.options.mk>

.if ${PORT_OPTIONS:MOPT1}
CMAKE_ARGS+= -DTEST:BOOL=true -DDEBUG:BOOL=true
.else
CMAKE_ARGS+= -DOPTIMIZE:BOOL=true
```

```
.endif
```

See Section 5.12.3.7, "*OPT*_CMAKE_BOOL and *OPT*_CMAKE_BOOL_OFF" for a shorter helper when the value is boolean.

5.12.3.7. *OPT*_CMAKE_BOOL and *OPT*_CMAKE_BOOL_OFF

When option *OPT* is selected, for each *entry* in *OPT*_CMAKE_BOOL then -D*entry*:BOOL=true is appended to CMAKE_ARGS . When option *OPT* is *not* selected, -D*entry*:BOOL=false is appended to CONFIGURE_ARGS. *OPT*_C-MAKE_BOOL_OFF is the oposite, -D*entry*:BOOL=false is appended to CMAKE_ARGS when the option is selected, and -D*entry*:BOOL=true when the option is *not* selected. For example:

```
OPTIONS_DEFINE= OPT1
OPT1_CMAKE_BOOL= TEST DEBUG
OPT1_CMAKE_BOOL_OFF= OPTIMIZE
```

is equivalent to:

```
OPTIONS_DEFINE= OPT1

.include <bsd.port.options.mk>

.if ${PORT_OPTIONS:MOPT1}
CMAKE_ARGS+= -DTEST:BOOL=true -DDEBUG:BOOL=true \
  -DOPTIMIZE:BOOL=false
.else
CMAKE_ARGS+= -DTEST:BOOL=false -DDEBUG:BOOL=false \
  -DOPTIMIZE:BOOL=true
.endif
```

5.12.3.8. *OPT*_QMAKE_ON and *OPT*_QMAKE_OFF

When option *OPT* is selected, the value of *OPT*_QMAKE_ON, if defined, is appended to QMAKE_ARGS . *OPT*_QMAKE_OFF works the same way, but when OPT is *not* selected. For example:

```
OPTIONS_DEFINE= OPT1
OPT1_QMAKE_ON= -DTEST:BOOL=true
OPT1_QMAKE_OFF= -DPRODUCTION:BOOL=true
```

is equivalent to:

```
OPTIONS_DEFINE= OPT1

.include <bsd.port.options.mk>

.if ${PORT_OPTIONS:MOPT1}
QMAKE_ARGS+= -DTEST:BOOL=true
.else
QMAKE_ARGS+= -DPRODUCTION:BOOL=true
.endif
```

5.12.3.9. *OPT*_IMPLIES

Provides a way to add dependencies between options.

When *OPT* is selected, all the options listed in this variable will be selected too. Using the *OPT*_CONFIGURE_ENABLE described earlier to illustrate:

```
OPTIONS_DEFINE= OPT1 OPT2
OPT1_IMPLIES= OPT2

OPT1_CONFIGURE_ENABLE= opt1
OPT2_CONFIGURE_ENABLE= opt2
```

Is equivalent to:

```
OPTIONS_DEFINE= OPT1 OPT2

.include <bsd.port.options.mk>

.if ${PORT_OPTIONS:MOPT1}
CONFIGURE_ARGS+= --enable-opt1
.else
CONFIGURE_ARGS+= --disable-opt1
.endif

.if ${PORT_OPTIONS:MOPT2} || ${PORT_OPTIONS:MOPT1}
CONFIGURE_ARGS+= --enable-opt2
.else
CONFIGURE_ARGS+= --disable-opt2
.endif
```

Example 5.21. Simple Use of *OPT_IMPLIES*

This port has a X11 option, and a GNOME option that needs the X11 option to be selected to build.

```
OPTIONS_DEFINE= X11 GNOME
OPTIONS_DEFAULT= X11

X11_USE= xorg=xi,xextproto
GNOME_USE= gnome=gtk30
GNOME_IMPLIES= X11
```

5.12.3.10. *OPT_PREVENTS* and *OPT_PREVENTS_MSG*

Provides a way to add conflicts between options.

When *OPT* is selected, all the options listed in this variable must be un-selected. If *OPT*_PREVENTS_MSG is also selected, its content will be shown, explaining why they conflict. For example:

```
OPTIONS_DEFINE= OPT1 OPT2
OPT1_PREVENTS= OPT2
OPT1_PREVENTS_MSG= OPT1 and OPT2 enable conflicting options
```

Is roughly equivalent to:

```
OPTIONS_DEFINE= OPT1 OPT2

.include <bsd.port.options.mk>

.if ${PORT_OPTIONS:MOPT2} && ${PORT_OPTIONS:MOPT1}
BROKEN= Option OPT1 conflicts with OPT2 (select only one)
.endif
```

The only difference is that the first one will write an error after running make config, suggesting changing the selected options.

Example 5.22. Simple Use of *OPT_PREVENTS*

This port has X509 and SCTP options. Both options add patches, but the patches conflict with each other, so they cannot be selected at the same time.

```
OPTIONS_DEFINE= X509 SCTP
```

```
SCTP_PATCHFILES= ${PORTNAME}-6.8p1-sctp-2573.patch.gz:-p1
SCTP_CONFIGURE_WITH= sctp

X509_PATCH_SITES= http://www.roumenpetrov.info/openssh/x509/:x509
X509_PATCHFILES= ${PORTNAME}-7.0p1+x509-8.5.diff.gz:-p1:x509
X509_PREVENTS=   SCTP
X509_PREVENTS_MSG= X509 and SCTP patches conflict
```

5.12.3.11. *OPT*_VARS and *OPT*_VARS_OFF

Provides a generic way to set and append to variables.

Warning

Before using *OPT*_VARS and *OPT*_VARS_OFF , see if there is already a more specific helper available in Section 5.12.3.13, "Generic Variables Replacement, *OPT_VARIABLE* and *OP-T_VARIABLE* _OFF".

When option *OPT* is selected, and *OPT*_VARS defined, *key=value* and *key+=value* pairs are evaluated from *OPT*_VARS . An = cause the existing value of KEY to be overwritten, an += appends to the value. *OPT*_VARS_OFF works the same way, but when OPT is *not* selected.

```
OPTIONS_DEFINE= OPT1 OPT2 OPT3
OPT1_VARS= also_build+=bin1
OPT2_VARS= also_build+=bin2
OPT3_VARS= bin3_build=yes
OPT3_VARS_OFF= bin3_build=no

MAKE_ARGS= ALSO_BUILD="${ALSO_BUILD}" BIN3_BUILD="${BIN3_BUILD}"
```

is equivalent to:

```
OPTIONS_DEFINE= OPT1 OPT2

MAKE_ARGS= ALSO_BUILD="${ALSO_BUILD}" BIN3_BUILD="${BIN3_BUILD}"

.include <bsd.port.options.mk>

.if ${PORT_OPTIONS:MOPT1}
ALSO_BUILD+= bin1
.endif

.if ${PORT_OPTIONS:MOPT2}
ALSO_BUILD+= bin2
.endif

.if ${PORT_OPTIONS:MOPT2}
BIN3_BUILD= yes
.else
BIN3_BUILD= no
.endif
```

Tip

Values containing whitespace must be enclosed in quotes:

```
OPT_VARS= foo="bar baz"
```

This is due to the way make(1) variable expansion deals with whitespace. When OPT_VARS=
foo=bar baz is expanded, the variable ends up containing two strings, foo=bar and baz.
But the submitter probably intended there to be only one string, foo=bar baz . Quoting the
value prevents whitespace from being used as a delimiter.

5.12.3.12. Dependencies, *OPT_DEPTYPE* and *OPT_DEPTYPE*_OFF

For any of these dependency types:

- PKG_DEPENDS

- EXTRACT_DEPENDS

- PATCH_DEPENDS

- FETCH_DEPENDS

- BUILD_DEPENDS

- LIB_DEPENDS

- RUN_DEPENDS

When option *OPT* is selected, the value of *OPT_DEPTYPE*, if defined, is appended to *DEPTYPE*. *OPT_DEPTYPE*_OFF works
the same, but when OPT is *not* selected. For example:

```
OPTIONS_DEFINE= OPT1
OPT1_LIB_DEPENDS= liba.so:devel/a
OPT1_LIB_DEPENDS_OFF= libb.so:devel/b
```

is equivalent to:

```
OPTIONS_DEFINE= OPT1

.include <bsd.port.options.mk>

.if ${PORT_OPTIONS:MOPT1}
LIB_DEPENDS+= liba.so:devel/a
.else
LIB_DEPENDS+= libb.so:devel/b
.endif
```

5.12.3.13. Generic Variables Replacement, *OPT_VARIABLE* and *OPT_VARIABLE*_OFF

For any of these variables:

- ALL_TARGET

- BROKEN

- CATEGORIES

- CFLAGS

- CONFIGURE_ENV

- CONFLICTS

- CONFLICTS_BUILD

- CONFLICTS_INSTALL

- CPPFLAGS

- CXXFLAGS

- DESKTOP_ENTRIES

- DISTFILES

- EXTRA_PATCHES

- EXTRACT_ONLY

- GH_ACCOUNT

- GH_PROJECT

- GH_SUBDIR

- GH_TAGNAME

- GH_TUPLE

- IGNORE

- INFO

- INSTALL_TARGET

- LDFLAGS

- LIBS

- MAKE_ARGS

- MAKE_ENV

- MASTER_SITES

- PATCHFILES

- PATCH_SITES

- PLIST_DIRS

- PLIST_DIRSTRY

- PLIST_FILES

- PLIST_SUB

- PORTDOCS

- PORTEXAMPLES

- SUB_FILES

- SUB_LIST

- `TEST_TARGET`

- `USES`

When option *OPT* is selected, the value of *OPT_ABOVEVARIABLE*, if defined, is appended to *ABOVEVARIABLE*. *OPT_ABOVEVARIABLE*_OFF works the same way, but when OPT is *not* selected. For example:

```
OPTIONS_DEFINE= OPT1
OPT1_USES= gmake
OPT1_CFLAGS_OFF= -DTEST
```

is equivalent to:

```
OPTIONS_DEFINE= OPT1

.include <bsd.port.options.mk>

.if ${PORT_OPTIONS:MOPT1}
USES+=  gmake
.else
CFLAGS+= -DTEST
.endif
```

Note

Some variables are not in this list, in particular `PKGNAMEPREFIX` and `PKGNAMESUFFIX`. This is intentional. A port *must not* change its name when its option set changes.

Warning

Some of these variables, at least `ALL_TARGET` and `INSTALL_TARGET`, have their default values set *after* the options are processed.

With these lines in the `Makefile`:

```
ALL_TARGET= all
```

```
DOCS_ALL_TARGET= doc
```

If the `DOCS` option is enabled, `ALL_TARGET` will have a final value of `all  doc`; if the option is disabled, it would have a value of `all`.

With only the options helper line in the `Makefile`:

```
DOCS_ALL_TARGET= doc
```

If the `DOCS` option is enabled, `ALL_TARGET` will have a final value of `doc`; if the option is disabled, it would have a value of `all`.

5.12.3.14. Additional Build Targets, *TARGET-OPT*-on and *TARGET-OPT*-off

These `Makefile` targets can accept optional extra build targets:

- `pre-fetch`

- `do-fetch`

- post-fetch

- pre-extract

- do-extract

- post-extract

- pre-patch

- do-patch

- post-patch

- pre-configure

- do-configure

- post-configure

- pre-build

- do-build

- post-build

- pre-install

- do-install

- post-install

- post-stage

- pre-package

- do-package

- post-package

When option *OPT* is selected, the target *TARGET-OPT*-on, if defined, is executed after *TARGET*. *TARGET-OPT*-off works the same way, but when OPT is *not* selected. For example:

```
OPTIONS_DEFINE= OPT1

post-patch-OPT1-on:
 @${REINPLACE_CMD} -e '/opt1/d' ${WRKSRC}/Makefile
post-patch-OPT1-off:
 @${REINPLACE_CMD} -e '/opt1/s|/usr/bin/|${LOCALBASE}/bin/|' ${WRKSRC}/Makefile
```

is equivalent to:

```
OPTIONS_DEFINE= OPT1

.include <bsd.port.options.mk>

post-patch:
.if ${PORT_OPTIONS:MOPT1}
 @${REINPLACE_CMD} -e '/opt1/d' ${WRKSRC}/Makefile
.else
 @${REINPLACE_CMD} -e '/opt1/s|/usr/bin/|${LOCALBASE}/bin/|' ${WRKSRC}/Makefile
.endif
```

5.13. Specifying the Working Directory

Each port is extracted into a working directory, which must be writable. The ports system defaults to having DIST-
FILES unpack in to a directory called ${DISTNAME}. In other words, if the Makefile has:

```
PORTNAME= foo
PORTVERSION= 1.0
```

then the port's distribution files contain a top-level directory, foo-1.0, and the rest of the files are located under
that directory.

A number of variables can be overridden if that is not the case.

5.13.1. WRKSRC

The variable lists the name of the directory that is created when the application's distfiles are extracted. If our
previous example extracted into a directory called foo (and not foo-1.0) write:

```
WRKSRC= ${WRKDIR}/foo
```

or possibly

```
WRKSRC= ${WRKDIR}/${PORTNAME}
```

5.13.2. WRKSRC_SUBDIR

If the source files needed for the port are in a subdirectory of the extracted distribution file, set WRKSRC_SUBDIR
to that directory.

```
WRKSRC_SUBDIR= src
```

5.13.3. NO_WRKSUBDIR

If the port does not extract in to a subdirectory at all, then set NO_WRKSUBDIR to indicate that.

```
NO_WRKSUBDIR= yes
```

Note

Because WRKDIR is the only directory that is supposed to be writable during the build, and is
used to store many files recording the status of the build, the port's extraction will be forced
into a subdirectory.

5.14. Conflict Handling

There are three different variables to register a conflict between packages and ports: CONFLICTS, CONFLICTS_INS-
TALL and CONFLICTS_BUILD.

Note

The conflict variables automatically set the variable IGNORE, which is more fully documented
in Section 12.14, "Marking a Port Not Installable with BROKEN, FORBIDDEN, or IGNORE".

When removing one of several conflicting ports, it is advisable to retain CONFLICTS in those other ports for a few months to cater for users who only update once in a while.

5.14.1. CONFLICTS_INSTALL

If the package cannot coexist with other packages (because of file conflicts, runtime incompatibilities, etc.), list the other package names in CONFLICTS_INSTALL. Use shell globs like * and ? here. Enumerate package names in there, not port names or origins. Please make sure that CONFLICTS_INSTALL does not match this port's package itself. Otherwise enforcing its installation with FORCE_PKG_REGISTER will no longer work. CONFLICTS_INSTALL check is done after the build stage and prior to the install stage.

5.14.2. CONFLICTS_BUILD

If the port cannot be built when other specific ports are already installed, list the other port names in CONFLIC-TS_BUILD. Use shell globs like * and ? here. Use package names, not port names or origins. CONFLICTS_BUILD check is done prior to the build stage. Build conflicts are not recorded in the resulting package.

5.14.3. CONFLICTS

If the port cannot be built if a certain port is already installed and the resulting package cannot coexist with the other package, list the other package name in CONFLICTS. use shell globs like * and ? here. Enumerate package names in there, not port names or origins. Please make sure that CONFLICTS does not match this port's package itself. Otherwise enforcing its installation with FORCE_PKG_REGISTER will no longer work. CONFLICTS check is done prior to the build stage and prior to the install stage.

5.15. Installing Files

Important

The install phase is very important to the end user because it adds files to their system. All the additional commands run in the port Makefile's *-install targets should be echoed to the screen. *Do not* silence these commands with @ or .SILENT.

5.15.1. INSTALL_* Macros

Use the macros provided in bsd.port.mk to ensure correct modes of files in the port's *-install targets. Set ownership directly in pkg-plist with the corresponding entries, such as @(*owner,group,*), @owner *owner*, and @group *group*. These operators work until overridden, or until the end of pkg-plist, so remember to reset them after they are no longer needed. The default ownership is root:wheel . See Section 7.6.13, "Base Keywords" for more information.

- INSTALL_PROGRAM is a command to install binary executables.

- INSTALL_SCRIPT is a command to install executable scripts.

- INSTALL_LIB is a command to install shared libraries (but not static libraries).

- INSTALL_KLD is a command to install kernel loadable modules. Some architectures do not like having the modules stripped, so use this command instead of INSTALL_PROGRAM.

- INSTALL_DATA is a command to install sharable data, including static libraries.

- INSTALL_MAN is a command to install manpages and other documentation (it does not compress anything).

These variables are set to the install(1) command with the appropriate flags for each situation.

Important

Do not use INSTALL_LIB to install static libraries, because stripping them renders them useless. Use INSTALL_DATA instead.

5.15.2. Stripping Binaries and Shared Libraries

Installed binaries should be stripped. Do not strip binaries manually unless absolutely required. The INSTALL_PROGRAM macro installs and strips a binary at the same time. The INSTALL_LIB macro does the same thing to shared libraries.

When a file must be stripped, but neither INSTALL_PROGRAM nor INSTALL_LIB macros are desirable, ${STRIP_CMD} strips the program or shared library. This is typically done within the post-install target. For example:

```
post-install:
 ${STRIP_CMD} ${STAGEDIR}${PREFIX}/bin/xdl
```

When multiple files need to be stripped:

```
post-install:
.for l in geometry media body track world
 ${STRIP_CMD} ${STAGEDIR}${PREFIX}/lib/lib${PORTNAME}-${l}.so.0
.endfor
```

Use file(1) on a file to determine if it has been stripped. Binaries are reported by file(1) as **stripped**, or **not stripped**. Additionally, strip(1) will detect programs that have already been stripped and exit cleanly.

5.15.3. Installing a Whole Tree of Files

Sometimes, a large number of files must be installed while preserving their hierarchical organization. For example, copying over a whole directory tree from WRKSRC to a target directory under PREFIX. Note that PREFIX, EXAMPLESDIR, DATADIR, and other path variables must always be prepended with STAGEDIR to respect staging (see Section 6.1, "Staging").

Two macros exist for this situation. The advantage of using these macros instead of cp is that they guarantee proper file ownership and permissions on target files. The first macro, COPYTREE_BIN, will set all the installed files to be executable, thus being suitable for installing into PREFIX/bin. The second macro, COPYTREE_SHARE, does not set executable permissions on files, and is therefore suitable for installing files under PREFIX/share target.

```
post-install:
 ${MKDIR} ${STAGEDIR}${EXAMPLESDIR}
 (cd ${WRKSRC}/examples && ${COPYTREE_SHARE} . ${STAGEDIR}${EXAMPLESDIR})
```

This example will install the contents of the examples directory in the vendor distfile to the proper examples location of the port.

```
post-install:
 ${MKDIR} ${STAGEDIR}${DATADIR}/summer
 (cd ${WRKSRC}/temperatures && ${COPYTREE_SHARE} "June July August" ↵
${STAGEDIR}${DATADIR}/summer)
```

And this example will install the data of summer months to the summer subdirectory of a DATADIR.

Additional find arguments can be passed via the third argument to COPYTREE_* macros. For example, to install all files from the first example except Makefiles, one can use these commands.

```
post-install:
```

```
${MKDIR} ${STAGEDIR}${EXAMPLESDIR}
(cd ${WRKSRC}/examples && \
${COPYTREE_SHARE} . ${STAGEDIR}${EXAMPLESDIR} "! -name Makefile")
```

These macros do not add the installed files to pkg-plist . They must be added manually. For optional documentation (PORTDOCS, see Section 5.15.4, "Install Additional Documentation") and examples (PORTEXAMPLES), the %%PORT-DOCS%% or %%PORTEXAMPLES%% prefixes must be prepended in pkg-plist .

5.15.4. Install Additional Documentation

If the software has some documentation other than the standard man and info pages that is useful for the user, install it under DOCSDIR This can be done, like the previous item, in the post-install target.

Create a new directory for the port. The directory name is DOCSDIR . This usually equals PORTNAME. However, if the user might want different versions of the port to be installed at the same time, the whole PKGNAME can be used.

Since only the files listed in pkg-plist are installed, it is safe to always install documentation to STAGEDIR (see Section 6.1, "Staging"). Hence .if blocks are only needed when the installed files are large enough to cause significant I/O overhead.

```
post-install:
 ${MKDIR} ${STAGEDIR}${DOCSDIR}
 ${INSTALL_MAN} ${WRKSRC}/docs/xvdocs.ps ${STAGEDIR}${DOCSDIR}
```

On the other hand, if there is a DOCS option in the port, install the documentation in a post-install-DOCS-on target. These targets are described in Section 5.12.3.14, "Additional Build Targets, *TARGET-OPT*-on and *TARGET-OPT*-off*".

Here are some handy variables and how they are expanded by default when used in the Makefile:

- DATADIR gets expanded to PREFIX/share/PORTNAME .

- DATADIR_REL gets expanded to share/PORTNAME .

- DOCSDIR gets expanded to PREFIX/share/doc/PORTNAME .

- DOCSDIR_REL gets expanded to share/doc/PORTNAME .

- EXAMPLESDIR gets expanded to PREFIX/share/examples/PORTNAME .

- EXAMPLESDIR_REL gets expanded to share/examples/PORTNAME .

 Note

The DOCS option only controls additional documentation installed in DOCSDIR . It does not apply to standard man pages and info pages. Things installed in DATADIR and EXAMPLESDIR are controlled by DATA and EXAMPLES options, respectively.

These variables are exported to PLIST_SUB . Their values will appear there as pathnames relative to PREFIX if possible. That is, share/doc/PORTNAME will be substituted for %%DOCSDIR%% in the packing list by default, and so on. (See more on pkg-plist substitution here.)

All conditionally installed documentation files and directories are included in pkg-plist with the %%PORTDOCS%% prefix, for example:

```
%%PORTDOCS%%%%DOCSDIR%%/AUTHORS
%%PORTDOCS%%%%DOCSDIR%%/CONTACT
```

As an alternative to enumerating the documentation files in pkg-plist , a port can set the variable PORTDOCS to a list of file names and shell glob patterns to add to the final packing list. The names will be relative to DOCSDIR . Therefore, a port that utilizes PORTDOCS, and uses a non-default location for its documentation, must set DOCSDIR accordingly. If a directory is listed in PORTDOCS or matched by a glob pattern from this variable, the entire subtree of contained files and directories will be registered in the final packing list. If the DOCS option has been unset then files and directories listed in PORTDOCS would not be installed or added to port packing list. Installing the documentation at PORTDOCS as shown above remains up to the port itself. A typical example of utilizing PORTDOCS looks as follows:

```
PORTDOCS= README.* ChangeLog docs/*
```

Note

The equivalents of PORTDOCS for files installed under DATADIR and EXAMPLESDIR are PORTDATA and PORTEXAMPLES, respectively.

The contents of pkg-message are displayed upon installation. See the section on using pkg-message for details. pkg-message does not need to be added to pkg-plist .

5.15.5. Subdirectories Under PREFIX

Try to let the port put things in the right subdirectories of PREFIX. Some ports lump everything and put it in the subdirectory with the port's name, which is incorrect. Also, many ports put everything except binaries, header files and manual pages in a subdirectory of lib, which does not work well with the BSD paradigm. Many of the files must be moved to one of these directories: etc (setup/configuration files), libexec (executables started internally), sbin (executables for superusers/managers), info (documentation for info browser) or share (architecture independent files). See hier(7) for details; the rules governing /usr pretty much apply to /usr/local too. The exception are ports dealing with USENET "news". They may use PREFIX/news as a destination for their files.

Chapter 6. Special Considerations

This section explains the most common things to consider when creating a port.

6.1. Staging

bsd.port.mk expects ports to work with a "stage directory". This means that a port must not install files directly to the regular destination directories (that is, under PREFIX, for example) but instead into a separate directory from which the package is then built. In many cases, this does not require root privileges, making it possible to build packages as an unprivileged user. With staging, the port is built and installed into the stage directory, STAGEDIR. A package is created from the stage directory and then installed on the system. Automake tools refer to this concept as DESTDIR, but in FreeBSD, DESTDIR has a different meaning (see Section 9.4, "PREFIX and DESTDIR").

> Note
>
> No port *really* needs to be root. It can mostly be avoided by using USES=uidfix. If the port still runs commands like chown(8), chgrp(1), or forces owner or group with install(1) then use USES=fakeroot to fake those calls. Some patching of the port's Makefiles will be needed.

Meta ports, or ports that do not install files themselves but only depend on other ports, must avoid needlessly extracting the mtree(8) to the stage directory. This is the basic directory layout of the package, and these empty directories will be seen as orphans. To prevent mtree(8) extraction, add this line:

```
NO_MTREE= yes
```

> Tip
>
> Metaports should use USES=metaport. It sets up defaults for ports that do not fetch, build, or install anything.

Staging is enabled by prepending STAGEDIR to paths used in the pre-install, do-install, and post-install targets (see the examples through the book). Typically, this includes PREFIX, ETCDIR, DATADIR, EXAMPLESDIR, MAN-PREFIX, DOCSDIR, and so on. Directories should be created as part of the post-install target. Avoid using absolute paths whenever possible.

When creating a symlink, STAGEDIR is prepended to the target path only. For example:

```
${LN} -sf libfoo.so.42  ${STAGEDIR}${PREFIX}/lib/libfoo.so
```

The source path ${PREFIX}/lib/libfoo.so.42 looks fine but could, in fact, be incorrect. Absolute paths can point to a wrong location, like when a remote file system has been mounted with NFS under a non-root mount point. Relative paths are less fragile, and often much shorter.

Ports that install kernel modules must prepend STAGEDIR to their destination, by default /boot/modules.

6.2. Bundled Libraries

This section explains why bundled dependencies are considered bad and what to do about them.

6.2.1. Why Bundled Libraries Are Bad

Some software requires the porter to locate third-party libraries and add the required dependencies to the port. Other software bundles all necessary libraries into the distribution file. The second approach seems easier at first, but there are some serious drawbacks:

This list is loosely based on the Fedora and Gentoo wikis, both licensed under the CC-BY-SA 3.0 license.

Security
> If vulnerabilities are found in the upstream library and fixed there, they might not be fixed in the library bundled with the port. One reason could be that the author is not aware of the problem. This means that the porter must fix them, or upgrade to a non-vulnerable version, and send a patch to the author. This all takes time, which results in software being vulnerable longer than necessary. This in turn makes it harder to coordinate a fix without unnecessarily leaking information about the vulnerability.

Bugs
> This problem is similar to the problem with security in the last paragraph, but generally less severe.

Forking
> It is easier for the author to fork the upstream library once it is bundled. While convenient on first sight, it means that the code diverges from upstream making it harder to address security or other problems with the software. A reason for this is that patching becomes harder.
>
> Another problem of forking is that because code diverges from upstream, bugs get solved over and over again instead of just once at a central location. This defeats the idea of open source software in the first place.

Symbol collision
> When a library is installed on the system, it might collide with the bundled version. This can cause immediate errors at compile or link time. It can also cause errors when running the program which might be harder to track down. The latter problem could be caused because the versions of the two libraries are incompatible.

Licensing
> When bundling projects from different sources, license issues can arise more easily, especially when licenses are incompatible.

Waste of resources
> Bundled libraries waste resources on several levels. It takes longer to build the actual application, especially if these libraries are already present on the system. At run-time, they can take up unnecessary memory when the system-wide library is already loaded by one program and the bundled library is loaded by another program.

Waste of effort
> When a library needs patches for FreeBSD, these patches have to be duplicated again in the bundled library. This wastes developer time because the patches might not apply cleanly. It can also be hard to notice that these patches are required in the first place.

6.2.2. What to do About Bundled Libraries

Whenever possible, use the unbundled version of the library by adding a LIB_DEPENDS to the port. If such a port does not exist yet, consider creating it.

Only use bundled libraries if the upstream has a good track record on security and using unbundled versions leads to overly complex patches.

Note

In some very special cases, for example emulators, like Wine, a port has to bundle libraries, because they are in a different architecture, or they have been modified to fit the software's use. In that case, those libraries should not be exposed to other ports for linking. Add BUN-DLE_LIBS=yes to the port's Makefile. This will tell pkg(8) to not compute provided libraries.

> Always ask the Ports Management Team <portmgr@FreeBSD.org> before adding this to a port.

6.3. Shared Libraries

If the port installs one or more shared libraries, define a USE_LDCONFIG make variable, which will instruct a bs-d.port.mk to run ${LDCONFIG} -m on the directory where the new library is installed (usually PREFIX/lib) during post-install target to register it into the shared library cache. This variable, when defined, will also facilitate addition of an appropriate @exec /sbin/ldconfig -m and @unexec /sbin/ldconfig -R pair into pkg-plist, so that a user who installed the package can start using the shared library immediately and de-installation will not cause the system to still believe the library is there.

```
USE_LDCONFIG= yes
```

The default directory can be overridden by setting USE_LDCONFIG to a list of directories into which shared libraries are to be installed. For example, if the port installs shared libraries into PREFIX/lib/foo and PREFIX/lib/bar use this in Makefile:

```
USE_LDCONFIG= ${PREFIX}/lib/foo ${PREFIX}/lib/bar
```

Please double-check, often this is not necessary at all or can be avoided through -rpath or setting LD_RUN_PATH during linking (see lang/moscow_ml for an example), or through a shell-wrapper which sets LD_LIBRARY_PATH before invoking the binary, like www/seamonkey does.

When installing 32-bit libraries on 64-bit system, use USE_LDCONFIG32 instead.

If the software uses autotools, and specifically libtool, add USES=libtool .

When the major library version number increments in the update to the new port version, all other ports that link to the affected library must have their PORTREVISION incremented, to force recompilation with the new library version.

6.4. Ports with Distribution Restrictions or Legal Concerns

Licenses vary, and some of them place restrictions on how the application can be packaged, whether it can be sold for profit, and so on.

> **Important**
>
> It is the responsibility of a porter to read the licensing terms of the software and make sure that the FreeBSD project will not be held accountable for violating them by redistributing the source or compiled binaries either via FTP/HTTP or CD-ROM. If in doubt, please contact the FreeBSD ports mailing list.

In situations like this, the variables described in the next sections can be set.

6.4.1. NO_PACKAGE

This variable indicates that we may not generate a binary package of the application. For instance, the license may disallow binary redistribution, or it may prohibit distribution of packages created from patched sources.

However, the port's DISTFILES may be freely mirrored on FTP/HTTP. They may also be distributed on a CD-ROM (or similar media) unless NO_CDROM is set as well.

If the binary package is not generally useful, and the application must always be compiled from the source code, use NO_PACKAGE. For example, if the application has configuration information that is site specific hard coded into it at compile time, set NO_PACKAGE.

Set NO_PACKAGE to a string describing the reason why the package cannot be generated.

6.4.2. NO_CDROM

This variable alone indicates that, although we are allowed to generate binary packages, we may put neither those packages nor the port's DISTFILES onto a CD-ROM (or similar media) for resale. However, the binary packages and the port's DISTFILES will still be available via FTP/HTTP.

If this variable is set along with NO_PACKAGE, then only the port's DISTFILES will be available, and only via FTP/HTTP.

Set NO_CDROM to a string describing the reason why the port cannot be redistributed on CD-ROM. For instance, use this if the port's license is for "non-commercial" use only.

6.4.3. NOFETCHFILES

Files defined in NOFETCHFILES are not fetchable from any of MASTER_SITES . An example of such a file is when the file is supplied on CD-ROM by the vendor.

Tools which check for the availability of these files on MASTER_SITES have to ignore these files and not report about them.

6.4.4. RESTRICTED

Set this variable alone if the application's license permits neither mirroring the application's DISTFILES nor distributing the binary package in any way.

Do not set NO_CDROM or NO_PACKAGE along with RESTRICTED, since the latter variable implies the former ones.

Set RESTRICTED to a string describing the reason why the port cannot be redistributed. Typically, this indicates that the port contains proprietary software and that the user will need to manually download the DISTFILES, possibly after registering for the software or agreeing to accept the terms of an EULA.

6.4.5. RESTRICTED_FILES

When RESTRICTED or NO_CDROM is set, this variable defaults to ${DISTFILES} ${PATCHFILES}, otherwise it is empty. If only some of the distribution files are restricted, then set this variable to list them.

6.4.6. LEGAL_TEXT

If the port has legal concerns not addressed by the above variables, set LEGAL_TEXT to a string explaining the concern. For example, if special permission was obtained for FreeBSD to redistribute the binary, this variable must indicate so.

6.4.7. /usr/ports/LEGAL and LEGAL

A port which sets any of the above variables must also be added to /usr/ports/LEGAL . The first column is a glob which matches the restricted distfiles. The second column is the port's origin. The third column is the output of make -VLEGAL .

6.4.8. Examples

The preferred way to state "the distfiles for this port must be fetched manually" is as follows:

```
.if !exists(${DISTDIR}/${DISTNAME}${EXTRACT_SUFX})
IGNORE= may not be redistributed because of licensing reasons. Please visit some-
website to accept their license and download ${DISTFILES} into ${DISTDIR}
```

```
.endif
```

This both informs the user, and sets the proper metadata on the user's machine for use by automated programs.

Note that this stanza must be preceded by an inclusion of `bsd.port.pre.mk`.

6.5. Building Mechanisms

6.5.1. Building Ports in Parallel

The FreeBSD ports framework supports parallel building using multiple `make` sub-processes, which allows SMP systems to utilize all of their available CPU power, allowing port builds to be faster and more effective.

This is achieved by passing `-jX` flag to make(1) running on vendor code. This is the default build behavior of ports. Unfortunately, not all ports handle parallel building well and it may be required to explicitly disable this feature by adding the `MAKE_JOBS_UNSAFE=yes` variable. It is used when a port is known to be broken with `-jX`.

6.5.2. `make`, `gmake`, `fmake`, and `imake`

Several differing `make` implementations exist. Ported software often requires a particular implementation, like GNU `make`, known in FreeBSD as `gmake`, or `fmake`, the legacy FreeBSD `make`.

If the port uses GNU `make`, add `gmake` to `USES`. If the legacy FreeBSD `make` is needed, add `fmake` there.

`MAKE_CMD` can be used to reference the specific command configured by the `USES` setting in the port's `Makefile`. In rare cases when more than one `make` implementation is listed in `USES`, the variables `GMAKE` (for the GNU version) or `FMAKE` (for the legacy FreeBSD version) are available. Only use `MAKE_CMD` within the application `Makefile`s in `WRKSRC` to call the `make` implementation expected by the ported software.

If the port is an X application that uses imake to create `Makefile`s from `Imakefile`s, set `USES= imake ..` See the USES=imake section of Chapter 15, *Using USES Macros* for more details.

If the port's source `Makefile` has something other than `all` as the main build target, set `ALL_TARGET` accordingly. The same goes for `install` and `INSTALL_TARGET`.

6.5.3. `configure` Script

If the port uses the `configure` script to generate `Makefile` from `Makefile.in`, set `GNU_CONFIGURE=yes`. To give extra arguments to the `configure` script (the default argument is `--prefix=${PREFIX}  --infodir=${PREFIX}/${IN-FO_PATH}  --mandir=${MANPREFIX}/man  --build=${CONFIGURE_TARGET}`), set those extra arguments in `CON-FIGURE_ARGS`. Extra environment variables can be passed using `CONFIGURE_ENV`.

Table 6.1. Variables for Ports That Use `configure`

Variable	Means
GNU_CONFIGURE	The port uses `configure` script to prepare build.
HAS_CONFIGURE	Same as `GNU_CONFIGURE`, except default configure target is not added to `CONFIGURE_ARGS`.
CONFIGURE_ARGS	Additional arguments passed to `configure` script.
CONFIGURE_ENV	Additional environment variables to be set for `configure` script run.
CONFIGURE_TARGET	Override default configure target. Default value is `${MACHINE_ARCH}-portbld-freebsd${OSREL}` .

6.5.4. Using cmake

For ports that use CMake, define USES= cmake , or USES= cmake:outsource to build in a separate directory (see below).

Table 6.2. Variables for Ports That Use cmake

Variable	Means
CMAKE_ARGS	Port specific CMake flags to be passed to the cmake binary.
CMAKE_BUILD_TYPE	Type of build (CMake predefined build profiles). Default is Release, or Debug if WITH_DEBUG is set.
CMAKE_ENV	Environment variables to be set for the cmake binary. Default is ${CONFIGURE_ENV}.
CMAKE_SOURCE_PATH	Path to the source directory. Default is ${WRKSRC} .

Table 6.3. Variables the Users Can Define for cmake Builds

Variable	Means
CMAKE_VERBOSE	Enable verbose build output. Default not set, unless BATCH or PACKAGE_BUILDING are set.
CMAKE_NOCOLOR	Disables color build output. Default not set, unless BATCH or PACKAGE_BUILDING are set.

CMake supports these build profiles: Debug, Release, RelWithDebInfo and MinSizeRel. Debug and Release profiles respect system *FLAGS , RelWithDebInfo and MinSizeRel will set CFLAGS to -O2 -g and -Os -DNDEBUG correspondingly. The lower-cased value of CMAKE_BUILD_TYPE is exported to PLIST_SUB and must be used if the port installs *.cmake depending on the build type (see deskutils/strigi for an example). Please note that some projects may define their own build profiles and/or force particular build type by setting CMAKE_BUILD_TYPE in CMakeLists.txt. To make a port for such a project respect CFLAGS and WITH_DEBUG, the CMAKE_BUILD_TYPE definitions must be removed from those files.

Most CMake-based projects support an out-of-source method of building. The out-of-source build for a port can be requested by using the :outsource suffix. When enabled, CONFIGURE_WRKSRC, BUILD_WRKSRC and INSTALL_WRKSRC will be set to ${WRKDIR}/.build and this directory will be used to keep all files generated during configuration and build stages, leaving the source directory intact.

Example 6.1. USES= cmake Example

This snippet demonstrates the use of CMake for a port. CMAKE_SOURCE_PATH is not usually required, but can be set when the sources are not located in the top directory, or if only a subset of the project is intended to be built by the port.

```
USES=    cmake:outsource
CMAKE_SOURCE_PATH= ${WRKSRC}/subproject
```

6.5.5. Using scons

If the port uses SCons, define USE_SCONS=yes.

Table 6.4. Variables for Ports That Use `scons`

Variable	Means
SCONS_ARGS	Port specific SCons flags passed to the SCons environment.
SCONS_BUILDENV	Variables to be set in system environment.
SCONS_ENV	Variables to be set in SCons environment.
SCONS_TARGET	Last argument passed to SCons, similar to `MAKE_TARGET`.

To make third party `SConstruct` respect everything that is passed to SCons in `SCONS_ENV` (that is, most importantly, `CC/CXX/CFLAGS/CXXFLAGS`), patch `SConstruct` so build `Environment` is constructed like this:

```
env = Environment(**ARGUMENTS)
```

It may be then modified with `env.Append` and `env.Replace`.

6.6. Using GNU Autotools

6.6.1. Introduction

The various GNU autotools provide an abstraction mechanism for building a piece of software over a wide variety of operating systems and machine architectures. Within the Ports Collection, an individual port can make use of these tools via a simple construct:

```
USE_AUTOTOOLS= tool[:env] ...
```

At the time of writing, *tool* can be one of `autoconf`, `autoheader`, `automake`, `aclocal`, `libtoolize`. It can also be one the older legacy of `autoconf213`, `autoheader213`, `automake14`, `aclocal14`.

env is used to specify that the environmental variables are needed. It also adds a build dependency on the tool. The relevant tool is *not* ran as part of the `run-autotools` target.

Multiple tools can be specified at once, either by including them all on a single line, or using the += Makefile construct.

6.6.2. `libtool` and `libtoolize`

Ports shipping with their own copy of libtool (search for a file named ltmain.sh) need to have `USES=libtool`. If a port has `USE_AUTOTOOLS=libtoolize` it probably also needs `USES=libtool`. See the USES=libtool section in Chapter 15, *Using USES Macros* for more details.

6.6.3. `libltdl.so`

Some ports make use of the `libltdl.so` library package, which is part of the `libtool` suite. Use of this library does not automatically necessitate the use of `libtool` itself. If the port needs `libltdl.so`, add a dependency on it:

```
LIB_DEPENDS= libltdl.so:devel/libltdl
```

6.6.4. `autoconf` and `autoheader`

Some ports do not contain a configure script, but do contain an autoconf template in `configure.ac`. Use these assignments to let `autoconf` create the configure script, and also have `autoheader` create template headers for use by the configure script.

```
USE_AUTOTOOLS= autoconf[:env]
```

and

```
USE_AUTOTOOLS= autoheader
```

which also implies the use of `autoconf`.

The additional optional variables AUTOCONF_ARGS and AUTOHEADER_ARGS can be overridden by the port `Makefile` if specifically requested. Most ports are unlikely to need this. See `bsd.autotools.mk` for further details.

6.6.5. `automake` **and** `aclocal`

Some packages only contain `Makefile.am`. These have to be converted into `Makefile.in` using `automake`, and the further processed by `configure` to generate an actual `Makefile`.

Similarly, packages occasionally do not ship with an included `aclocal.m4`, again required to build the software. This can be achieved with `aclocal`, which scans `configure.ac` or `configure.in`.

`aclocal` has a similar relationship to `automake` as `autoheader` does to `autoconf`, described in the previous section. `aclocal` implies the use of `automake`, thus we have:

```
USE_AUTOTOOLS= automake[:env]
```

and

```
USE_AUTOTOOLS= aclocal
```

As with `autoconf` and `autoheader`, both `automake` and `aclocal` have optional argument variables, AUTOMAKE_ARGS and ACLOCAL_ARGS respectively, which may be overridden by the port `Makefile` if required.

6.7. Using GNU gettext

6.7.1. Basic Usage

If the port requires `gettext`, set USES= `gettext`, and the port will inherit a dependency on `libintl.so` from devel/gettext. Other values for `gettext` usage are listed in USES=gettext.

A rather common case is a port using `gettext` and `configure`. Generally, GNU `configure` should be able to locate `gettext` automatically.

```
USES= gettext
GNU_CONFIGURE= yes
```

If it ever fails to, hints at the location of `gettext` can be passed in CPPFLAGS and LDFLAGS as follows:

```
USES= gettext
CPPFLAGS+= -I${LOCALBASE}/include
LDFLAGS+= -L${LOCALBASE}/lib

GNU_CONFIGURE= yes
```

6.7.2. Optional Usage

Some software products allow for disabling NLS. For example, through passing `--disable-nls` to `configure`. In that case, the port must use `gettext` conditionally, depending on the status of the NLS option. For ports of low to medium complexity, use this idiom:

```
GNU_CONFIGURE= yes

OPTIONS_DEFINE= NLS
OPTIONS_SUB= yes

NLS_USES= gettext
NLS_CONFIGURE_ENABLE= nls

.include <bsd.port.mk>
```

Or using the older way of using options:

```
GNU_CONFIGURE=  yes

OPTIONS_DEFINE=  NLS

.include <bsd.port.options.mk>

.if ${PORT_OPTIONS:MNLS}
USES+=   gettext
PLIST_SUB+=  NLS=""
.else
CONFIGURE_ARGS+= --disable-nls
PLIST_SUB+=  NLS="@comment "
.endif

.include <bsd.port.mk>
```

The next item on the to-do list is to arrange so that the message catalog files are included in the packing list conditionally. The `Makefile` part of this task is already provided by the idiom. It is explained in the section on advanced pkg-plist practices. In a nutshell, each occurrence of `%%NLS%%` in `pkg-plist` will be replaced by "`@comment `" if NLS is disabled, or by a null string if NLS is enabled. Consequently, the lines prefixed by `%%NLS%%` will become mere comments in the final packing list if NLS is off; otherwise the prefix will be just left out. Then insert `%%NLS%%` before each path to a message catalog file in `pkg-plist`. For example:

```
%%NLS%%share/locale/fr/LC_MESSAGES/foobar.mo
%%NLS%%share/locale/no/LC_MESSAGES/foobar.mo
```

In high complexity cases, more advanced techniques may be needed, such as dynamic packing list generation.

6.7.3. Handling Message Catalog Directories

There is a point to note about installing message catalog files. The target directories for them, which reside under `LOCALBASE/share/locale`, must not be created and removed by a port. The most popular languages have their respective directories listed in `PORTSDIR/Templates/BSD.local.dist`. The directories for many other languages are governed by the devel/gettext port. Consult its `pkg-plist` and see whether the port is going to install a message catalog file for a unique language.

6.8. Using Perl

If `MASTER_SITES` is set to `CPAN`, the correct subdirectory is usually selected automatically. If the default subdirectory is wrong, `CPAN/Module` can be used to change it. `MASTER_SITES` can also be set to the old `MASTER_SITE_PERL_CPAN`, then the preferred value of `MASTER_SITE_SUBDIR` is the top-level hierarchy name. For example, the recommended value for `p5-Module-Name` is `Module`. The top-level hierarchy can be examined at cpan.org. This keeps the port working when the author of the module changes.

The exception to this rule is when the relevant directory does not exist or the distfile does not exist in that directory. In such case, using author's id as `MASTER_SITE_SUBDIR` is allowed. The `CPAN:AUTHOR` macro can be used, which will be translated to the hashed author directory. For example, `CPAN:AUTHOR` will be converted to `authors/id/A/AU/AUTHOR`.

When a port needs Perl support, it must set `USES=perl5` with the optional `USE_PERL5` described in the perl5 USES description.

Table 6.5. Read-Only Variables for Ports That Use Perl

Read only variables	Means
PERL	The full path of the Perl 5 interpreter, either in the system or installed from a port, but without the version

Read only variables	Means
	number. Use this when the software needs the path to the Perl interpreter. To replace "#!"lines in scripts, use USES=shebangfix.
PERL_VERSION	The full version of Perl installed (for example, 5.8.9).
PERL_LEVEL	The installed Perl version as an integer of the form MNNNPP (for example, 500809).
PERL_ARCH	Where Perl stores architecture dependent libraries. Defaults to ${ARCH}-freebsd.
PERL_PORT	Name of the Perl port that is installed (for example, perl5).
SITE_PERL	Directory name where site specific Perl packages go. This value is added to PLIST_SUB.

Note

Ports of Perl modules which do not have an official website must link to cpan.org in the WWW line of pkg-descr. The preferred URL form is http://search.cpan.org/dist/Module-Name/ (including the trailing slash).

Note

Do not use ${SITE_PERL} in dependency declarations. Doing so assumes that perl5.mk has been included, which is not always true. Ports depending on this port will have incorrect dependencies if this port's files move later in an upgrade. The right way to declare Perl module dependencies is shown in the example below.

Example 6.2. Perl Dependency Example

```
p5-IO-Tee>=0.64:devel/p5-IO-Tee
```

For Perl ports that install manual pages, the macro PERL5_MAN3 can be used inside pkg-plist. For example,

```
lib/perl5/5.14/man/man3/AnyEvent::I3.3.gz
```

can be replaced with

```
%%PERL5_MAN3%%/AnyEvent::I3.3.gz
```

Note

There are no PERL5_MANx macros for the other sections (x in 1, 2 and 4 to 9) because those get installed in the regular directories.

6.9. Using X11

6.9.1. X.Org Components

The X11 implementation available in The Ports Collection is X.Org. If the application depends on X components, set USE_XORG to the list of required components. Available components, at the time of writing, are:

bigreqsproto compositeproto damageproto dmx dmxproto dri2proto dri3proto evieproto fixesproto
fontcacheproto fontenc fontsproto fontutil glproto ice inputproto kbproto libfs oldx pciaccess
pixman presentproto printproto randrproto recordproto renderproto resourceproto scrnsaverproto sm
trapproto videoproto x11 xau xaw xaw6 xaw7 xbitmaps xcb xcmiscproto xcomposite xcursor xdamage
xdmcp xevie xext xextproto xf86bigfontproto xf86dgaproto xf86driproto xf86miscproto xf86rushproto
xf86vidmodeproto xfixes xfont xfontcache xft xi xinerama xineramaproto xkbfile xkbui xmu xmuu
xorg-macros xorg-server xp xpm xprintapputil xprintutil xproto xproxymngproto xrandr xrender xres
xscrnsaver xshmfence xt xtrans xtrap xtst xv xvmc xxf86dga xxf86misc xxf86vm .

Always up-to-date list can be found in /usr/ports/Mk/bsd.xorg.mk .

The Mesa Project is an effort to provide free OpenGL implementation. To specify a dependency on various components of this project, use USE_GL. Valid options are: egl, gl, glesv2, glew, glu, glut, glw and linux. For backwards compatibility, the value of yes maps to glu.

Example 6.3. USE_XORG Example

```
USE_XORG= xrender xft xkbfile xt xaw
USE_GL= glu
```

Table 6.6. Variables for Ports That Use X

USES= imake	The port uses imake.
XMKMF	Set to the path of xmkmf if not in the PATH. Defaults to xmkmf -a.

Example 6.4. Using X11-Related Variables

```
# Use some X11 libraries
USE_XORG= x11 xpm
```

6.9.2. Ports That Require Motif

If the port requires a Motif library, define USES= motif in the Makefile. Default Motif implementation is x11-toolkits/open-motif. Users can choose x11-toolkits/lesstif instead by setting WANT_LESSTIF in their make.conf .

MOTIFLIB will be set by motif.mk to reference the appropriate Motif library. Please patch the source of the port to use ${MOTIFLIB} wherever the Motif library is referenced in the original Makefile or Imakefile.

There are two common cases:

• If the port refers to the Motif library as -lXm in its Makefile or Imakefile, substitute ${MOTIFLIB} for it.

- If the port uses XmClientLibs in its Imakefile, change it to ${MOTIFLIB} ${XTOOLLIB} ${XLIB} .

Note that MOTIFLIB (usually) expands to -L/usr/local/lib -lXm -lXp or /usr/local/lib/libXm.a , so there is no need to add -L or -l in front.

6.9.3. X11 Fonts

If the port installs fonts for the X Window System, put them in LOCALBASE/lib/X11/fonts/local .

6.9.4. Getting a Fake DISPLAY with Xvfb

Some applications require a working X11 display for compilation to succeed. This pose a problem for machines that operate headless. When this variable is used, the build infrastructure will start the virtual framebuffer X server. The working DISPLAY is then passed to the build. See USES=display for the possible arguments.

```
USES= display
```

6.9.5. Desktop Entries

Desktop entries (a Freedesktop standard) provide a way to automatically adjust desktop features when a new program is installed, without requiring user intervention. For example, newly-installed programs automatically appear in the application menus of compatible desktop environments. Desktop entries originated in the GNOME desktop environment, but are now a standard and also work with KDE and Xfce. This bit of automation provides a real benefit to the user, and desktop entries are encouraged for applications which can be used in a desktop environment.

6.9.5.1. Using Predefined .desktop Files

Ports that include predefined *.desktop must include those files in pkg-plist and install them in the $LOCALBASE/share/applications directory. The INSTALL_DATA macro is useful for installing these files.

6.9.5.2. Updating Desktop Database

If a port has a MimeType entry in its *portname*.desktop, the desktop database must be updated after install and deinstall. To do this, define USES= desktop-file-utils.

6.9.5.3. Creating Desktop Entries with DESKTOP_ENTRIES

Desktop entries can be easily created for applications by using DESKTOP_ENTRIES. A file named *name*.desktop will be created, installed, and added to pkg-plist automatically. Syntax is:

```
DESKTOP_ENTRIES= "NAME" "COMMENT" "ICON" "COMMAND" "CATEGORY" StartupNotify
```

The list of possible categories is available on the Freedesktop website. StartupNotify indicates whether the application is compatible with *startup notifications*. These are typically a graphic indicator like a clock that appear at the mouse pointer, menu, or panel to give the user an indication when a program is starting. A program that is compatible with startup notifications clears the indicator after it has started. Programs that are not compatible with startup notifications would never clear the indicator (potentially confusing and infuriating the user), and must have StartupNotify set to false so the indicator is not shown at all.

Example:

```
DESKTOP_ENTRIES= "ToME" "Roguelike game based on JRR Tolkien's work" \
    "${DATADIR}/xtra/graf/tome-128.png" \
    "tome -v -g" "Application;Game;RolePlaying;" \
    false
```

6.10. Using GNOME

6.10.1. Introduction

This chapter explains the GNOME framework as used by ports. The framework can be loosely divided into the base components, GNOME desktop components, and a few special macros that simplify the work of port maintainers.

While developing a port or changing one, please set

```
DEVELOPER=yes
```

in the environment or in /etc/make.conf . This causes the ports framework to enable additional checks.

6.10.2. Using USE_GNOME

Adding this variable to the port allows the use of the macros and components defined in bsd.gnome.mk. The code in bsd.gnome.mk adds the needed build-time, run-time or library dependencies or the handling of special files. GNOME applications under FreeBSD use the USE_GNOME infrastructure. Include all the needed components as a space-separated list. The USE_GNOME components are divided into these virtual lists: basic components, GNOME 3 components and legacy components. If the port needs only GTK3 libraries, this is the shortest way to define it:

```
USE_GNOME= gtk30
```

USE_GNOME components automatically add the dependencies they need. Please see Section 6.11, "GNOME Components" for an exhaustive list of all USE_GNOME components and which other components they imply and their dependencies.

Here is an example Makefile for a GNOME port that uses many of the techniques outlined in this document. Please use it as a guide for creating new ports.

```
# $FreeBSD$

PORTNAME= regexxer
PORTVERSION= 0.10
CATEGORIES= devel textproc gnome
MASTER_SITES= GNOME

MAINTAINER= kwm@FreeBSD.org
COMMENT= Interactive tool for performing search and replace operations

USES=   gettext gmake pathfix pkgconfig tar:xz
GNU_CONFIGURE= yes
USE_GNOME= gnomeprefix intlhack gtksourceviewmm3
CPPFLAGS+=  -I${LOCALBASE}/include
LDFLAGS+=  -L${LOCALBASE}/lib
INSTALLS_ICONS= yes

GLIB_SCHEMAS=  org.regexxer.gschema.xml

.include <bsd.port.mk>
```

Note

The USE_GNOME macro without any arguments does not add any dependencies to the port. USE_GNOME cannot be set after bsd.port.pre.mk.

6.10.3. Variables

This section explains which macros are available and how they are used. Like they are used in the above example. The Section 6.11, "GNOME Components" has a more in-depth explanation. USE_GNOME has to be set for these macros to be of use.

INSTALLS_ICONS

    GTK+ ports which install Freedesktop-style icons to `${LOCALBASE}/share/icons` should use this macro to ensure that the icons are cached and will display correctly. The cache file is named `icon-theme.cache` . Do not include that file in `pkg-plist` . This macro handles that automatically. This macro is not needed for Qt, which use a internal method.

GLIB_SCHEMAS

    List of all the glib schema files the port installs. The macro will add the files to the port plist and handle the registration of these files on install and deinstall.

    The glib schema files are written in XML and end with the `gschema.xml` extension. They are installed in the `share/glib-2.0/schemas/` directory. These schema files contain all application config values with there default settings. The actual database used by the applications is built by glib-compile-schema, which is run by the GLIB_SCHEMAS macro.

```
GLIB_SCHEMAS=foo.gschema.xml
```

> ### Note
>
> Do not add glib schemas to the `pkg-plist` . If they are listed in `pkg-plist` , they will not be registered and the applications might not work properly.

GCONF_SCHEMAS

    List all the gconf schema files. The macro will add the schema files to the port plist and will handle their registration on install and deinstall.

    GConf is the XML-based database that virtually all GNOME applications use for storing their settings. These files are installed into the `etc/gconf/schemas` directory. This database is defined by installed schema files that are used to generate `%gconf.xml` key files. For each schema file installed by the port, there be an entry in the `Makefile`:

```
GCONF_SCHEMAS=my_app.schemas my_app2.schemas my_app3.schemas
```

> ### Note
>
> Gconf schemas are listed in the GCONF_SCHEMAS macro rather than `pkg-plist` . If they are listed in `pkg-plist` , they will not be registered and the applications might not work properly.

INSTALLS_OMF

    Open Source Metadata Framework (OMF) files are commonly used by GNOME 2 applications. These files contain the application help file information, and require special processing by ScrollKeeper/rarian. To properly register OMF files when installing GNOME applications from packages, make sure that `omf` files are listed in `pkg-plist` and that the port `Makefile` has INSTALLS_OMF defined:

```
INSTALLS_OMF=yes
```

When set, `bsd.gnome.mk` automatically scans `pkg-plist` and adds appropriate `@exec` and `@unexec` directives for each `.omf` to track in the OMF registration database.

6.11. GNOME Components

For further help with a GNOME port, look at some of the existing ports for examples. The FreeBSD GNOME page has contact information if more help is needed. The components are divided into GNOME components that are currently in use and legacy components. If the component supports argument, they are listed between parenthesis in the description. The first is the default. "Both" is shown if the component defaults to adding to both build and run dependencies.

Table 6.7. GNOME Components

Component	Associated program	Description
atk	accessibility/atk	Accessibility toolkit (ATK)
atkmm	accessibility/atkmm	c++ bindings for atk
cairo	graphics/cairo	Vector graphics library with cross-device output support
cairomm	graphics/cairomm	c++ bindings for cairo
dconf	devel/dconf	Configuration database system (both, build, run)
evolutiondataserver3	databases/evolution-data-server	Data backends for the Evolution integrated mail/PIM suite
gdkpixbuf2	graphics/gdk-pixbuf2	Graphics library for GTK+
glib20	devel/glib20	GNOME core library glib20
glibmm	devel/glibmm	c++ bindings for glib20
gnomecontrolcenter3	sysutils/gnome-control-center	GNOME 3 Control Center
gnomedesktop3	x11/gnome-desktop	GNOME 3 desktop UI library
gsound	audio/gsound	GObject library for playing system sounds (both, build, run)
gtk-update-icon-cache	graphics/gtk-update-icon-cache	Gtk-update-icon-cache utility from the Gtk+ toolkit
gtk20	x11-toolkits/gtk20	Gtk+ 2 toolkit
gtk30	x11-toolkits/gtk30	Gtk+ 3 toolkit
gtkmm20	x11-toolkits/gtkmm20	c++ bindings 2.0 for the gtk20 toolkit
gtkmm24	x11-toolkits/gtkmm24	c++ bindings 2.4 for the gtk20 toolkit
gtkmm30	x11-toolkits/gtkmm30	c++ bindings 3.0 for the gtk30 toolkit
gtksourceview2	x11-toolkits/gtksourceview2	Widget that adds syntax highlighting to GtkTextView
gtksourceview3	x11-toolkits/gtksourceview3	Text widget that adds syntax highlighting to the GtkTextView widget
gtksourceviewmm3	x11-toolkits/gtksourceviewmm3	c++ bindings for the gtksourceview3 library
gvfs	devel/gvfs	GNOME virtual file system
intltool	textproc/intltool	Tool for internationalization (also see intlhack)

Component	Associated program	Description
introspection	devel/gobject-introspection	Basic introspection bindings and tools to generate introspection bindings. Most of the time :build is enough, :both/:run is only need for applications that use introspection bindings. (both, build, run)
libgda5	databases/libgda5	Provides uniform access to different kinds of data sources
libgda5-ui	databases/libgda5-ui	UI library from the libgda5 library
libgdamm5	databases/libgdamm5	c++ bindings for the libgda5 library
libgsf	devel/libgsf	Extensible I/O abstraction for dealing with structured file formats
librsvg2	graphics/librsvg2	Library for parsing and rendering SVG vector-graphic files
libsigc++20	devel/libsigc++20	Callback Framework for C++
libxml++26	textproc/libxml++26	c++ bindings for the libxml2 library
libxml2	textproc/libxml2	XML parser library (both, build, run)
libxslt	textproc/libxslt	XSLT C library (both, build, run)
metacity	x11-wm/metacity	Window manager from GNOME
nautilus3	x11-fm/nautilus	GNOME file manager
pango	x11-toolkits/pango	Open-source framework for the layout and rendering of i18n text
pangomm	x11-toolkits/pangomm	c++ bindings for the pango library
py3gobject3	devel/py3-gobject3	Python 3, GObject 3.0 bindings
pygobject3	devel/py-gobject3	Python 2, GObject 3.0 bindings
vte3	x11-toolkits/vte3	Terminal widget with improved accessibility and I18N support

Table 6.8. GNOME Macro Components

Component	Description
gnomeprefix	Supply configure with some default locations.
intlhack	Same as intltool, but patches to make sure share/locale/ is used. Please only use when intltool alone is not enough.
referencehack	This macro is there to help splitting of the API or reference documentation into its own port.

Table 6.9. GNOME Legacy Components

Component	Associated program	Description
atspi	accessibility/at-spi	Assistive Technology Service Provider Interface
esound	audio/esound	Enlightenment sound package
gal2	x11-toolkits/gal2	Collection of widgets taken from GNOME 2 gnumeric

Component	Associated program	Description
gconf2	devel/gconf2	Configuration database system for GNOME 2
gconfmm26	devel/gconfmm26	c++ bindings for gconf2
gdkpixbuf	graphics/gdk-pixbuf	Graphics library for GTK+
glib12	devel/glib12	glib 1.2 core library
gnomedocutils	textproc/gnome-doc-utils	GNOME doc utils
gnomemimedata	misc/gnome-mime-data	MIME and Application database for GNOME 2
gnomesharp20	x11-toolkits/gnome-sharp20	GNOME 2 interfaces for the .NET runtime
gnomespeech	accessibility/gnome-speech	GNOME 2 text-to-speech API
gnomevfs2	devel/gnome-vfs	GNOME 2 Virtual File System
gtk12	x11-toolkits/gtk12	Gtk+ 1.2 toolkit
gtkhtml3	www/gtkhtml3	Lightweight HTML rendering/printing/editing engine
gtkhtml4	www/gtkhtml4	Lightweight HTML rendering/printing/editing engine
gtksharp20	x11-toolkits/gtk-sharp20	GTK+ and GNOME 2 interfaces for the .NET runtime
gtksourceview	x11-toolkits/gtksourceview	Widget that adds syntax highlighting to GtkTextView
libartgpl2	graphics/libart_lgpl	Library for high-performance 2D graphics
libbonobo	devel/libbonobo	Component and compound document system for GNOME 2
libbonoboui	x11-toolkits/libbonoboui	GUI frontend to the libbonobo component of GNOME 2
libgda4	databases/libgda4	Provides uniform access to different kinds of data sources
libglade2	devel/libglade2	GNOME 2 glade library
libgnome	x11/libgnome	Libraries for GNOME 2, a GNU desktop environment
libgnomecanvas	graphics/libgnomecanvas	Graphics library for GNOME 2
libgnomekbd	x11/libgnomekbd	GNOME 2 keyboard shared library
libgnomeprint	print/libgnomeprint	Gnome 2 print support library
libgnomeprintui	x11-toolkits/libgnomeprintui	Gnome 2 print support library
libgnomeui	x11-toolkits/libgnomeui	Libraries for the GNOME 2 GUI, a GNU desktop environment
libgtkhtml	www/libgtkhtml	Lightweight HTML rendering/printing/editing engine
libgtksourceviewmm	x11-toolkits/libgtksourceviewmm	c++ binding of GtkSourceView
libidl	devel/libIDL	Library for creating trees of CORBA IDL file

Component	Associated program	Description
libsigc++12	devel/libsigc++12	Callback Framework for C++
libwnck	x11-toolkits/libwnck	Library used for writing pagers and taskslists
libwnck3	x11-toolkits/libwnck3	Library used for writing pagers and taskslists
orbit2	devel/ORBit2	High-performance CORBA ORB with support for the C language
pygnome2	x11-toolkits/py-gnome2	Python bindings for GNOME 2
pygobject	devel/py-gobject	Python 2, GObject 2.0 bindings
pygtk2	x11-toolkits/py-gtk2	Set of Python bindings for GTK+
pygtksourceview	x11-toolkits/py-gtksourceview	Python bindings for GtkSourceView 2
vte	x11-toolkits/vte	Terminal widget with improved accessibility and I18N support

Table 6.10. Deprecated Components: Do Not Use

Component	Description
HAVE_GNOME	Deprecated, do not use. Was used to check if a component was installed. This was used for ports that did not have --enable/--disable switches for their configure script. But the building of parts of a port without a implicit request is discouraged.
WANT_GNOME	Deprecated, do not use. Was used by ports that needed USE_GNOME for optional dependencies, which where defined after bsd.port.pre.mk. Since USE_GNOME can be used after the inclusion of bsd.port.options.mk, there is little need for this macro any more.
pangox-compat	pangox-compat has been deprecated and split off from the pango package.

6.12. Using Qt

6.12.1. Ports That Require Qt

The Ports Collection provides support for Qt 4 and Qt 5 frameworks with USE_QTx, where x is 4 or 5. Set USE_QTx to the list of required Qt components (libraries, tools, plugins). The Qt 4 and Qt 5 frameworks are quite similar. The main difference is the set of supported components.

The Qt framework exports a number of variables which can be used by ports, some of them listed below:

Table 6.11. Variables Provided to Ports That Use Qt

QT_PREFIX	Set to the path where Qt was installed (${LOCALBASE}).
QMAKE	Full path to qmake binary.
LRELEASE	Full path to lrelease utility.
MOC	Full path to moc.
RCC	Full path to rcc.

UIC	Full path to uic.
QT_INCDIR	Qt include directory.
QT_LIBDIR	Qt libraries path.
QT_PLUGINDIR	Qt plugins path.

When using the Qt framework, these settings are deployed:

```
CONFIGURE_ARGS+= --with-qt-includes=${QT_INCDIR} \
    --with-qt-libraries=${QT_LIBDIR} \
    --with-extra-libs=${LOCALBASE}/lib \
    --with-extra-includes=${LOCALBASE}/include

CONFIGURE_ENV+= QTDIR="${QT_PREFIX}" QMAKE="${QMAKE}" \
  MOC="${MOC}" RCC="${RCC}" UIC="${UIC}" \
  QMAKESPEC="${QMAKESPEC}"

PLIST_SUB+= QT_INCDIR=${QT_INCDIR_REL} \
  QT_LIBDIR=${QT_LIBDIR_REL} \
  QT_PLUGINDIR=${QT_PLUGINDIR_REL}
```

Some configure scripts do not support the arguments above. To suppress modification of CONFIGURE_ENV and CON-FIGURE_ARGS, set QT_NONSTANDARD.

6.12.2. Component Selection

Individual Qt tool and library dependencies must be specified in USE_QT*x*. Every component can be suffixed with _build or _run, the suffix indicating whether the dependency on the component is at buildtime or runtime. If unsuffixed, the component will be depended on at both build- and runtime. Usually, library components are specified unsuffixed, tool components are mostly specified with the _build suffix and plugin components are specified with the _run suffix. The most commonly used components are listed below (all available components are listed in _USE_QT_ALL , _USE_QT4_ONLY, and _USE_QT5_ONLY in /usr/ports/Mk/bsd.qt.mk):

Table 6.12. Available Qt Library Components

Name	Description
core	core library (Qt 5 only)
corelib	core library (Qt 4 only)
dbus	Qt DBus library
gui	graphical user interface library
network	network library
opengl	Qt OpenGL library
script	script library
sql	SQL library
testlib	unit testing library
webkit	Qt WebKit library
xml	Qt XML library

To determine the libraries an application depends on, run ldd on the main executable after a successful compilation.

Table 6.13. Available Qt Tool Components

Name	Description
qmake	Makefile generator/build utility

Name	Description
buildtools	build tools (moc, rcc), needed for almost every Qt application (Qt 5 only)
linguisttools	localization tools: lrelease, lupdate (Qt 5 only)
linguist	localization tools: lrelease, lupdate (Qt 4 only)
moc	meta object compiler, needed for almost every Qt application at buildtime (Qt 4 only)
rcc	resource compiler, needed if the application comes with *.rc or *.qrc files (Qt 4 only)
uic	user interface compiler, needed if the application comes with *.ui files, in practice, every Qt application with a GUI (Qt 4 only)

Table 6.14. Available Qt Plugin Components

Name	Description
iconengines	SVG icon engine plugin, needed if the application ships SVG icons (Qt 4 only)
imageformats	plugins for TGA, TIFF, and MNG image formats

Example 6.5. Selecting Qt 4 Components

In this example, the ported application uses the Qt 4 graphical user interface library, the Qt 4 core library, all of the Qt 4 code generation tools and Qt 4's Makefile generator. Since the gui library implies a dependency on the core library, corelib does not need to be specified. The Qt 4 code generation tools moc, uic and rcc, as well as the Makefile generator qmake are only needed at buildtime, thus they are specified with the _build suffix:

```
USE_QT4= gui moc_build qmake_build rcc_build uic_build
```

6.12.3. Using qmake

If the application provides a qmake project file (*.pro), define USES= qmake along with USE_QT x. Note that USES= qmake already implies a build dependency on qmake, therefore the qmake component can be omitted from USE_QT x. Similar to CMake, qmake supports out-of-source builds, which can be enabled by specifying the outsource argument (see USES= qmake example).

Table 6.15. Variables for Ports That Use qmake

Variable	Means
QMAKE_ARGS	Port specific qmake flags to be passed to the qmake binary.
QMAKE_ENV	Environment variables to be set for the qmake binary. The default is ${CONFIGURE_ENV}.
QMAKE_SOURCE_PATH	Path to qmake project files (.pro). The default is ${WRKSRC} if an out-of-source build is requested, empty otherwise.

> ### Example 6.6. USES= qmake Example
>
> This snippet demonstrates the use of qmake for a Qt 4 port:
>
> ```
> USES=   qmake:outsource
> USE_QT4= moc_build
> ```
>
> For a Qt 5 port:
>
> ```
> USES=   qmake:outsource
> USE_QT5= buildtools_build
> ```

Qt applications are often written to be cross-platform and often X11/Unix is not the platform they are developed on, which in turn leads to certain loose ends, like:

* *Missing additional include paths.* Many applications come with system tray icon support, but neglect to look for includes and/or libraries in the X11 directories. To add directories to qmake's include and library search paths via the command line, use:

```
QMAKE_ARGS+= INCLUDEPATH+=${LOCALBASE}/include \
   LIBS+=-L${LOCALBASE}/lib
```

* *Bogus installation paths.* Sometimes data such as icons or .desktop files are by default installed into directories which are not scanned by XDG-compatible applications. editors/texmaker is an example for this - look at patch-texmaker.pro in the files directory of that port for a template on how to remedy this directly in the qmake project file.

6.13. Using KDE

6.13.1. KDE 4 Variable Definitions

If the application depends on KDE 4, set USES+=kde:4 and USE_KDE to the list of required components. _build and _run suffixes can be used to force components dependency type (for example, baseapps_run). If no suffix is set, a default dependency type will be used. To force both types, add the component twice with both suffixes (for example, automoc4_build automoc4_run). The most commonly used components are listed below (up-to-date components are documented at the top of /usr/ports/Mk/bsd.kde4.mk):

Table 6.16. Available KDE 4 Components

Name	Description
kdehier	Hierarchy of common KDE directories
kdelibs	KDE core libraries
kdeprefix	If set, port will be installed into ${KDE_PREFIX}
automoc4	Build tool to automatically generate moc files
akonadi	Storage server for KDE PIM data
soprano	Library for Resource Description Framework (RDF)
strigi	Strigi desktop search library
libkcddb	KDE CDDB (compact disc database) library
libkcompactdisc	KDE library for interfacing with audio CDs
libkdeedu	Libraries used by educational applications

Name	Description
libkdcraw	KDE LibRaw library
libkexiv2	KDE Exiv2 library
libkipi	KDE Image Plugin Interface
libkonq	Konqueror core library
libksane	KDE SANE ("Scanner Access Now Easy") library
pimlibs	Personal information management libraries
kate	Advanced text editor framework
marble	Virtual globe and world atlas
okular	Universal document viewer
korundum	KDE Ruby bindings
perlkde	KDE Perl bindings
pykde4	KDE Python bindings
pykdeuic4	PyKDE user interface compiler
smokekde	KDE SMOKE libraries

KDE 4 ports are installed into KDE_PREFIX. This is achieved by specifying the kdeprefix component, which over-rides the default PREFIX. The ports, however, respect any PREFIX set via the MAKEFLAGS environment variable and/or make arguments. Currently KDE_PREFIX is identical to the default PREFIX, ${LOCALBASE}.

Example 6.7. USE_KDE Example

This is a simple example for a KDE 4 port. USES= cmake:outsource instructs the port to utilize CMake, a configuration tool widely used by KDE 4 projects (see Section 6.5.4, "Using cmake" for detailed usage). USE_KDE brings dependency on KDE libraries and makes port using automoc4 at build stage. Required KDE components and other dependencies can be determined through configure log. USE_KDE does not imply USE_QT4. If a port requires some Qt 4 components, specify them in USE_QT4.

```
USES= cmake:outsource kde:4
USE_KDE= kdelibs kdeprefix automoc4
USE_QT4= moc_build qmake_build rcc_build uic_build
```

6.14. Using Java

6.14.1. Variable Definitions

If the port needs a Java™ Development Kit (JDK™) to either build, run or even extract the distfile, then define USE_JAVA.

There are several JDKs in the ports collection, from various vendors, and in several versions. If the port must use a particular version, specify it using the JAVA_VERSION variable. The most current version is java/openjdk8, with java/openjdk6 and java/openjdk7 also available.

Table 6.17. Variables Which May be Set by Ports That Use Java

Variable	Means
USE_JAVA	Define for the remaining variables to have any effect.

Variable	Means
JAVA_VERSION	List of space-separated suitable Java versions for the port. An optional "+" allows specifying a range of versions (allowed values: 1.5[+] 1.6[+] 1.7[+]).
JAVA_OS	List of space-separated suitable JDK port operating systems for the port (allowed values: native linux).
JAVA_VENDOR	List of space-separated suitable JDK port vendors for the port (allowed values: freebsd bsdjava sun openjdk).
JAVA_BUILD	When set, add the selected JDK port to the build dependencies.
JAVA_RUN	When set, add the selected JDK port to the run dependencies.
JAVA_EXTRACT	When set, add the selected JDK port to the extract dependencies.

Below is the list of all settings a port will receive after setting USE_JAVA:

Table 6.18. Variables Provided to Ports That Use Java

Variable	Value
JAVA_PORT	The name of the JDK port (for example, java/openjdk6).
JAVA_PORT_VERSION	The full version of the JDK port (for example, 1.6.0). Only the first two digits of this version number are needed, use ${JAVA_PORT_VERSION:C/^([0-9])\.([0-9])(.*)$/\1.\2/} .
JAVA_PORT_OS	The operating system used by the JDK port (for example, 'native').
JAVA_PORT_VENDOR	The vendor of the JDK port (for example, 'openjdk').
JAVA_PORT_OS_DESCRIPTION	Description of the operating system used by the JDK port (for example, 'Native').
JAVA_PORT_VENDOR_DESCRIPTION	Description of the vendor of the JDK port (for example, 'OpenJDK BSD Porting Team').
JAVA_HOME	Path to the installation directory of the JDK (for example, '/usr/local/openjdk6').
JAVAC	Path to the Java compiler to use (for example, '/usr/local/openjdk6/bin/javac').
JAR	Path to the jar tool to use (for example, '/usr/local/openjdk6/bin/jar' or '/usr/local/bin/fastjar').
APPLETVIEWER	Path to the appletviewer utility (for example, '/usr/local/openjdk6/bin/appletviewer').
JAVA	Path to the java executable. Use this for executing Java programs (for example, '/usr/local/openjdk6/bin/java').
JAVADOC	Path to the javadoc utility program.
JAVAH	Path to the javah program.
JAVAP	Path to the javap program.
JAVA_KEYTOOL	Path to the keytool utility program.

Variable	Value
JAVA_N2A	Path to the native2ascii tool.
JAVA_POLICYTOOL	Path to the policytool program.
JAVA_SERIALVER	Path to the serialver utility program.
RMIC	Path to the RMI stub/skeleton generator, rmic.
RMIREGISTRY	Path to the RMI registry program, rmiregistry.
RMID	Path to the RMI daemon program rmid.
JAVA_CLASSES	Path to the archive that contains the JDK class files, ${JAVA_HOME}/jre/lib/rt.jar .

Use the java-debug make target to get information for debugging the port. It will display the value of many of the previously listed variables.

Additionally, these constants are defined so all Java ports may be installed in a consistent way:

Table 6.19. Constants Defined for Ports That Use Java

Constant	Value
JAVASHAREDIR	The base directory for everything related to Java. Default: ${PREFIX}/share/java .
JAVAJARDIR	The directory where JAR files is installed. Default: ${JAVASHAREDIR}/classes .
JAVALIBDIR	The directory where JAR files installed by other ports are located. Default: ${LOCALBASE}/share/java/classes .

The related entries are defined in both PLIST_SUB (documented in Section 7.1, "Changing pkg-plist Based on Make Variables") and SUB_LIST .

6.14.2. Building with Ant

When the port is to be built using Apache Ant, it has to define USE_ANT . Ant is thus considered to be the sub-make command. When no do-build target is defined by the port, a default one will be set that runs Ant according to MAKE_ENV , MAKE_ARGS and ALL_TARGET. This is similar to the USES= gmake mechanism, which is documented in Section 6.5, "Building Mechanisms".

6.14.3. Best Practices

When porting a Java library, the port has to install the JAR file(s) in ${JAVAJARDIR}, and everything else under ${JAVASHAREDIR}/${PORTNAME}   (except for the documentation, see below). To reduce the packing file size, reference the JAR file(s) directly in the Makefile. Use this statement (where *myport*.jar is the name of the JAR file installed as part of the port):

```
PLIST_FILES+= ${JAVAJARDIR}/myport.jar
```

When porting a Java application, the port usually installs everything under a single directory (including its JAR dependencies). The use of ${JAVASHAREDIR}/${PORTNAME}   is strongly encouraged in this regard. It is up the porter to decide whether the port installs the additional JAR dependencies under this directory or uses the already installed ones (from ${JAVAJARDIR}).

When porting a Java™ application that requires an application server such as www/tomcat7 to run the service, it is quite common for a vendor to distribute a .war. A .war is a Web application ARchive and is extracted when called by the application. Avoid adding a .war to pkg-plist . It is not considered best practice. An application server will expand war archive, but not clean it up properly if the port is removed. A more desirable way of working with this file is to extract the archive, then install the files, and lastly add these files to pkg-plist .

```
TOMCATDIR= ${LOCALBASE}/apache-tomcat-7.0
WEBAPPDIR= myapplication

post-extract:
 @${MKDIR} ${WRKDIR}/${PORTDIRNAME}
 @${TAR} xf ${WRKDIR}/myapplication.war -C ${WRKDIR}/${PORTDIRNAME}

do-install:
 cd ${WRKDIR} && \
 ${INSTALL} -d -o ${WWWOWN} -g ${WWWGRP} ${TOMCATDIR}/webapps/${PORTDIRNAME}
 cd ${WRKDIR}/${PORTDIRNAME} && ${COPYTREE_SHARE} \* ${WEBAPPDIR}/${PORTDIRNAME}
```

Regardless of the type of port (library or application), the additional documentation is installed in the same location as for any other port. The JavaDoc tool is known to produce a different set of files depending on the version of the JDK that is used. For ports that do not enforce the use of a particular JDK, it is therefore a complex task to specify the packing list (pkg-plist). This is one reason why porters are strongly encouraged to use PORTDOCS. Moreover, even if the set of files that will be generated by javadoc can be predicted, the size of the resulting pkg-plist advocates for the use of PORTDOCS.

The default value for DATADIR is ${PREFIX}/share/${PORTNAME}. It is a good idea to override DATADIR to ${JAVASHAREDIR}/${PORTNAME} for Java ports. Indeed, DATADIR is automatically added to PLIST_SUB (documented in Section 7.1, "Changing pkg-plist Based on Make Variables") so use %%DATADIR%% directly in pkg-plist.

As for the choice of building Java ports from source or directly installing them from a binary distribution, there is no defined policy at the time of writing. However, people from the FreeBSD Java Project encourage porters to have their ports built from source whenever it is a trivial task.

All the features that have been presented in this section are implemented in bsd.java.mk. If the port needs more sophisticated Java support, please first have a look at the bsd.java.mk Subversion log as it usually takes some time to document the latest features. Then, if the needed support that is lacking would be beneficial to many other Java ports, feel free to discuss it on the FreeBSD Java Language mailing list.

Although there is a java category for PRs, it refers to the JDK porting effort from the FreeBSD Java project. Therefore, submit the Java port in the ports category as for any other port, unless the issue is related to either a JDK implementation or bsd.java.mk.

Similarly, there is a defined policy regarding the CATEGORIES of a Java port, which is detailed in Section 5.3, "Categorization".

6.15. Web Applications, Apache and PHP

6.15.1. Apache

Table 6.20. Variables for Ports That Use Apache

USE_APACHE	The port requires Apache. Possible values: yes (gets any version), 22, 24, 22-24, 22+, etc. The default APACHE version is 22. More details are available in ports/Mk/bsd.apache.mk and at wiki.freebsd.org/Apache/.
APXS	Full path to the apxs binary. Can be overridden in the port.
HTTPD	Full path to the httpd binary. Can be overridden in the port.
APACHE_VERSION	The version of present Apache installation (read-only variable). This variable is only available after inclusion of bsd.port.pre.mk. Possible values: 22, 24.

APACHEMODDIR	Directory for Apache modules. This variable is automatically expanded in `pkg-plist`.
APACHEINCLUDEDIR	Directory for Apache headers. This variable is automatically expanded in `pkg-plist`.
APACHEETCDIR	Directory for Apache configuration files. This variable is automatically expanded in `pkg-plist`.

Table 6.21. Useful Variables for Porting Apache Modules

MODULENAME	Name of the module. Default value is `PORTNAME`. Example: `mod_hello`
SHORTMODNAME	Short name of the module. Automatically derived from `MODULENAME`, but can be overridden. Example: `hello`
AP_FAST_BUILD	Use `apxs` to compile and install the module.
AP_GENPLIST	Also automatically creates a `pkg-plist`.
AP_INC	Adds a directory to a header search path during compilation.
AP_LIB	Adds a directory to a library search path during compilation.
AP_EXTRAS	Additional flags to pass to `apxs`.

6.15.2. Web Applications

Web applications must be installed into PREFIX/www/ *appname*. This path is available both in `Makefile` and in `pkg-plist` as `WWWDIR`, and the path relative to `PREFIX` is available in `Makefile` as `WWWDIR_REL`.

The user and group of web server process are available as `WWWOWN` and `WWWGRP`, in case the ownership of some files needs to be changed. The default values of both are `www`. Use `WWWOWN?= myuser` and `WWWGRP?= mygroup` if the port needs different values. This allows the user to override them easily.

Important

Use `WWWOWN` and `WWWGRP` sparingly. Remember that every file the web server can write to is a security risk waiting to happen.

Do not depend on Apache unless the web app explicitly needs Apache. Respect that users may wish to run a web application on a web server other than Apache.

6.15.3. PHP

PHP web applications declare their dependency on it with `USES=php`. See Section 15.63, "php" for more information.

6.15.4. PEAR Modules

Porting PEAR modules is a very simple process.

Add `USES=pear` to the port's `Makefile`. The framework will install the relevant files in the right places and automatically generate the plist at install time.

Example 6.8. Example Makefile for PEAR Class

```
PORTNAME=       Date
PORTVERSION= 1.4.3
CATEGORIES= devel www pear

MAINTAINER= example@domain.com
COMMENT= PEAR Date and Time Zone Classes

USES= pear

.include <bsd.port.mk>
```

6.15.4.1. Horde Modules

In the same way, porting Horde modules is a simple process.

Add USES=horde to the port's Makefile. The framework will install the relevant files in the right places and automatically generate the plist at install time.

The USE_HORDE_BUILD and USE_HORDE_RUN variables can be used to add buildtime and runtime dependencies on other Horde modules. See Mk/Uses/horde.mk for a complete list of available modules.

Example 6.9. Example Makefile for Horde Module

```
PORTNAME= Horde_Core
PORTVERSION= 2.14.0
CATEGORIES= devel www pear

MAINTAINER= horde@FreeBSD.org
COMMENT= Horde Core Framework libraries

OPTIONS_DEFINE= KOLAB SOCKETS
KOLAB_DESC= Enable Kolab server support
SOCKETS_DESC= Depend on sockets PHP extension

USES= horde
USE_PHP= session

USE_HORDE_BUILD= Horde_Role
USE_HORDE_RUN= Horde_Role Horde_History Horde_Pack \
  Horde_Text_Filter Horde_View

KOLAB_USE= HORDE_RUN=Horde_Kolab_Server,Horde_Kolab_Session
SOCKETS_USE= PHP=sockets

.include <bsd.port.mk>
```

6.16. Using Python

The Ports Collection supports parallel installation of multiple Python versions. Ports must use a correct python interpreter, according to the user-settable PYTHON_VERSION . Most prominently, this means replacing the path to python executable in scripts with the value of PYTHON_CMD .

Ports that install files under PYTHON_SITELIBDIR must use the pyXY- package name prefix, so their package name embeds the version of Python they are installed into.

```
PKGNAMEPREFIX= ${PYTHON_PKGNAMEPREFIX}
```

Table 6.22. Most Useful Variables for Ports That Use Python

USES=python	The port needs Python. The minimal required version can be specified with values such as 2.7+. Version ranges can also be specified by separating two version numbers with a dash: USES=python:3.2-3.3
USE_PYTHON=distutils	Use Python distutils for configuring, compiling, and installing. This is required when the port comes with setup.py. This overrides the do-build and do-install targets and may also override do-configure if GNU_CONFIGURE is not defined.
USE_PYTHON=autoplist	Create the packaging list automatically. This also requires USE_PYTHON=distutils to be set.
USE_PYTHON=concurrent	The port will use an unique prefix, typically PYTHON_PKGNAMEPREFIX for certain directories, such as EXAMPLESDIR and DOCSDIR and also will append a suffix, the python version from PYTHON_VER, to binaries and scripts to be installed. This allows ports to be installed for different Python versions at the same time, which otherwise would install conflicting files.
PYTHON_PKGNAMEPREFIX	Used as a PKGNAMEPREFIX to distinguish packages for different Python versions. Example: py27-
PYTHON_SITELIBDIR	Location of the site-packages tree, that contains installation path of Python (usually LOCALBASE). PYTHON_SITELIBDIR can be very useful when installing Python modules.
PYTHONPREFIX_SITELIBDIR	The PREFIX-clean variant of PYTHON_SITELIBDIR. Always use %%PYTHON_SITELIBDIR%% in pkg-plist when possible. The default value of %%PYTHON_SITELIBDIR%% is lib/python%%PYTHON_VERSION%%/site-packages
PYTHON_CMD	Python interpreter command line, including version number.
PYNUMERIC	Dependency line for numeric extension.
PYNUMPY	Dependency line for the new numeric extension, numpy. (PYNUMERIC is deprecated by upstream vendor).
PYXML	Dependency line for XML extension (not needed for Python 2.0 and higher as it is also in base distribution).

A complete list of available variables can be found in /usr/ports/Mk/Uses/python.mk .

Example 6.10. Makefile for a Simple Python Module

```
PORTNAME= sample
PORTVERSION= 1.2.3
CATEGORIES= devel

MAINTAINER= john@doe.tld
```

```
COMMENT= Python sample module

USES=   python
USE_PYTHON= autoplist distutils

.include <bsd.port.mk>
```

Some Python applications claim to have DESTDIR support (which would be required for staging) but it is broken (Mailman up to 2.1.16, for instance). This can be worked around by recompiling the scripts. This can be done, for example, in the **post-build** target. Assuming the Python scripts are supposed to reside in PYTHONPREFIX_SITELIB-DIR after installation, this solution can be applied:

```
(cd ${STAGEDIR}${PREFIX} \
  && ${PYTHON_CMD} ${PYTHON_LIBDIR}/compileall.py \
  -d ${PREFIX} -f ${PYTHONPREFIX_SITELIBDIR:S;${PREFIX}/;;})
```

This recompiles the sources with a path relative to the stage directory, and prepends the value of PREFIX to the file name recorded in the byte-compiled output file by -d. -f is required to force recompilation, and the :S;${PRE-FIX}/;; strips prefixes from the value of PYTHONPREFIX_SITELIBDIR to make it relative to PREFIX.

6.17. Using Tcl/Tk

The Ports Collection supports parallel installation of multiple Tcl/Tk versions. Ports should try to support at least the default Tcl/Tk version and higher with USES=tcl. It is possible to specify the desired version of tcl by appending :*xx*, for example, USES=tcl:85.

Table 6.23. The Most Useful Read-Only Variables for Ports That Use Tcl/Tk

TCL_VER	chosen major.minor version of Tcl
TCLSH	full path of the Tcl interpreter
TCL_LIBDIR	path of the Tcl libraries
TCL_INCLUDEDIR	path of the Tcl C header files
TK_VER	chosen major.minor version of Tk
WISH	full path of the Tk interpreter
TK_LIBDIR	path of the Tk libraries
TK_INCLUDEDIR	path of the Tk C header files

See the USES=tcl and USES=tk of Chapter 15, *Using USES Macros* for a full description of those variables. A complete list of those variables is available in /usr/ports/Mk/Uses/tcl.mk .

6.18. Using Emacs

This section is yet to be written.

6.19. Using Ruby

Table 6.24. Useful Variables for Ports That Use Ruby

Variable	Description
USE_RUBY	Adds build and run dependencies on Ruby.
USE_RUBY_EXTCONF	The port uses **extconf.rb** to configure.

Variable	Description
USE_RUBY_SETUP	The port uses setup.rb to configure.
RUBY_SETUP	Override the name of the setup script from setup.rb. Another common value is install.rb.

This table shows the selected variables available to port authors via the ports infrastructure. These variables are used to install files into their proper locations. Use them in pkg-plist as much as possible. Do not redefine these variables in the port.

Table 6.25. Selected Read-Only Variables for Ports That Use Ruby

Variable	Description	Example value
RUBY_PKGNAMEPREFIX	Used as a PKGNAMEPREFIX to distinguish packages for different Ruby versions.	ruby19-
RUBY_VERSION	Full version of Ruby in the form of x.y.z[.p].	1.9.3.484
RUBY_SITELIBDIR	Architecture independent libraries installation path.	/usr/local/lib/ruby/site_ruby/1.9
RUBY_SITEARCHLIBDIR	Architecture dependent libraries installation path.	/usr/local/lib/ruby/site_ruby/1.9/amd64-freebsd10
RUBY_MODDOCDIR	Module documentation installation path.	/usr/local/share/doc/ruby19/patsy
RUBY_MODEXAMPLESDIR	Module examples installation path.	/usr/local/share/examples/ruby19/patsy

A complete list of available variables can be found in /usr/ports/Mk/bsd.ruby.mk .

6.20. Using SDL

USE_SDL is used to autoconfigure the dependencies for ports which use an SDL based library like devel/sdl12 and graphics/sdl_image.

These SDL libraries for version 1.2 are recognized:

- sdl: devel/sdl12

- console: devel/sdl_console

- gfx: graphics/sdl_gfx

- image: graphics/sdl_image

- mixer: audio/sdl_mixer

- mm: devel/sdlmm

- net: net/sdl_net

- pango: x11-toolkits/sdl_pango

- sound: audio/sdl_sound

- **ttf:** graphics/sdl_ttf

These SDL libraries for version 2.0 are recognized:

- **sdl:** devel/sdl20

- **gfx:** graphics/sdl2_gfx

- **image:** graphics/sdl2_image

- **mixer:** audio/sdl2_mixer

- **net:** net/sdl2_net

- **ttf:** graphics/sdl2_ttf

Therefore, if a port has a dependency on net/sdl_net and audio/sdl_mixer, the syntax will be:

```
USE_SDL= net mixer
```

The dependency devel/sdl12, which is required by net/sdl_net and audio/sdl_mixer, is automatically added as well.

Using `USE_SDL` with entries for SDL 1.2, it will automatically:

- Add a dependency on sdl12-config to `BUILD_DEPENDS`

- Add the variable `SDL_CONFIG` to `CONFIGURE_ENV`

- Add the dependencies of the selected libraries to `LIB_DEPENDS`

Using `USE_SDL` with entries for SDL 2.0, it will automatically:

- Add a dependency on sdl2-config to `BUILD_DEPENDS`

- Add the variable `SDL2_CONFIG` to `CONFIGURE_ENV`

- Add the dependencies of the selected libraries to `LIB_DEPENDS`

6.21. Using wxWidgets

This section describes the status of the wxWidgets libraries in the ports tree and its integration with the ports system.

6.21.1. Introduction

There are many versions of the wxWidgets libraries which conflict between them (install files under the same name). In the ports tree this problem has been solved by installing each version under a different name using version number suffixes.

The obvious disadvantage of this is that each application has to be modified to find the expected version. Fortunately, most of the applications call the `wx-config` script to determine the necessary compiler and linker flags. The script is named differently for every available version. Majority of applications respect an environment variable, or accept a configure argument, to specify which `wx-config` script to call. Otherwise they have to be patched.

6.21.2. Version Selection

To make the port use a specific version of wxWidgets there are two variables available for defining (if only one is defined the other will be set to a default value):

Table 6.26. Variables to Select wxWidgets Versions

Variable	Description	Default value
USE_WX	List of versions the port can use	All available versions
USE_WX_NOT	List of versions the port cannot use	None

The available wxWidgets versions and the corresponding ports in the tree are:

Table 6.27. Available wxWidgets Versions

Version	Port
2.4	x11-toolkits/wxgtk24
2.6	x11-toolkits/wxgtk26
2.8	x11-toolkits/wxgtk28

Note

The versions starting from 2.5 also come in Unicode version and are installed by a slave port named like the normal one plus a -unicode suffix, but this can be handled with variables (see Section 6.21.4, "Unicode").

The variables in Table 6.26, "Variables to Select wxWidgets Versions" can be set to one or more of these combinations separated by spaces:

Table 6.28. wxWidgets Version Specifications

Description	Example
Single version	2.4
Ascending range	2.4+
Descending range	2.6-
Full range (must be ascending)	2.4-2.6

There are also some variables to select the preferred versions from the available ones. They can be set to a list of versions, the first ones will have higher priority.

Table 6.29. Variables to Select Preferred wxWidgets Versions

Name	Designed for
WANT_WX_VER	the port
WITH_WX_VER	the user

6.21.3. Component Selection

There are other applications that, while not being wxWidgets libraries, are related to them. These applications can be specified in WX_COMPS. These components are available:

Table 6.30. Available wxWidgets Components

Name	Description	Version restriction
wx	main library	none
contrib	contributed libraries	none
python	wxPython (Python bindings)	2.4-2.6

Name	Description	Version restriction
mozilla	wxMozilla	2.4
svg	wxSVG	2.6

The dependency type can be selected for each component by adding a suffix separated by a semicolon. If not present then a default type will be used (see Table 6.32, "Default wxWidgets Dependency Types"). These types are available:

Table 6.31. Available wxWidgets Dependency Types

Name	Description
build	Component is required for building, equivalent to BUILD_DEPENDS
run	Component is required for running, equivalent to RUN_DEPENDS
lib	Component is required for building and running, equivalent to LIB_DEPENDS

The default values for the components are detailed in this table:

Table 6.32. Default wxWidgets Dependency Types

Component	Dependency type
wx	lib
contrib	lib
python	run
mozilla	lib
svg	lib

Example 6.11. Selecting wxWidgets Components

This fragment corresponds to a port which uses wxWidgets version 2.4 and its contributed libraries.

```
USE_WX= 2.4
WX_COMPS= wx contrib
```

6.21.4. Unicode

The wxWidgets library supports Unicode since version 2.5. In the ports tree both versions are available and can be selected with these variables:

Table 6.33. Variables to Select Unicode in wxWidgets Versions

Variable	Description	Designed for
WX_UNICODE	The port works *only* with the Unicode version	the port
WANT_UNICODE	The port works with both versions but prefers the Unicode one	the port
WITH_UNICODE	The port will use the Unicode version	the user

Variable	Description	Designed for
WITHOUT_UNICODE	The port will use the normal version if supported (when WX_UNICODE is not defined)	the user

 Warning

Do not use WX_UNICODE for ports that can use both Unicode and normal versions. If the port needs to use Unicode by default, define WANT_UNICODE instead.

6.21.5. Detecting Installed Versions

To detect an installed version, define WANT_WX. If it is not set to a specific version then the components will have a version suffix. HAVE_WX will be filled after detection.

Example 6.12. Detecting Installed wxWidgets Versions and Components

This fragment can be used in a port that uses wxWidgets if it is installed, or an option is selected.

```
WANT_WX= yes

.include <bsd.port.pre.mk>

.if defined(WITH_WX) || !empty(PORT_OPTIONS:MWX) || !empty(HAVE_WX:Mwx-2.4)
USE_WX=   2.4
CONFIGURE_ARGS+= --enable-wx
.endif
```

This fragment can be used in a port that enables wxPython support if it is installed or if an option is selected, in addition to wxWidgets, both version 2.6.

```
USE_WX=  2.6
WX_COMPS= wx
WANT_WX= 2.6

.include <bsd.port.pre.mk>

.if defined(WITH_WXPYTHON) || !empty(PORT_OPTIONS:MWXPYTHON) || !empty
(HAVE_WX:Mpython)
WX_COMPS+=   python
CONFIGURE_ARGS+= --enable-wxpython
.endif
```

6.21.6. Defined Variables

These variables are available in the port (after defining one from Table 6.26, "Variables to Select wxWidgets Versions").

Table 6.34. Variables Defined for Ports That Use wxWidgets

Name	Description
WX_CONFIG	The path to the wxWidgets wx-config script (with different name)

Name	Description
`WXRC_CMD`	The path to the wxWidgets `wxrc` program (with different name)
`WX_VERSION`	The wxWidgets version that is going to be used (for example, `2.6`)
`WX_UNICODE`	If not defined but Unicode is going to be used then it will be defined

6.21.7. Processing in `bsd.port.pre.mk`

Define `WX_PREMK` to be able to use the variables right after including `bsd.port.pre.mk`.

> **Important**
>
> When defining `WX_PREMK`, then the version, dependencies, components and defined variables will not change if modifying the wxWidgets port variables *after* including `bsd.port.pre.mk`.

Example 6.13. Using wxWidgets Variables in Commands

This fragment illustrates the use of `WX_PREMK` by running the `wx-config` script to obtain the full version string, assign it to a variable and pass it to the program.

```
USE_WX=  2.4
WX_PREMK= yes

.include <bsd.port.pre.mk>

.if exists(${WX_CONFIG})
VER_STR!= ${WX_CONFIG} --release

PLIST_SUB+= VERSION="${VER_STR}"
.endif
```

> **Note**
>
> The wxWidgets variables can be safely used in commands when they are inside targets without the need of `WX_PREMK`.

6.21.8. Additional `configure` Arguments

Some GNU `configure` scripts cannot find wxWidgets with just the `WX_CONFIG` environment variable set, requiring additional arguments. `WX_CONF_ARGS` can be used for provide them.

Table 6.35. Legal Values for `WX_CONF_ARGS`

Possible value	Resulting argument
`absolute`	`--with-wx-config=${WX_CONFIG}`

Possible value	Resulting argument	
`relative`	`--with-wx=${LOCALBASE}` `fig=${WX_CONFIG:T}`	`--with-wx-con-`

6.22. Using Lua

This section describes the status of the Lua libraries in the ports tree and its integration with the ports system.

6.22.1. Introduction

There are many versions of the Lua libraries and corresponding interpreters, which conflict between them (install files under the same name). In the ports tree this problem has been solved by installing each version under a different name using version number suffixes.

The obvious disadvantage of this is that each application has to be modified to find the expected version. But it can be solved by adding some additional flags to the compiler and linker.

6.22.2. Version Selection

A port using Lua only needs to have this line:

```
USES= lua
```

If a specific version of Lua is needed, instructions on how to select it are given in the USES=lua part of Chapter 15, *Using USES Macros*.

6.22.3. Defined Variables

These variables are available in the port.

Table 6.36. Variables Defined for Ports That Use Lua

Name	Description
LUA_VER	The Lua version that is going to be used (for example, 5.1)
LUA_VER_STR	The Lua version without the dots (for example, 51)
LUA_PREFIX	The prefix where Lua (and components) is installed
LUA_SUBDIR	The directory under ${PREFIX}/bin, ${PREFIX}/share and ${PREFIX}/lib where Lua is installed
LUA_INCDIR	The directory where Lua and tolua header files are installed
LUA_LIBDIR	The directory where Lua and tolua libraries are installed
LUA_MODLIBDIR	The directory where Lua module libraries (.so) are installed
LUA_MODSHAREDIR	The directory where Lua modules (.lua) are installed
LUA_PKGNAMEPREFIX	The package name prefix used by Lua modules
LUA_CMD	The path to the Lua interpreter
LUAC_CMD	The path to the Lua compiler

6.23. Using `iconv`

After 2013-10-08 (254273), FreeBSD 10-CURRENT and newer versions have a native `iconv` in the operating system. On earlier versions, converters/libiconv was used as a dependency.

For software that needs `iconv`, define USES=iconv. FreeBSD versions before 10-CURRENT on 2013-08-13 (254273) do not have a native `iconv`. On these earlier versions, a dependency on converters/libiconv will be added automatically.

When a port defines USES=iconv, these variables will be available:

Variable name	Purpose	Value before Free-BSD 10-CURRENT 254273 (2013-08-13)	Value after Free-BSD 10-CURRENT 254273 (2013-08-13)
ICONV_CMD	Directory where the `iconv` binary resides	`${LOCALBASE}/bin/iconv`	`/usr/bin/iconv`
ICONV_LIB	`ld` argument to link to libiconv (if needed)	`-liconv`	(empty)
ICONV_PREFIX	Directory where the `iconv` implementation resides (useful for configure scripts)	`${LOCALBASE}`	`/usr`
ICONV_CONFIGURE_ARG	Preconstructed configure argument for configure scripts	`--with-libiconv-prefix=${LOCALBASE}`	(empty)
ICONV_CONFIGURE_BASE	Preconstructed configure argument for configure scripts	`--with-libiconv=${LOCALBASE}`	(empty)

These two examples automatically populate the variables with the correct value for systems using converters/libiconv or the native `iconv` respectively:

Example 6.14. Simple `iconv` Usage

```
USES=  iconv
LDFLAGS+= -L${LOCALBASE}/lib ${ICONV_LIB}
```

Example 6.15. `iconv` Usage with `configure`

```
USES=  iconv
CONFIGURE_ARGS+=${ICONV_CONFIGURE_ARG}
```

As shown above, ICONV_LIB is empty when a native `iconv` is present. This can be used to detect the native `iconv` and respond appropriately.

Sometimes a program has an `ld` argument or search path hardcoded in a `Makefile` or configure script. This approach can be used to solve that problem:

Example 6.16. Fixing Hardcoded `-liconv`

```
USES=  iconv

post-patch:
 @${REINPLACE_CMD} -e 's/-liconv/${ICONV_LIB}/' ${WRKSRC}/Makefile
```

In some cases it is necessary to set alternate values or perform operations depending on whether there is a native iconv. `bsd.port.pre.mk` must be included before testing the value of `ICONV_LIB`:

Example 6.17. Checking for Native `iconv` Availability

```
USES=  iconv

.include <bsd.port.pre.mk>

post-patch:
.if empty(ICONV_LIB)
 # native iconv detected
 @${REINPLACE_CMD} -e 's|iconv||' ${WRKSRC}/Config.sh
.endif

.include <bsd.port.post.mk>
```

6.24. Using Xfce

Ports that need Xfce libraries or applications set `USES=xfce`.

Specific Xfce library and application dependencies are set with values assigned to `USE_XFCE`. They are defined in `/usr/ports/Mk/Uses/xfce.mk` . The possible values are:

garcon
    sysutils/garcon

libexo
    x11/libexo

libgui
    x11-toolkits/libxfce4gui

libmenu
    x11/libxfce4menu

libutil
    x11/libxfce4util

panel
    x11-wm/xfce4-panel

thunar
    x11-fm/thunar

xfconf
    x11/xfce4-conf

Example 6.18. USES=xfce Example

```
USES= xfce
USE_XFCE= libmenu
```

Example 6.19. Using Xfce's Own GTK3 Widgets

In this example, the ported application uses the GTK3-specific widgets x11/libxfce4menu and x11/xfce4-conf.

```
USES= xfce:gtk3
USE_XFCE= libmenu xfconf
```

Tip

Xfce components included this way will automatically include any dependencies they need. It is no longer necessary to specify the entire list. If the port only needs x11-wm/xfce4-panel, use:

```
USES= xfce
USE_XFCE= panel
```

There is no need to list the components x11-wm/xfce4-panel needs itself like this:

```
USES= xfce
USE_XFCE= libexo libmenu libutil panel
```

However, Xfce components and non-Xfce dependencies of the port must be included explicitly. Do not count on an Xfce component to provide a sub-dependency other than itself for the main port.

6.25. Using Mozilla

Table 6.37. Variables for Ports That Use Mozilla

USE_GECKO	Gecko backend the port can handle. Possible values: libxul (libxul.so), seamonkey (libgtkembedmoz.so, deprecated, must not be used any more).
USE_FIREFOX	The port requires Firefox as a runtime dependency. Possible values: yes (get default version), 40, 36, 35. Default dependency is on version 40.
USE_FIREFOX_BUILD	The port requires Firefox as a buildtime dependency. Possible values: see USE_FIREFOX. This automatically sets USE_FIREFOX and assigns the same value.

USE_SEAMONKEY	The port requires SeaMonkey as a runtime dependency. Possible values: **yes** (get default version), **20**, **11** (deprecated, must not be used any more). Default dependency is on version **20**.
USE_SEAMONKEY_BUILD	The port requires SeaMonkey as a buildtime dependency. Possible values: see USE_SEAMONKEY. This automatically sets USE_SEAMONKEY and assigns the same value.
USE_THUNDERBIRD	The port requires Thunderbird as a runtime dependency. Possible values: **yes** (get default version), **31**, **30** (deprecated, must not be used any more). Default dependency is on version **31**.
USE_THUNDERBIRD_BUILD	The port requires Thunderbird as a buildtime dependency. Possible values: see USE_THUNDERBIRD. This automatically sets USE_THUNDERBIRD and assigns the same value.

A complete list of available variables can be found in `/usr/ports/Mk/bsd.gecko.mk` .

6.26. Using Databases

Table 6.38. Variables for Ports Using Databases

Variable	Means
USE_BDB	Obsolete. Replaced by `USES=bdb`
USE_MYSQL	Obsolete. Replaced by `USES=mysql`
USE_PGSQL	Obsolete. Replaced by `USES=pgsql` .
USE_SQLITE	Obsolete. Replaced by `USES=sqlite`

6.27. Starting and Stopping Services (rc Scripts)

`rc.d` scripts are used to start services on system startup, and to give administrators a standard way of stopping, starting and restarting the service. Ports integrate into the system `rc.d` framework. Details on its usage can be found in the rc.d Handbook chapter. Detailed explanation of the available commands is provided in rc(8) and rc.subr(8). Finally, there is an article on practical aspects of `rc.d` scripting.

With a mythical port called *doorman*, which needs to start a *doormand* daemon. Add the following to the `Makefile`:

```
USE_RC_SUBR= doormand
```

Multiple scripts may be listed and will be installed. Scripts must be placed in the `files` subdirectory and a `.in` suffix must be added to their filename. Standard `SUB_LIST` expansions will be ran against this file. Use of the `%%PREFIX%%` and `%%LOCALBASE%%` expansions is strongly encouraged as well. More on `SUB_LIST` in the relevant section.

As of FreeBSD 6.1-RELEASE, local `rc.d` scripts (including those installed by ports) are included in the overall rcorder(8) of the base system.

An example simple `rc.d` script to start the doormand daemon:

```
#!/bin/sh

# $FreeBSD$
#
# PROVIDE: doormand
# REQUIRE: LOGIN
```

```
# KEYWORD: shutdown
#
# Add these lines to /etc/rc.conf.local or /etc/rc.conf
# to enable this service:
#
# doormand_enable (bool): Set to NO by default.
#     Set it to YES to enable doormand .
# doormand_config (path): Set to %%PREFIX%%/etc/doormand/doormand.cf
#     by default.

. /etc/rc.subr

name=doormand
rcvar=doormand_enable

load_rc_config $name

: ${doormand_enable:="NO"}
: ${doormand_config="%%PREFIX%%/etc/doormand/doormand.cf "}

command=%%PREFIX%%/sbin/${name}
pidfile=/var/run/${name}.pid

command_args="-p $pidfile -f $doormand_config "

run_rc_command "$1"
```

Unless there is a very good reason to start the service earlier, or it runs as a particular user (other than root), all ports scripts must use:

```
REQUIRE: LOGIN
```

If the startup script launches a daemon that must be shutdown, the following will trigger a stop of the service on system shutdown:

```
KEYWORD: shutdown
```

If the script is not starting a persistent service this is not necessary.

For optional configuration elements the "=" style of default variable assignment is preferable to the ":=" style here, since the former sets a default value only if the variable is unset, and the latter sets one if the variable is unset *or* null. A user might very well include something like:

```
doormand_flags=""
```

in their rc.conf.local, and a variable substitution using ":=" would inappropriately override the user's intention. The _enable variable is not optional, and must use the ":" for the default.

6.27.1. Pre-Commit Checklist

Before contributing a port with an rc.d script, and more importantly, before committing one, please consult this checklist to be sure that it is ready.

The devel/rclint port can check for most of these, but it is not a substitute for proper review.

1. If this is a new file, does it have a .sh extension? If so, that must be changed to just *file* .in since rc.d files may not end with that extension.

2. Does the file have a $FreeBSD$ tag?

3. Do the name of the file (minus .in), the PROVIDE line, and $*name* all match? The file name matching PROVIDE makes debugging easier, especially for rcorder(8) issues. Matching the file name and $*name* makes it easier to figure out which variables are relevant in rc.conf[.local]. It is also a policy for all new scripts, including those in the base system.

4. Is the REQUIRE line set to LOGIN? This is mandatory for scripts that run as a non-root user. If it runs as root, is there a good reason for it to run prior to LOGIN? If not, it must run after so that local scrips can be loosely grouped to a point in rcorder(8) after most everything in the base is already running.

5. Does the script start a persistent service? If so, it must have KEYWORD: shutdown.

6. Make sure there is no KEYWORD: FreeBSD present. This has not been necessary nor desirable for years. It is also an indication that the new script was copy/pasted from an old script, so extra caution must be given to the review.

7. If the script uses an interpreted language like perl, python, or ruby, make certain that command_interpreter is set appropriately, for example, for Perl, by adding PERL=${PERL} to SUB_LIST and using %%PERL%%. Otherwise,

    ```
    # service name stop
    ```

    will probably not work properly. See service(8) for more information.

8. Have all occurrences of /usr/local been replaced with %%PREFIX%%?

9. Do the default variable assignments come after load_rc_config?

10. Are there default assignments to empty strings? They should be removed, but double-check that the option is documented in the comments at the top of the file.

11. Are things that are set in variables actually used in the script?

12. Are options listed in the default *name*_flags things that are actually mandatory? If so, they must be in command_args. The -d option is a red flag (pardon the pun) here, since it is usually the option to "daemonize" the process, and therefore is actually mandatory.

13. *name*_flags must never be included in command_args (and vice versa, although that error is less common).

14. Does the script execute any code unconditionally? This is frowned on. Usually these things must be dealt with through a start_precmd .

15. All boolean tests must use the checkyesno function. No hand-rolled tests for [Yy][Ee][Ss] , etc.

16. If there is a loop (for example, waiting for something to start) does it have a counter to terminate the loop? We do not want the boot to be stuck forever if there is an error.

17. Does the script create files or directories that need specific permissions, for example, a pid that needs to be owned by the user that runs the process? Rather than the traditional touch(1)/chown(8)/chmod(1) routine, consider using install(1) with the proper command line arguments to do the whole procedure with one step.

6.28. Adding Users and Groups

Some ports require a particular user account to be present, usually for daemons that run as that user. For these ports, choose a *unique* UID from 50 to 999 and register it in ports/UIDs (for users) and ports/GIDs (for groups). The unique identification should be the same for users and groups.

Please include a patch against these two files when requiring a new user or group to be created for the port.

Then use USERS and GROUPS in Makefile, and the user will be automatically created when installing the port.

```
USERS= pulse
GROUPS= pulse pulse-access pulse-rt
```

The current list of reserved UIDs and GIDs can be found in ports/UIDs and ports/GIDs .

6.29. Ports That Rely on Kernel Sources

Some ports (such as kernel loadable modules) need the kernel source files so that the port can compile. Here is the correct way to determine if the user has them installed:

```
USES= kmod
```

Apart from this check, the kmod feature takes care of most items that these ports need to take into account.

Chapter 7. Advanced pkg-plist Practices

7.1. Changing pkg-plist Based on Make Variables

Some ports, particularly the p5- ports, need to change their pkg-plist depending on what options they are configured with (or version of perl, in the case of p5- ports). To make this easy, any instances in pkg-plist of %%OSREL%%, %%PERL_VER%%, and %%PERL_VERSION%% will be substituted appropriately. The value of %%OSREL%% is the numeric revision of the operating system (for example, 4.9). %%PERL_VERSION%% and %%PERL_VER%% is the full version number of perl (for example, 5.8.9). Several other %%VARS%% related to port's documentation files are described in the relevant section.

To make other substitutions, set PLIST_SUB with a list of *VAR=VALUE* pairs and instances of %%*VAR*%% will be substituted with *VALUE* in pkg-plist.

For instance, if a port installs many files in a version-specific subdirectory, use a placeholder for the version so that pkg-plist does not have to be regenerated every time the port is updated. For example:

```
OCTAVE_VERSION= ${PORTREVISION}
PLIST_SUB= OCTAVE_VERSION=${OCTAVE_VERSION}
```

in the Makefile and use %%OCTAVE_VERSION%% wherever the version shows up in pkg-plist. When the port is upgraded, it will not be necessary to edit dozens (or in some cases, hundreds) of lines in pkg-plist.

If files are installed conditionally on the options set in the port, the usual way of handling it is prefixing pkg-plist lines with a %%OPT%% for lines needed when the option is enabled, or %%NO_OPT%% when the option is disabled, and adding OPTIONS_SUB=yes to the Makefile. See Section 5.12.3.1, "OPTIONS_SUB" for more information.

For instance, if there are files that are only installed when the X11 option is enabled, and Makefile has:

```
OPTIONS_DEFINE= X11
OPTIONS_SUB= yes
```

In pkg-plist, put %%X11%% in front of the lines only being installed when the option is enabled, like this:

```
%%X11%%bin/foo-gui
```

This substitution will be done between the pre-install and do-install targets, by reading from PLIST and writing to TMPPLIST (default: WRKDIR/.PLIST.mktmp). So if the port builds PLIST on the fly, do so in or before pre-install. Also, if the port needs to edit the resulting file, do so in post-install to a file named TMPPLIST.

Another way of modifying a port's packing list is based on setting the variables PLIST_FILES and PLIST_DIRS. The value of each variable is regarded as a list of pathnames to write to TMPPLIST along with PLIST contents. While names listed in PLIST_FILES and PLIST_DIRS are subject to %%*VAR*%% substitution as described above, it is better to use the ${*VAR*} directly. Except for that, names from PLIST_FILES will appear in the final packing list unchanged, while @dir will be prepended to names from PLIST_DIRS. To take effect, PLIST_FILES and PLIST_DIRS must be set before TMPPLIST is written, that is, in pre-install or earlier.

From time to time, using OPTIONS_SUB is not enough. In those cases, adding a specific *TAG* to PLIST_SUB inside the Makefile with a special value of @comment, makes package tools to ignore the line. For instance, if some files are only installed when the X11 option is on and the architecture is i386:

```
.include <bsd.port.pre.mk>

.if ${PORT_OPTIONS:MX11} && ${ARCH} == "i386"
PLIST_SUB+= X11I386=""
.else
```

```
PLIST_SUB+= X11I386="@comment "
.endif
```

7.2. Empty Directories

7.2.1. Cleaning Up Empty Directories

When being de-installed, a port has to remove empty directories it created. Most of these directories are removed automatically by pkg(8), but for directories created outside of ${PREFIX}, or empty directories, some more work needs to be done. This is usually accomplished by adding @dir lines for those directories. Subdirectories must be deleted before deleting parent directories.

```
[...-]
@dir /var/games/oneko/saved-games
@dir /var/games/oneko
```

7.2.2. Creating Empty Directories

Empty directories created during port installation need special attention. They must be present when the package is created. If they are not created by the port code, create them in the Makefile:

```
post-stage:
 ${MKDIR} ${STAGEDIR}${PREFIX}/some/directory
```

Add the directory to pkg-plist like any other. For example:

```
@dir some/directory
```

7.3. Configuration Files

If the port installs configuration files to PREFIX/etc (or elsewhere) do *not* list them in pkg-plist. That will cause pkg delete to remove files that have been carefully edited by the user, and a re-installation will wipe them out.

Instead, install sample files with a *filename*.sample extension. The @sample macro automates this, see Section 7.6.9, "@sample *file* [*file*]" for what it does exactly. For each sample file, add a line to pkg-plist:

```
@sample etc/orbit.conf.sample
```

If there is a very good reason not to install a working configuration file by default, only list the sample filename in pkg-plist, without the @sample followed by a space part, and add a message pointing out that the user must copy and edit the file before the software will work.

> Tip
>
> When a port installs its configuration in a subdirectory of ${PREFIX}/etc, use ETCDIR, which defaults to ${PREFIX}/etc/${PORTNAME}, it can be overridden in the ports Makefile if there is a convention for the port to use some other directory. The %%ETCDIR%% macro will be used in its stead in pkg-plist.

> Note
>
> The sample configuration files should always have the .sample suffix. If for some historical reason using the standard suffix is not possible, or if the sample files come from some other directory, use this construct:

```
@sample etc/orbit.conf-dist etc/orbit.conf
```

or

```
@sample %%EXAMPLESDIR%%/orbit.conf etc/orbit.conf
```

The format is @sample *sample-file actual-config-file.*

7.4. Dynamic Versus Static Package List

A *static package list* is a package list which is available in the Ports Collection either as `pkg-plist` (with or without variable substitution), or embedded into the `Makefile` via `PLIST_FILES` and `PLIST_DIRS`. Even if the contents are auto-generated by a tool or a target in the Makefile *before* the inclusion into the Ports Collection by a committer (for example, using `make makeplist>`), this is still considered a static list, since it is possible to examine it without having to download or compile the distfile.

A *dynamic package list* is a package list which is generated at the time the port is compiled based upon the files and directories which are installed. It is not possible to examine it before the source code of the ported application is downloaded and compiled, or after running a `make clean`.

While the use of dynamic package lists is not forbidden, maintainers should use static package lists wherever possible, as it enables users to grep(1) through available ports to discover, for example, which port installs a certain file. Dynamic lists should be primarily used for complex ports where the package list changes drastically based upon optional features of the port (and thus maintaining a static package list is infeasible), or ports which change the package list based upon the version of dependent software used. For example, ports which generate docs with Javadoc.

7.5. Automated Package List Creation

First, make sure the port is almost complete, with only `pkg-plist` missing. Running `make makeplist` will show an example for `pkg-plist`. The output of `makeplist` must be double checked for correctness as it tries to automatically guess a few things, and can get it wrong.

User configuration files should be installed as *filename*.sample, as it is described in Section 7.3, "Configuration Files". `info/dir` must not be listed and appropriate `install-info` lines must be added as noted in the info files section. Any libraries installed by the port must be listed as specified in the shared libraries section.

7.5.1. Expanding `PLIST_SUB` With Regular Expressions

Strings to be replaced sometimes need to be very specific to avoid undesired replacements. This is a common problem with shorter values.

To address this problem, for each *PLACEHOLDER=value*, a *PLACEHOLDER*_regex= *regex* can be set, with the *regex* part matching *value* more precisely.

Example 7.1. Using PLIST_SUB With Regular Expressions

Perl ports can install architecture dependant files in a specific tree. On FreeBSD to ease porting, this tree is called mach. For example, a port that installs a file whose path contains mach could have that part of the path string replaced with the wrong values. Consider this `Makefile`:

```
PORTNAME= Machine-Build
PORTVERSION= 1
```

```
CATEGORIES= devel perl5
MASTER_SITES= CPAN
PKGNAMEPREFIX= p5-

MAINTAINER= perl@FreeBSD.org
COMMENT= Building machine

USES=   perl5
USE_PERL5= configure

PLIST_SUB= PERL_ARCH=mach
```

The files installed by the port are:

```
/usr/local/bin/machine-build
/usr/local/lib/perl5/site_perl/man/man1/machine-build.1.gz
/usr/local/lib/perl5/site_perl/man/man3/Machine::Build.3.gz
/usr/local/lib/perl5/site_perl/Machine/Build.pm
/usr/local/lib/perl5/site_perl/mach/5.20/Machine/Build/Build.so
```

Runnig make makeplist wrongly generates:

```
bin/%%PERL_ARCH%%ine-build
%%PERL5_MAN1%%/%%PERL_ARCH%%ine-build.1.gz
%%PERL5_MAN3%%/Machine::Build.3.gz
%%SITE_PERL%%/Machine/Build.pm
%%SITE_PERL%%/%%PERL_ARCH%%/%%PERL_VER%%/Machine/Build/Build.so
```

Change the PLIST_SUB line from the Makefile to:

```
PLIST_SUB= PERL_ARCH=mach \
  PERL_ARCH_regex=\bmach\b
```

Now make makeplist correctly generates:

```
bin/machine-build
%%PERL5_MAN1%%/machine-build.1.gz
%%PERL5_MAN3%%/Machine::Build.3.gz
%%SITE_PERL%%/Machine/Build.pm
%%SITE_PERL%%/%%PERL_ARCH%%/%%PERL_VER%%/Machine/Build/Build.so
```

7.6. Expanding Package List with Keywords

All keywords can also take optional arguments in parentheses. The arguments are owner, group, and mode. This argument is used on the file or directory referenced. To change the owner, group, and mode of a configuration file, use:

```
@sample(games,games,640) etc/config.sample
```

The arguments are optional. If only the group and mode need to be changed, use:

```
@sample(,games,660) etc/config.sample
```

7.6.1. @desktop-file-utils

Will run update-desktop-database -q after installation and deinstallation.

7.6.2. @fc directory

Add a @dir entry for the directory passed as an argument, and run fc-cache -fs on that directory after installation and deinstallation.

7.6.3. @fcfontsdir **directory**

Add a @dir entry for the directory passed as an argument, and run fc-cache -fs , mkfontscale and mkfontdir on that directory after installation and deinstallation. Additionally, on deinstallation, it removes the fonts.scale and fonts.dir cache files if they are empty. This keyword is equivalent to adding both @fc *directory* and @fontsdir *directory*.

7.6.4. @fontsdir **directory**

Add a @dir entry for the directory passed as an argument, and run mkfontscale and mkfontdir on that directory after installation and deinstallation. Additionally, on deinstallation, it removes the fonts.scale and fonts.dir cache files if they are empty.

7.6.5. @glib-schemas

Runs glib-compile-schemas on installation and deinstallation.

7.6.6. @info **file**

Add the file passed as argument to the plist, and updates the info document index on installation and deinstallation. Additionally, it removes the index if empty on deinstallation. This should never be used manually, but always through INFO. See Section 5.11, "Info Files" for more information.

7.6.7. @kld **directory**

Runs kldxref on the directory on installation and deinstallation. Additionally, on deinstallation, it will remove the directory if empty.

7.6.8. @rmtry **file**

Will remove the file on deinstallation, and not give an error if the file is not there.

7.6.9. @sample **file [file]**

This is used to handle installation of configuration files, through example files bundled with the package. The "actual", non-sample, file is either the second filename, if present, or the first filename without the .sample extension.

This does three things. First, add the first file passed as argument, the sample file, to the plist. Then, on installation, if the actual file is not found, copy the sample file to the actual file. And finally, on deinstallation, remove the actual file if it has not been modified. See Section 7.3, "Configuration Files" for more information.

7.6.10. @shared-mime-info **directory**

Runs update-mime-database on the directory on installation and deinstallation.

7.6.11. @shell **file**

Add the file passed as argument to the plist.

On installation, add the full path to *file* to /etc/shells , while making sure it is not added twice. On deinstallation, remove it from /etc/shells .

7.6.12. @terminfo

Do not use by itself. If the port installs *.terminfo files, add USES=terminfo to its Makefile.

On installation and deinstallation, if tic is present, refresh ${PREFIX}/share/misc/terminfo.db from the *.terminfo files in ${PREFIX}/share/misc .

7.6.13. Base Keywords

There are a few keywords that are hardcoded, and documented in pkg-create(8). For the sake of completeness, they are also documented here.

7.6.13.1. @ [file]

The empty keyword is a placeholder to use when the file's owner, group, or mode need to be changed. For example, to set the group of the file to games and add the setgid bit, add:

```
@(,games,2755) sbin/daemon
```

7.6.13.2. @preexec command, @postexec command, @preunexec command, @postunexec command

Execute *command* as part of the package installation or deinstallation process.

@preexec *command*
> Execute *command* as part of the pre-install scripts.

@postexec *command*
> Execute *command* as part of the post-install scripts.

@preunexec *command*
> Execute *command* as part of the pre-deinstall scripts.

@postunexec *command*
> Execute *command* as part of the post-deinstall scripts.

If *command* contains any of these sequences somewhere in it, they are expanded inline. For these examples, assume that @cwd is set to /usr/local and the last extracted file was bin/emacs .

%F
> Expand to the last filename extracted (as specified). In the example case bin/emacs .

%D
> Expand to the current directory prefix, as set with @cwd. In the example case /usr/local .

%B
> Expand to the basename of the fully qualified filename, that is, the current directory prefix plus the last file-spec, minus the trailing filename. In the example case, that would be /usr/local/bin .

%f
> Expand to the filename part of the fully qualified name, or the converse of %B. In the example case, emacs .

7.6.13.3. @mode mode

Set default permission for all subsequently extracted files to *mode*. Format is the same as that used by chmod(1). Use without an arg to set back to default permissions (mode of the file while being packed).

> **Important**
>
> This must be a numeric mode, like 644, 4755, or 600. It cannnot be a relative mode like u+s.

7.6.13.4. @owner user

Set default ownership for all subsequent files to *user*. Use without an argument to set back to default ownership (root).

7.6.13.5. @group **group**

Set default group ownership for all subsequent files to *group*. Use without an arg to set back to default group ownership (`wheel`).

7.6.13.6. @comment **string**

This line is ignored when packing.

7.6.13.7. @dir **directory**

Declare directory name. By default, directories created under `PREFIX` by a package installation are automatically removed. Use this when an empty directory under `PREFIX` needs to be created, or when the directory needs to have non default owner, group, or mode. Directories outside of `PREFIX` need to be registered. For example, `/var/db/${PORTNAME}` needs to have a `@dir` entry whereas `${PREFIX}/share/${PORTNAME}` does not if it contains files or uses the default owner, group, and mode.

7.6.13.8. @exec **command,** @unexec **command (Deprecated)**

Execute *command* as part of the installation or deinstallation process. Please use Section 7.6.13.2, "@preexec *command*, @postexec *command*, @preunexec *command*, @postunexec *command*" instead.

7.6.13.9. @dirrm **directory (Deprecated)**

Declare directory name to be deleted at deinstall time. By default, directories created under `PREFIX` by a package installation are deleted when the package is deinstalled.

7.6.13.10. @dirrmtry **directory (Deprecated)**

Declare directory name to be removed, as for `@dirrm`, but does not issue a warning if the directory cannot be removed.

7.6.14. Creating New Keywords

Package list files can be extended by keywords that are defined in the `${PORTSDIR}/Keywords` directory. The settings for each keyword are stored in a UCL file named *keyword*.`ucl`. The file must contain at least one of these sections:

- `attributes`

- `action`

- `pre-install`

- `post-install`

- `pre-deinstall`

- `post-deinstall`

- `pre-upgrade`

- `post-upgrade`

7.6.14.1. attributes

Changes the owner, group, or mode used by the keyword. Contains an associative array where the possible keys are `owner`, `group`, and `mode`. The values are, respectively, a user name, a group name, and a file mode. For example:

```
attributes: { owner: "games", group: "games", mode: 0555 }
```

7.6.14.2. action

Defines what happens to the keyword's parameter. Contains an array where the possible values are:

setprefix
> Set the prefix for the next plist entries.

dir
> Register a directory to be created on install and removed on deinstall.

dirrm
> Register a directory to be deleted on deinstall. Deprecated.

dirrmtry
> Register a directory to try and deleted on deinstall. Deprecated.

file
> Register a file.

setmode
> Set the mode for the next plist entries.

setowner
> Set the owner for the next plist entries.

setgroup
> Set the group for the next plist entries.

comment
> Does not do anything, equivalent to not entering an action section.

ignore_next
> Ignore the next entry in the plist.

7.6.14.3. arguments

If set to true, adds argument handling, splitting the whole line, %@, into numbered arguments, %1, %2, and so on. For example, for this line:

```
@foo some.content other.content
```

%1 and %2 will contain:

```
some.content
other.content
```

It also affects how the action entry works. When there is more than one argument, the argument number must be specified. For example:

```
actions: [file(1)]
```

7.6.14.4. pre-install, post-install, pre-deinstall, post-deinstall, pre-upgrade, post-upgrade

These keywords contains a sh(1) script to be executed before or after installation, deinstallation, or upgrade of the package. In addition to the usual @exec %foo placeholders described in Section 7.6.13.2, "@preexec *command*, @postexec *command*, @preunexec *command*, @postunexec *command*", there is a new one, %@, which represents the argument of the keyword.

7.6.14.5. Custom Keyword Examples

Example 7.2. Example of a `@dirrmtryecho` Keyword

This keyword does two things, it adds a `@dirrmtry` *directory* line to the packing list, and echoes the fact that the directory is removed when deinstalling the package.

```
actions: [dirrmtry]
post-deinstall: <<EOD
  echo "Directory %D/%@ removed."
EOD
```

Example 7.3. Real Life Example, How `@sample` is Implemented

This keyword does three things. It adds the first *filename* passed as an argument to `@sample` to the packing list, it adds to the `post-install` script instructions to copy the sample to the actual configuration file if it does not already exist, and it adds to the `post-deinstall` instructions to remove the configuration file if it has not been modified.

```
actions: [file(1)]
arguments: true
post-install: <<EOD
  case "%1" in
  /*) sample_file="%1" -;;
  *) sample_file="%D/%1" -;;
  esac
  target_file="${sample_file%.sample}"
  set -- %@
  if [ $# -eq 2 -]; then
      target_file=${2}
  fi
  case "${target_file}" in
  /*) target_file="${target_file}" -;;
  *) target_file="%D/${target_file}" -;;
  esac
  if ! [ -f "${target_file}" -]; then
    /bin/cp -p "${sample_file}" "${target_file}" && \
      /bin/chmod u+w "${target_file}"
  fi
EOD
pre-deinstall: <<EOD
  case "%1" in
  /*) sample_file="%1" -;;
  *) sample_file="%D/%1" -;;
  esac
  target_file="${sample_file%.sample}"
  set -- %@
  if [ $# -eq 2 -]; then
      set -- %@
      target_file=${2}
  fi
  case "${target_file}" in
  /*) target_file="${target_file}" -;;
  *) target_file="%D/${target_file}" -;;
  esac
  if cmp -s "${target_file}" "${sample_file}"; then
    rm -f "${target_file}"
  else
```

```
    echo "You may need to manually remove ${target_file} if it is no longer ↵
needed."
  fi
EOD
```

Chapter 8. pkg-*

There are some tricks we have not mentioned yet about the pkg-* files that come in handy sometimes.

8.1. pkg-message

To display a message when the package is installed, place the message in pkg-message. This capability is often useful to display additional installation steps to be taken after a pkg install or to display licensing information.

When some lines about the build-time knobs or warnings have to be displayed, use ECHO_MSG. pkg-message is only for post-installation steps. Likewise, the distinction between ECHO_MSG is for printing informational text to the screen and ECHO_CMD is for command pipelining:

```
update-etc-shells:
 @${ECHO_MSG} "updating /etc/shells"
 @${CP} /etc/shells /etc/shells.bak
 @( ${GREP} -v ${PREFIX}/bin/bash /etc/shells.bak; \
   ${ECHO_CMD} ${PREFIX}/bin/bash) >/etc/shells
 @${RM} /etc/shells.bak
```

> Note
>
> Do not add an entry for pkg-message in pkg-plist.

8.2. pkg-install

If the port needs to execute commands when the binary package is installed with pkg add or pkg install, use pkg-install. This script will automatically be added to the package. It will be run twice by pkg, the first time as ${SH} pkg-install ${PKGNAME} PRE-INSTALL before the package is installed, and the second time as ${SH} pkg-install ${PKGNAME} POST-INSTALL after it has been installed. $2 can be tested to determine which mode the script is being run in. The PKG_PREFIX environmental variable will be set to the package installation directory.

8.3. pkg-deinstall

This script executes when a package is removed.

This script will be run twice by pkg delete The first time as ${SH} pkg-deinstall ${PKGNAME} DEINSTALL before the port is de-installed and the second time as ${SH} pkg-deinstall ${PKGNAME} POST-DEINSTALL after the port has been de-installed. $2 can be tested to determine which mode the script is being run in. The PKG_PREFIX environmental variable will be set to the package installation directory

8.4. Changing the Names of pkg-*

All the names of pkg-* are defined using variables that can be changed in the Makefile if needed. This is especially useful when sharing the same pkg-* files among several ports or when it is necessary to write to one of these files. See writing to places other than WRKDIR for why it is a bad idea to write directly into the directory containing the pkg-* files.

Here is a list of variable names and their default values. (PKGDIR defaults to ${MASTERDIR}.)

Variable	Default value
DESCR	${PKGDIR}/pkg-descr
PLIST	${PKGDIR}/pkg-plist
PKGINSTALL	${PKGDIR}/pkg-install
PKGDEINSTALL	${PKGDIR}/pkg-deinstall
PKGMESSAGE	${PKGDIR}/pkg-message

8.5. Making Use of SUB_FILES and SUB_LIST

SUB_FILES and SUB_LIST are useful for dynamic values in port files, such as the installation PREFIX in pkg-message.

SUB_FILES specifies a list of files to be automatically modified. Each *file* in the SUB_FILES list must have a corresponding *file*.in present in FILESDIR. A modified version will be created as ${WRKDIR}/ *file*. Files defined as a value of USE_RC_SUBR (or the deprecated USE_RCORDER) are automatically added to SUB_FILES. For the files pkg-message, pkg-install, and pkg-deinstall, the corresponding Makefile variable is automatically set to point to the processed version.

SUB_LIST is a list of VAR=VALUE pairs. For each pair, %%VAR%% will be replaced with VALUE in each file listed in SUB_FILES. Several common pairs are automatically defined: PREFIX, LOCALBASE, DATADIR, DOCSDIR, EXAMPLESDIR, WWWDIR, and ETCDIR. Any line beginning with @comment followed by a space, will be deleted from resulting files after a variable substitution.

This example replaces %%ARCH%% with the system architecture in a pkg-message:

```
SUB_FILES= pkg-message
SUB_LIST= ARCH=${ARCH}
```

Note that for this example, pkg-message.in must exist in FILESDIR.

Example of a good pkg-message.in:

```
Now it is time to configure this package.
Copy %%PREFIX%%/share/examples/putsy/%%ARCH%%.conf into your home directory
as .putsy.conf and edit it.
```

Chapter 9. Testing the Port

9.1. Running `make describe`

Several of the FreeBSD port maintenance tools, such as portupgrade(1), rely on a database called `/usr/ports/INDEX` which keeps track of such items as port dependencies. `INDEX` is created by the top-level `ports/Makefile` via `make index`, which descends into each port subdirectory and executes `make describe` there. Thus, if `make describe` fails in any port, no one can generate `INDEX`, and many people will quickly become unhappy.

Note

It is important to be able to generate this file no matter what options are present in `make.conf`, so please avoid doing things such as using `.error` statements when (for instance) a dependency is not satisfied. (See Section 12.16, "Avoid Use of the `.error` Construct".)

If `make describe` produces a string rather than an error message, everything is probably safe. See `bsd.port.mk` for the meaning of the string produced.

Also note that running a recent version of `portlint` (as specified in the next section) will cause `make describe` to be run automatically.

9.2. Portlint

Do check the port with `portlint` before submitting or committing it. `portlint` warns about many common errors, both functional and stylistic. For a new (or repocopied) port, `portlint -A` is the most thorough; for an existing port, `portlint -C` is sufficient.

Since `portlint` uses heuristics to try to figure out errors, it can produce false positive warnings. In addition, occasionally something that is flagged as a problem really cannot be done in any other way due to limitations in the ports framework. When in doubt, the best thing to do is ask on FreeBSD ports mailing list.

9.3. Port Tools

The ports-mgmt/porttools program is part of the Ports Collection.

`port` is the front-end script, which can help simplify the testing job. Whenever a new port or an update to an existing one needs testing, use `port test` to test the port, including the `portlint` checking. This command also detects and lists any files that are not listed in `pkg-plist`. For example:

```
# port test /usr/ports/net/csup
```

9.4. `PREFIX` and `DESTDIR`

`PREFIX` determines where the port will be installed. It defaults to `/usr/local`, but can be set by the user to a custom path like `/opt`. The port must respect the value of this variable.

`DESTDIR`, if set by the user, determines the complete alternative environment, usually a jail or an installed system mounted somewhere other than `/`. A port will actually install into `DESTDIR/PREFIX`, and register with the package database in DESTDIR/var/db/pkg . As DESTDIR is handled automatically by the ports infrastructure with chroot(8). There is no need for modifications or any extra care to write DESTDIR-compliant ports.

The value of PREFIX will be set to LOCALBASE (defaulting to /usr/local). If USE_LINUX_PREFIX is set, PREFIX will be LINUXBASE (defaulting to /compat/linux).

Avoiding hard-coded /usr/local paths in the source makes the port much more flexible and able to cater to the needs of other sites. Often, this can be accomplished by replacing occurrences of /usr/local in the port's various Makefiles with ${PREFIX}. This variable is automatically passed down to every stage of the build and install processes.

Make sure the application is not installing things in /usr/local instead of PREFIX. A quick test for such hard-coded paths is:

```
% make clean; make package PREFIX=/var/tmp/`make -V PORTNAME`
```

If anything is installed outside of PREFIX, the package creation process will complain that it cannot find the files.

In addition, it is worth checking the same with the stage directory support (see Section 6.1, "Staging"):

```
% make stage && make check-plist && make stage-qa && make package
```

- check-plist checks for files missing from the plist, and files in the plist that are not installed by the port.

- stage-qa checks for common problems like bad shebang, symlinks pointing outside the stage directory, setuid files, and non-stripped libraries...

These tests will not find hard-coded paths inside the port's files, nor will it verify that LOCALBASE is being used to correctly refer to files from other ports. The temporarily-installed port in /var/tmp/`make -V PORTNAME` must be tested for proper operation to make sure there are no problems with paths.

PREFIX must not be set explicitly in a port's Makefile. Users installing the port may have set PREFIX to a custom location, and the port must respect that setting.

Refer to programs and files from other ports with the variables mentioned above, not explicit pathnames. For instance, if the port requires a macro PAGER to have the full pathname of less, do not use a literal path of /usr/local/bin/less . Instead, use ${LOCALBASE}:

```
-DPAGER=\"${LOCALBASE}/bin/less\"
```

The path with LOCALBASE is more likely to still work if the system administrator has moved the whole /usr/local tree somewhere else.

Tip

All these tests are done automatically when running poudriere testport or poudriere bulk -t. It is highly recommended that every ports contributor install and test their ports with it. See Section 9.5, "Poudriere" for more information.

9.5. Poudriere

For a ports contributor, Poudriere is one of the most important and helpful testing and build tools. Its main features include:

- Bulk building of the entire ports tree, specific subsets of the ports tree, or a single port including its dependencies

- Automatic packaging of build results

- Generation of build log files per port

- Providing a signed pkg(8) repository

- Testing of port builds before submitting a patch to the FreeBSD bug tracker or committing to the ports tree

- Testing for successful ports builds using different options

Because Poudriere performs its building in a clean jail(8) environment and uses zfs(8) features, it has several advantages over traditional testing on the host system:

- No pollution of the host environment: No leftover files, no accidental removals, no changes of existing configuration files.

- Verify `pkg-plist` for missing or superfluous entries

- Ports committers sometimes ask for a Poudriere log alongside a patch submission to assess whether the patch is ready for integration into the ports tree

It is also quite straightforward to set up and use, has no dependencies, and will run on any supported FreeBSD release. This section shows how to install, configure, and run Poudriere as part of the normal workflow of a ports contributor.

The examples in this section show a default file layout, as standard in FreeBSD. Substitute any local changes accordingly. The ports tree, represented by `${PORTSDIR}` , is located in `/usr/ports` . Both `${LOCALBASE}` and `${PRE-FIX}` are `/usr/local` by default.

9.5.1. Installing Poudriere

Poudriere is available in the ports tree in ports-mgmt/poudriere. It can be installed using pkg(8) or from ports:

```
# pkg install poudriere
```

or

```
# make -C /usr/ports/ports-mgmt/poudriere install clean
```

There is also a work-in-progress version of Poudriere which will eventually become the next release. It is available in ports-mgmt/poudriere-devel. This development version is used for the official FreeBSD package builds, so it is well tested. It often has newer interesting features. A ports committer will want to use the development version because it is what is used in production, and has all the new features that will make sure everything is exactly right. A contributor will not necessarily need those as the most important fixes are backported to released version. The main reason for the use of the development version to build the official package is because it is faster, in a way that will shorten a full build from 18 hours to 17 hours when using a high end 32 CPU server with 128GB of RAM. Those optimizations will not matter a lot when building ports on a desktop machine.

9.5.2. Setting Up Poudriere

The port installs a default configuration file, `/usr/local/etc/poudriere.conf` . Each parameter is documented in the configuration file and in poudriere(8). Here is a minimal example config file:

```
ZPOOL=tank
ZROOTFS=/poudriere
BASEFS=/poudriere
DISTFILES_CACHE=/usr/ports/distfiles
RESOLV_CONF=/etc/resolv.conf
FREEBSD_HOST=ftp://ftp.freebsd.org
SVN_HOST=svn.FreeBSD.org
```

ZPOOL
    The name of the ZFS storage pool which Poudriere shall use. Must be listed in the output of `zpool status` .

ZROOTFS

The root of Poudriere-managed file systems. This entry will cause Poudriere to create zfs(8) file systems under `tank/poudriere` .

BASEFS

The root mount point for Poudriere file systems. This entry will cause Poudriere to mount `tank/poudriere` to `/poudriere` .

DISTFILES_CACHE

Defines where distfiles are stored. In this example, Poudriere and the host share the distfiles storage directory. This avoids downloading tarballs which are already present on the system.

RESOLV_CONF

Use the host `/etc/resolv.conf` inside jails for DNS. This is needed so jails can resolve the URLs of distfiles when downloading. It is not needed when using a proxy. Refer to the default configuration file for proxy configuration.

FREEBSD_HOST

The FTP/HTTP server to use when the jails are installed from FreeBSD releases and updated with freebsd-update(8). Choose a server location which is close, for example if the machine is located in Australia, use `ftp.au.freebsd.org`.

SVN_HOST

The server from where jails are installed and updated when using Subversion. Also used for ports tree when not using portsnap(8). Again, choose a nearby location. A list of official Subversion mirrors can be found in the FreeBSD Handbook Subversion section.

9.5.3. Creating Poudriere Jails

Create the base jails which Poudriere will use for building:

```
# poudriere jail -c -j 93Ramd64 -v 9.3-RELEASE -a amd64
```

Fetch a `9.3-RELEASE` for `amd64` from the FTP server given by FREEBSD_HOST in `poudriere.conf` , create the zfs file system `tank/poudriere/jails/93Ramd64` , mount it on `/poudriere/jails/93Ramd64` and extract the 9.3-RELEASE tarballs into this file system.

```
# poudriere jail -c -j 10i386 -v stable/10 -a i386 -m svn+https
```

Create `tank/poudriere/jails/10i386` , mount it on `/poudriere/jails/10i386` , then check out the tip of the Subversion branch of FreeBSD-10-STABLE from SVN_HOST in `poudriere.conf` into `/poudriere/jails/10i386/usr/src`, then complete a `buildworld` and install it into `/poudriere/jails/10i386` .

Tip

If a specific Subversion revision is needed, append it to the version string. For example:

```
# poudriere jail -c -j 10i386 -v stable/10@123456 -a i386 -m svn+https
```

Note

While it is possible to build a newer version of FreeBSD on an older version, most of the time it will not run. For example, if a `stable/10` jail is needed, the host will have to run `stable/10` too. Running `10.0-RELEASE` is not enough.

Caution

The default svn protocol works but is not very secure. Using svn+https along with verifying the remote server's SSL fingerprint is advised. It will ensure that the files used for building the jail are from a trusted source.

A list of jails currently known to Poudriere can be shown with poudriere jail -l :

```
# poudriere jail -l
JAILNAME              VERSION            ARCH      METHOD
93Ramd64              9.3-RELEASE        amd64     ftp
10i386                10.0-STABLE        i386      svn+https
```

9.5.4. Keeping Poudriere Jails Updated

Managing updates is very straightforward. The command:

```
# poudriere jail -u -j JAILNAME
```

updates the specified jail to the latest version available. For FreeBSD releases, update to the latest patchlevel with freebsd-update(8). For FreeBSD versions built from source, update to the latest Subversion revision in the branch.

Tip

For jails employing a svn+* method, it is helpful to add -J NumberOfParallelBuildJobs to speed up the build by increasing the number of parallel compile jobs used. For example, if the building machine has 6 CPUs, use:

```
# poudriere jail -u -J 6 -j JAILNAME
```

9.5.5. Setting Up Ports Trees for Use with Poudriere

There are multiple ways to use ports trees in Poudriere. The most straightforward way is to have Poudriere create a default ports tree for itself:

```
# poudriere ports -c
```

This command creates tank/poudriere/ports/default , mount it on /poudriere/ports/default , and populate it using portsnap(8). Afterward it is included in the list of known ports trees:

```
# poudriere ports -l
PORTSTREE         METHOD         PATH
default           portsnap       /poudriere/ports/default
```

Note

Note that the "default" ports tree is special. Each of the build commands explained later will implicitly use this ports tree unless specifically specified otherwise. To use another tree, add -p treename to the commands.

While useful for regular bulk builds, having this default ports tree with the portsnap(8) method may not be the best way to deal with local modifications for a ports contributor. As with the creation of jails, it is possible to use a different method for creating the ports tree. To add an additional ports tree for testing local modifications and ports development, checking out the tree via Subversion is possible:

```
# poudriere ports -c -m svn+https -p subversive
```

Creates `tank/poudriere/ports/subversive` and mounts it on `/poudriere/ports/subversive` . It is then populated using Subversion. Finally, it is added to the list of known ports trees:

```
# poudriere ports -l
PORTSTREE       METHOD      PATH
default         portsnap    /poudriere/ports/default
subversive      svn+https   /poudriere/ports/subversive
```

Tip

The `svn` method allows extra qualifiers to tell Subversion exactly how to fetch data. This is explained in poudriere(8). For instance, `poudriere ports -c -m svn+ssh -p subversive` uses SSH for the checkout.

9.5.6. Using Manually Managed Ports Trees with Poudriere

Depending on the workflow, it can be extremely helpful to use ports trees which are maintained manually. For instance, if there is a local copy of the ports tree in `/work/ports` , point Poudriere to the location:

```
# poudriere ports -c -F -f none -M /work/ports -p development
```

This will be listed in the table of known trees:

```
# poudriere ports -l
PORTSTREE       METHOD      PATH
development     -           /work/ports
```

Note

The dash in the `METHOD` column means that Poudriere will not update or change this ports tree, ever. It is completely up to the user to maintain this tree, including all local modifications that may be used for testing new ports and submitting patches.

9.5.7. Keeping Poudriere Ports Trees Updated

As straightforward as with jails described earlier:

```
# poudriere ports -u -p PORTSTREE
```

Will update the given *PORTSTREE* , one tree given by the output of `poudriere -l` , to the latest revision available on the official servers.

Note

Ports trees without a method, see Section 9.5.6, "Using Manually Managed Ports Trees with Poudriere", cannot be updated like this. They must be updated manually by the porter.

9.5.8. Testing Ports

After jails and ports trees have been set up, the result of a contributor's modifications to the ports tree can be tested.

For example, local modifications to the www/firefox port located in `/work/ports/www/firefox` can be tested in the previously created 9.3-RELEASE jail:

```
# poudriere testport -j 93Ramd64 -p development -o www/firefox
```

This will build all dependencies of Firefox. If a dependency has been built previously and is still up-to-date, the pre-built package is installed. If a dependency has no up-to-date package, one will be built with default options in a jail. Then Firefox itself is built.

The complete build of every port is logged to `/poudriere/data/logs/bulk/93Ri386-development/` *build-time*`/logs`.

The directory name `93Ri386-development` is derived from the arguments to `-j` and `-p`, respectively. For convenience, a symbolic link `/poudriere/data/logs/bulk/93Ri386-development/latest` is also maintained. The link points to the latest *build-time* directory. Also in this directory is an `index.html` for observing the build process with a web browser.

By default, Poudriere cleans up the jails and leaves log files in the directories mentioned above. To ease investigation, jails can be kept running after the build by adding `-i` to `testport`:

```
# poudriere testport -j 93Ramd64 -p development -i -o www/firefox
```

After the build completes, and regardless of whether it was successful, a shell is provided within the jail. The shell is used to investigate further. Poudriere can be told to leave the jail running after the build finishes with `-I`. Poudriere will show the command to run when the jail is no longer needed. It is then possible to jexec(8) into it:

```
# poudriere testport -j 93Ramd64 -p development -I -o www/firefox
[...-]
=====>> Installing local Pkg repository to /usr/local/etc/pkg/repos
=====>> Leaving jail 93Ramd64-development-n running, mounted at /poudriere/data/.↺
m/93Ramd64-development/ref for interactive run testing
=====>> To enter jail: jexec 93Ramd64-development-n env -i TERM=$TERM /usr/bin/login -fp ↺
root
=====>> To stop jail: poudriere jail -k -j 93Ramd64 -p development
# jexec 93Ramd64-development-n env -i TERM=$TERM /usr/bin/login -fp root
# [do some stuff in the jail]
# exit
# poudriere jail -k -j 93Ramd64 -p development
=====>> Umounting file systems
```

An integral part of the FreeBSD ports build infrastructure is the ability to tweak ports to personal preferences with options. These can be tested with Poudriere as well. Adding the `-c`:

```
# poudriere testport -c -o www/firefox
```

Presents the port configuration dialog before the port is built. The ports given after `-o` in the format *category/portname* will use the specified options, all dependencies will use the default options. Testing dependent ports with non-default options can be accomplished using sets, see Section 9.5.9, "Using Sets".

Tip

When testing ports where `pkg-plist` is altered during build depending on the selected options, it is recommended to perform a test run with all options selected *and* one with all options deselected.

9.5.9. Using Sets

For all actions involving builds, a so-called *set* can be specified using -z *setname*. A set refers to a fully independent build. This allows, for instance, usage of `testport` with non-standard options for the dependent ports.

To use sets, Poudriere expects an existing directory structure similar to `PORT_DBDIR`, defaults to `/var/db/ports` in its configuration directory. This directory is then nullfs-mounted into the jails where the ports and their dependencies are built. Usually a suitable starting point can be obtained by recursively copying the existing `PORT_DBDIR` to `/usr/local/etc/poudriere.d/` *jailname-portname-setname*-options. This is described in detail in poudriere(8). For instance, testing www/firefox in a specific set named `devset`, add the -z `devset` parameter to the testport command:

```
# poudriere testport -j 93Ramd64 -p development -z devset -o www/firefox
```

This will look for the existence of these directories in this order:

- /usr/local/etc/poudriere.d/93Ramd64-development-devset-options

- /usr/local/etc/poudriere.d/93Ramd64-devset-options

- /usr/local/etc/poudriere.d/93Ramd64-development-options

- /usr/local/etc/poudriere.d/devset-options

- /usr/local/etc/poudriere.d/development-options

- /usr/local/etc/poudriere.d/93Ramd64-options

- /usr/local/etc/poudriere.d/options

From this list, Poudriere nullfs-mounts the *first existing* directory tree into the `/var/db/ports` directory of the build jails. Hence, all custom options are used for all the ports during this run of `testport`.

After the directory structure for a set is provided, the options for a particular port can be altered. For example:

```
# poudriere options -c www/firefox -z devset
```

The configuration dialog for www/firefox is shown, and options can be edited. The selected options are saved to the `devset` set.

> **Note**
>
> Poudriere is very flexible in the option configuration. They can be set for particular jails, ports trees, and for multiple ports by one command. Refer to poudriere(8) for details.

9.5.10. Providing a Custom `make.conf` File

Similar to using sets, Poudriere will also use a custom `make.conf` if it is provided. No special command line argument is necessary. Instead, Poudriere looks for existing files matching a name scheme derived from the command line. For instance:

```
# poudriere testport -j 93Ramd64 -p development -z devset -o www/firefox
```

causes Poudriere to check for the existence of these files in this order:

- /usr/local/etc/poudriere.d/make.conf

- /usr/local/etc/poudriere.d/devset-make.conf

- /usr/local/etc/poudriere.d/development-make.conf

- /usr/local/etc/poudriere.d/93Ramd64-make.conf

- /usr/local/etc/poudriere.d/93Ramd64-development-make.conf

- /usr/local/etc/poudriere.d/93Ramd64-devset-make.conf

- /usr/local/etc/poudriere.d/93Ramd64-development-devset-make.conf

Unlike with sets, all of the found files will be appended, *in that order*, into one make.conf inside the build jails. It is hence possible to have general make variables, intended to affect all builds in /usr/local/etc/poudriere.d/ make.conf . Special variables, intended to affect only certain jails or sets can be set in specialised make.conf files, such as /usr/local/etc/poudriere.d/93Ramd64-development-devset-make.conf .

Example 9.1. Using **make.conf** to Change Default Perl

To build a set with a non default Perl version, for example, 5.20, using a set named perl5-20, create a perl5-20-make.conf with this line:

```
DEFAULT_VERSIONS+= perl=5.20
```

Note

Note the use of += so that if the variable is already set in the default make.conf its content will not be overwritten.

9.5.11. Pruning no Longer Needed Distfiles

Poudriere comes with a built-in mechanism to remove outdated distfiles that are no longer used by any port of a given tree. The command

```
# poudriere distclean -p portstree
```

will scan the distfiles folder, DISTFILES_CACHE in poudriere.conf , versus the ports tree given by the -p *portstree* argument and prompt for removal of those distfiles. To skip the prompt and remove all unused files unconditionally, the -y argument can be added:

```
# poudriere distclean -p portstree -y
```

9.6. Tinderbox

As an avid ports contributor, take a look at Tinderbox. It is a powerful system for building and testing ports. Install Tinderbox using ports-mgmt/tinderbox port. Be sure to read supplied documentation since the configuration is not trivial.

Visit the Tinderbox website for more details.

Chapter 10. Upgrading a Port

When a port is not the most recent version available from the authors, update the local working copy of /usr/ports. The port might have already been updated to the new version.

When working with more than a few ports, it will probably be easier to use Subversion to keep the whole ports collection up-to-date, as described in the Handbook. This will have the added benefit of tracking all the port's dependencies.

The next step is to see if there is an update already pending. To do this, there are two options. There is a searchable interface to the FreeBSD Problem Report (PR) or bug database. Select Ports Tree in the Product dropdown, and enter the name of the port in the Summary field.

However, sometimes people forget to put the name of the port into the Summary field in an unambiguous fashion. In that case, try searching in the Comment field in the Detailed Bug Information section, or try the FreeBSD Ports Monitoring System (also known as portsmon). This system attempts to classify port PRs by portname. To search for PRs about a particular port, use the Overview of One Port.

If there is no pending PR, the next step is to send an email to the port's maintainer, as shown by make maintainer. That person may already be working on an upgrade, or have a reason to not upgrade the port right now (because of, for example, stability problems of the new version), and there is no need to duplicate their work. Note that unmaintained ports are listed with a maintainer of ports@FreeBSD.org, which is just the general ports mailing list, so sending mail there probably will not help in this case.

If the maintainer asks you to do the upgrade or there is no maintainer, then help out FreeBSD by preparing the update! Please do this by using the diff(1) command in the base system.

To create a suitable diff for a single patch, copy the file that needs patching to *something* .orig, save the changes to *something* and then create the patch:

```
% diff -u something .orig something > something.diff
```

Otherwise, either use the svn diff method (Section 10.1, "Using Subversion to Make Patches") or copy the contents of the port to an entire different directory and use the result of the recursive diff(1) output of the new and old ports directories (for example, if the modified port directory is called superedit and the original is in our tree as superedit.bak, then save the result of diff -ruN superedit.bak superedit). Either unified or context diff is fine, but port committers generally prefer unified diffs. Note the use of the -N option—this is the accepted way to force diff to properly deal with the case of new files being added or old files being deleted. Before sending us the diff, please examine the output to make sure all the changes make sense. (In particular, make sure to first clean out the work directories with make clean).

>
>
> ### Note
>
> If some files have been added, copied, moved, or removed, add this information to the problem report so that the committer picking up the patch will know what svn(1) commands to run.

To simplify common operations with patch files, use make makepatch as described in Section 4.4, "Patching". Other tools exists, like /usr/ports/Tools/scripts/patchtool.py . Before using it, please read /usr/ports/Tools/scripts/README.patchtool .

If the port is unmaintained, and you are actively using it, please consider volunteering to become its maintainer. FreeBSD has over 4000 ports without maintainers, and this is an area where more volunteers are always needed. (For a detailed description of the responsibilities of maintainers, refer to the section in the Developer's Handbook.)

To submit the diff, use the bug submit form (product `Ports & Packages`, component `Individual Port(s)`). If the submitter is also maintaining the port, be sure to put `[MAINTAINER]` at the beginning of the `Summary` line. Always include the category with the port name, followed by colon, and brief descripton of the issue. For example: *category/portname*: *add FOO option*, or if maintaining the port, `[MAINTAINER]` *category/portname*: *Update to X.Y*. Please mention any added or deleted files in the message, as they have to be explicitly specified to svn(1) when doing a commit. Do not compress or encode the diff.

Before submitting the bug, review the Writing the problem report section in the Problem Reports article. It contains far more information about how to write useful problem reports.

Important

If the upgrade is motivated by security concerns or a serious fault in the currently committed port, please notify the Ports Management Team <portmgr@FreeBSD.org> to request immediate rebuilding and redistribution of the port's package. Unsuspecting users of `pkg` will otherwise continue to install the old version via `pkg install` for several weeks.

Note

Please use diff(1) or `svn diff` to create updates to existing ports. Other formats include the whole file and make it impossible to see just what has changed. When diffs are not included, the entire update might be ignored.

Now that all of that is done, read about how to keep up-to-date in Chapter 14, *Keeping Up*.

10.1. Using Subversion to Make Patches

When possible, please submit a svn(1) diff. They are easier to handle than diffs between "new and old" directories. It is easier to see what has changed, and to update the diff if something was modified in the Ports Collection since the work on it began, or if the committer asks for something to be fixed. Also, a patch generated with `svn diff` can be easily applied with `svn patch` and will save some time to the committer.

```
% cd ~/my_wrkdir ❶
% svn co https://svn.FreeBSD.org /ports/head/dns/pdnsd ❷
% cd ~/my_wrkdir/pdnsd
```

❶   This can be anywhere, of course. Building ports is not limited to within /usr/ports/ .
❷   svn.FreeBSD.org is the FreeBSD public Subversion server. See Subversion mirror sites for more information.

While in the port directory, make any changes that are needed. If adding, copying, moving, or removing a file, use svn to track these changes:

```
% svn add new_file
% svn copy some_file file_copy
% svn move old_name new_name
% svn remove deleted_file
```

Make sure to check the port using the checklist in Section 3.4, "Testing the Port" and Section 3.5, "Checking the Port with portlint".

```
% svn status
% svn update ❶
```

❶ This will attempt to merge the differences between the patch and current repository version. Watch the output carefully. The letter in front of each file name indicates what was done with it. See Table 10.1, "Subversion Update File Prefixes" for a complete list.

Table 10.1. Subversion Update File Prefixes

U	The file was updated without problems.
G	The file was updated without problems (only when working against a remote repository).
M	The file had been modified, and was merged without conflicts.
C	The file had been modified, and was merged with conflicts.

If C is displayed as a result of **svn update**, it means something changed in the Subversion repository and svn(1) was not able to merge the local changes with those from the repository. It is always a good idea to inspect the changes anyway, since svn(1) does not know anything about the structure of a port, so it might (and probably will) merge things that do not make sense.

The last step is to make a unified diff(1) of the changes:

```
% svn diff > ../`make -VPKGNAME`.diff
```

Note

If files have been added, copied, moved, or removed, include the svn(1) **add**, **copy**, **move**, and **remove** commands that were used. **svn move** or **svn copy** must be run before the patch can be applied. **svn add** or **svn remove** must be run after the patch is applied.

Send the patch following the problem report submission guidelines.

Tip

The patch can be automatically generated and the PR pre-filled with the contact information by using **port submit**. See Section 9.3, "Port Tools" for more details.

10.2. UPDATING and MOVED

10.2.1. /usr/ports/UPDATING

If upgrading the port requires special steps like changing configuration files or running a specific program, it must be documented in this file. The format of an entry in this file is:

```
YYYYMMDD:
  AFFECTS: users of portcategory/portname
  AUTHOR: Your name <Your email address>

  Special instructions
```

Tip

When including exact portmaster, portupgrade, and/or pkg instructions, please make sure to get the shell escaping right. For example, do *not* use:

```
# pkg delete -g -f docbook-xml* docbook-sk* docbook[2345]??-* docbook-4*
```

As shown, the command will only work with bourne shells. Instead, use the form shown below, which will work with both bourne shell and c-shell:

```
# pkg delete -g -f docbook-xml\* docbook-sk\* docbook\[2345\]\?\?-\* ↵
docbook-4\*
```

Note

It is recommended that the AFFECTS line contains a glob matching all the ports affected by the entry so that automated tools can parse it as easily as possible. If an update concerns all the existing BIND 9 versions the AFFECTS content must be `users of dns/bind9*`, it must *not* be `users of BIND 9`

10.2.2. /usr/ports/MOVED

This file is used to list moved or removed ports. Each line in the file is made up of the name of the port, where the port was moved, when, and why. If the port was removed, the section detailing where it was moved can be left blank. Each section must be separated by the | (pipe) character, like so:

```
old name|new name (blank for deleted)|date of move|reason
```

The date must be entered in the form YYYY-MM-DD. New entries are added to the end of the list to keep it in chronological order, with the oldest entry at the top of the list.

If a port was removed but has since been restored, delete the line in this file that states that it was removed.

If a port was renamed and then renamed back to its original name, add a new one with the intermediate name to the old name, and remove the old entry as to not create a loop.

Note

Any changes must be validated with `Tools/scripts/MOVEDlint.awk`.

If using a ports directory other than /usr/ports, use:

```
% cd /home/user/ports
  % env PORTSDIR=$PWD Tools/scripts/MOVEDlint.awk
```

Chapter 11. Security

11.1. Why Security is So Important

Bugs are occasionally introduced to the software. Arguably, the most dangerous of them are those opening security vulnerabilities. From the technical viewpoint, such vulnerabilities are to be closed by exterminating the bugs that caused them. However, the policies for handling mere bugs and security vulnerabilities are very different.

A typical small bug affects only those users who have enabled some combination of options triggering the bug. The developer will eventually release a patch followed by a new version of the software, free of the bug, but the majority of users will not take the trouble of upgrading immediately because the bug has never vexed them. A critical bug that may cause data loss represents a graver issue. Nevertheless, prudent users know that a lot of possible accidents, besides software bugs, are likely to lead to data loss, and so they make backups of important data; in addition, a critical bug will be discovered really soon.

A security vulnerability is all different. First, it may remain unnoticed for years because often it does not cause software malfunction. Second, a malicious party can use it to gain unauthorized access to a vulnerable system, to destroy or alter sensitive data; and in the worst case the user will not even notice the harm caused. Third, exposing a vulnerable system often assists attackers to break into other systems that could not be compromised otherwise. Therefore closing a vulnerability alone is not enough: notify the audience of it in the most clear and comprehensive manner, which will allow them to evaluate the danger and take appropriate action.

11.2. Fixing Security Vulnerabilities

While on the subject of ports and packages, a security vulnerability may initially appear in the original distribution or in the port files. In the former case, the original software developer is likely to release a patch or a new version instantly. Update the port promptly with respect to the author's fix. If the fix is delayed for some reason, either mark the port as FORBIDDEN or introduce a patch file to the port. In the case of a vulnerable port, just fix the port as soon as possible. In either case, follow the standard procedure for submitting changes unless having rights to commit it directly to the ports tree.

 Important

Being a ports committer is not enough to commit to an arbitrary port. Remember that ports usually have maintainers, must be respected.

Please make sure that the port's revision is bumped as soon as the vulnerability has been closed. That is how the users who upgrade installed packages on a regular basis will see they need to run an update. Besides, a new package will be built and distributed over FTP and WWW mirrors, replacing the vulnerable one. Bump PORTREVISION unless PORTVERSION has changed in the course of correcting the vulnerability. That is, bump PORTREVISION if adding a patch file to the port, but do not bump it if updating the port to the latest software version and thus already touched PORTVERSION . Please refer to the corresponding section for more information.

11.3. Keeping the Community Informed

11.3.1. The VuXML Database

A very important and urgent step to take as early after a security vulnerability is discovered as possible is to notify the community of port users about the jeopardy. Such notification serves two purposes. First, if the danger is really severe it will be wise to apply an instant workaround. For example, stop the affected network service or even deinstall the port completely until the vulnerability is closed. Second, a lot of users tend to upgrade installed packages only occasionally. They will know from the notification that they *must* update the package without delay as soon as a corrected version is available.

Given the huge number of ports in the tree, a security advisory cannot be issued on each incident without creating a flood and losing the attention of the audience when it comes to really serious matters. Therefore security vulnerabilities found in ports are recorded in the FreeBSD VuXML database. The Security Officer Team members also monitor it for issues requiring their intervention.

Committers can update the VuXML database themselves, assisting the Security Officer Team and delivering crucial information to the community more quickly. Those who are not committers or have discovered an exceptionally severe vulnerability should not hesitate to contact the Security Officer Team directly, as described on the FreeBSD Security Information page.

The VuXML database is an XML document. Its source file `vuln.xml` is kept right inside the port security/vuxml. Therefore the file's full pathname will be `PORTSDIR/security/vuxml/vuln.xml`. Each time a security vulnerability is discovered in a port, please add an entry for it to that file. Until familiar with VuXML, the best thing to do is to find an existing entry fitting the case at hand, then copy it and use it as a template.

11.3.2. A Short Introduction to VuXML

The full-blown XML format is complex, and far beyond the scope of this book. However, to gain basic insight on the structure of a VuXML entry only the notion of tags is needed. XML tag names are enclosed in angle brackets. Each opening <tag> must have a matching closing </tag>. Tags may be nested. If nesting, the inner tags must be closed before the outer ones. There is a hierarchy of tags, that is, more complex rules of nesting them. This is similar to HTML. The major difference is that XML is eXtensible, that is, based on defining custom tags. Due to its intrinsic structure XML puts otherwise amorphous data into shape. VuXML is particularly tailored to mark up descriptions of security vulnerabilities.

Now consider a realistic VuXML entry:

```
<vuln vid="f4bc80f4-da62-11d8-90ea-0004ac98a7b9"> ❶
  <topic>Several vulnerabilities found in Foo</topic> ❷
  <affects>
    <package>
      <name>foo</name> ❸
      <name>foo-devel</name>
      <name>ja-foo</name>
      <range><ge>1.6</ge><lt>1.9</lt></range> ❹
      <range><ge>2.*</ge><lt>2.4_1</lt></range>
      <range><eq>3.0b1</eq></range>
    </package>
    <package>
      <name>openfoo</name> ❺
      <range><lt>1.10_7</lt></range> ❻
      <range><ge>1.2,1</ge><lt>1.3_1,1</lt></range>
    </package>
  </affects>
  <description>
    <body xmlns="http://www.w3.org/1999/xhtml">
      <p>J. Random Hacker reports:</p> ❼
      <blockquote
        cite="http://j.r.hacker.com/advisories/1">
        <p>Several issues in the Foo software may be exploited
          via carefully crafted QUUX requests.  These requests will
          permit the injection of Bar code, mumble theft, and the
          readability of the Foo administrator account.</p>
      </blockquote>
    </body>
  </description>
```

```
  <references> ❽
    <freebsdsa>SA-10:75.foo</freebsdsa> ❾
    <freebsdpr>ports/987654</freebsdpr> ❿
    <cvename>CAN-2010-0201</cvename> ⓫
    <cvename>CAN-2010-0466</cvename>
    <bid>96298</bid> ⓬
    <certsa>CA-2010-99</certsa> ⓭
    <certvu>740169</certvu> ⓮
    <uscertsa>SA10-99A</uscertsa> ⓯
    <uscertta>SA10-99A</uscertta> ⓰
    <mlist msgid="201075606@hacker.com">http://marc.theaimsgroup.com/?
l=bugtraq&amp;m=203886607825605</mlist> ⓱
    <url>http://j.r.hacker.com/advisories/1</url> ⓲
  </references>
  <dates>
    <discovery>2010-05-25</discovery> ⓳
    <entry>2010-07-13</entry> ⓴
    <modified>2010-09-17</modified> ㉑
  </dates>
</vuln>
```

The tag names are supposed to be self-explanatory so we shall take a closer look only at fields which needs to be filled in:

❶   This is the top-level tag of a VuXML entry. It has a mandatory attribute, vid, specifying a universally unique identifier (UUID) for this entry (in quotes). Generate a UUID for each new VuXML entry (and do not forget to substitute it for the template UUID unless writing the entry from scratch). use uuidgen(1) to generate a VuXML UUID.

❷   This is a one-line description of the issue found.

❸   The names of packages affected are listed there. Multiple names can be given since several packages may be based on a single master port or software product. This may include stable and development branches, localized versions, and slave ports featuring different choices of important build-time configuration options.

 Important

It is the submitter's responsibility to find all such related packages when writing a VuXML entry. Keep in mind that make search name=foo is helpful. The primary points to look for are:

- the foo-devel variant for a foo port;

- other variants with a suffix like -a4 (for print-related packages), -without-gui (for packages with X support disabled), or similar;

- jp-, ru-, zh-, and other possible localized variants in the corresponding national categories of the ports collection.

---

❹   Affected versions of the package(s) are specified there as one or more ranges using a combination of <lt>, <le>, <eq>, <ge>, and <gt> elements. Check that the version ranges given do not overlap.

In a range specification, * (asterisk) denotes the smallest version number. In particular, 2.* is less than 2.a. Therefore an asterisk may be used for a range to match all possible alpha, beta, and RC versions. For instance, <ge>2.*</ge><lt>3.*</lt> will selectively match every 2.x version while <ge>2.0</ge><lt>3.0</lt> will not since the latter misses 2.r3 and matches 3.b.

The above example specifies that affected are versions from 1.6 to 1.9 inclusive, versions 2.x before 2.4_1, and version 3.0b1.

❺ Several related package groups (essentially, ports) can be listed in the `<affected>` section. This can be used if several software products (say FooBar, FreeBar and OpenBar) grow from the same code base and still share its bugs and vulnerabilities. Note the difference from listing multiple names within a single `<package>` section.

❻ The version ranges have to allow for `PORTEPOCH` and `PORTREVISION` if applicable. Please remember that according to the collation rules, a version with a non-zero `PORTEPOCH` is greater than any version without `PORTEPOCH`, for example, 3.0,1 is greater than 3.1 or even than 8.9.

❼ This is a summary of the issue. XHTML is used in this field. At least enclosing `<p>` and `</p>` has to appear. More complex mark-up may be used, but only for the sake of accuracy and clarity: No eye candy please.

❽ This section contains references to relevant documents. As many references as apply are encouraged.

❾ This is a FreeBSD security advisory.

❿ This is a FreeBSD problem report.

⓫ This is a MITRE CVE identifier.

⓬ This is a SecurityFocus Bug ID.

⓭ This is a US-CERT security advisory.

⓮ This is a US-CERT vulnerability note.

⓯ This is a US-CERT Cyber Security Alert.

⓰ This is a US-CERT Technical Cyber Security Alert.

⓱ This is a URL to an archived posting in a mailing list. The attribute `msgid` is optional and may specify the message ID of the posting.

⓲ This is a generic URL. Only it if none of the other reference categories apply.

⓳ This is the date when the issue was disclosed (*YYYY-MM-DD*).

⓴ This is the date when the entry was added (*YYYY-MM-DD*).

㉑ This is the date when any information in the entry was last modified (*YYYY-MM-DD*). New entries must not include this field. Add it when editing an existing entry.

11.3.3. Testing Changes to the VuXML Database

This example describes a new entry for a vulnerability in the package `dropbear` that has been fixed in version `dropbear-2013.59`.

As a prerequisite, install a fresh version of security/vuxml port.

First, check whether there already is an entry for this vulnerability. If there were such an entry, it would match the previous version of the package, 2013.58 :

```
% pkg audit dropbear-2013.58
```

If there is none found, add a new entry for this vulnerability.

```
% cd ${PORTSDIR}/security/vuxml
% make newentry
```

Verify its syntax and formatting:

```
% make validate
```

Note

At least one of these packages needs to be installed: textproc/libxml2, textproc/jade.

Verify that the `<affected>` section of the entry will match the correct packages:

```
% pkg audit -f ${PORTSDIR}/security/vuxml/vuln.xml dropbear-2013.58
```

Make sure that the entry produces no spurious matches in the output.

Now check whether the right package versions are matched by the entry:

```
% pkg audit -f ${PORTSDIR}/security/vuxml/vuln.xml dropbear-2013.58 dropbear-2013.59
dropbear-2012.58 is vulnerable:
dropbear -- exposure of sensitive information, DoS
CVE: CVE-2013-4434
CVE: CVE-2013-4421
WWW: http://portaudit.FreeBSD.org/8c9b48d1-3715-11e3-a624-00262d8b701d.html

1 problem(s) in the installed packages found.
```

The former version matches while the latter one does not.

Chapter 12. Dos and Don'ts

12.1. Introduction

Here is a list of common dos and don'ts that are encountered during the porting process. Check the port against this list, but also check ports in the PR database that others have submitted. Submit any comments on ports as described in Bug Reports and General Commentary. Checking ports in the PR database will both make it faster for us to commit them, and prove that you know what you are doing.

12.2. WRKDIR

Do not write anything to files outside WRKDIR. WRKDIR is the only place that is guaranteed to be writable during the port build (see installing ports from a CDROM for an example of building ports from a read-only tree). The pkg-* files can be modified by redefining a variable rather than overwriting the file.

12.3. WRKDIRPREFIX

Make sure the port honors WRKDIRPREFIX. Most ports do not have to worry about this. In particular, when referring to a WRKDIR of another port, note that the correct location is WRKDIRPREFIXPORTSDIR/*subdir*/*name*/work not PORTSDIR/*subdir*/*name*/work or .CURDIR/../../*subdir*/*name*/work or some such.

Also, if defining WRKDIR, make sure to prepend ${WRKDIRPREFIX}${.CURDIR} in the front.

12.4. Differentiating Operating Systems and OS Versions

Some code needs modifications or conditional compilation based upon what version of FreeBSD Unix it is running under. The preferred way to tell FreeBSD versions apart are the __FreeBSD_version and __FreeBSD__ macros defined in sys/param.h. If this file is not included add the code,

```
#include <sys/param.h>
```

to the proper place in the .c file.

__FreeBSD__ is defined in all versions of FreeBSD as their major version number. For example, in FreeBSD 9.x, __FreeBSD__ is defined to be 9.

```
#if __FreeBSD__ >= 9
#  if __FreeBSD_version >= 901000
   /* 9.1+ release specific code here */
#  endif
#endif
```

A complete list of __FreeBSD_version values is available in Chapter 16, *__FreeBSD_version Values*.

12.5. Writing Something After bsd.port.mk

Do not write anything after the .include <bsd.port.mk> line. It usually can be avoided by including bsd.port.pre.mk somewhere in the middle of the Makefile and bsd.port.post.mk at the end.

Important

Include either the bsd.port.pre.mk/bsd.port.post.mk pair or bsd.port.mk only; do not mix these two usages.

bsd.port.pre.mk only defines a few variables, which can be used in tests in the Makefile, bsd.port.post.mk defines the rest.

Here are some important variables defined in bsd.port.pre.mk (this is not the complete list, please read bsd.port.mk for the complete list).

Variable	Description
ARCH	The architecture as returned by uname -m (for example, i386)
OPSYS	The operating system type, as returned by uname -s (for example, FreeBSD)
OSREL	The release version of the operating system (for example, 2.1.5 or 2.2.7)
OSVERSION	The numeric version of the operating system; the same as __FreeBSD_version.
LOCALBASE	The base of the "local" tree (for example, /usr/local)
PREFIX	Where the port installs itself (see more on PREFIX).

Note

When MASTERDIR is needed, always define it before including bsd.port.pre.mk.

Here are some examples of things that can be added after bsd.port.pre.mk:

```
# no need to compile lang/perl5 if perl5 is already in system
.if ${OSVERSION} > 300003
BROKEN= perl is in system
.endif
```

Always use tab instead of spaces after BROKEN=.

12.6. Use the exec **Statement in Wrapper Scripts**

If the port installs a shell script whose purpose is to launch another program, and if launching that program is the last action performed by the script, make sure to launch the program using the **exec** statement, for instance:

```
#!/bin/sh
exec %%LOCALBASE%%/bin/java -jar %%DATADIR%%/foo.jar "$@"
```

The **exec** statement replaces the shell process with the specified program. If **exec** is omitted, the shell process remains in memory while the program is executing, and needlessly consumes system resources.

12.7. Do Things Rationally

The Makefile should do things in a simple and reasonable manner. Making it a couple of lines shorter or more readable is always better. Examples include using a make .if construct instead of a shell if construct, not redefining do-extract if redefining EXTRACT* is enough, and using GNU_CONFIGURE instead of CONFIGURE_ARGS += --prefix=${PREFIX}.

If a lot of new code is needed to do something, there may already be an implementation of it in bsd.port.mk. While hard to read, there are a great many seemingly-hard problems for which bsd.port.mk already provides a shorthand solution.

12.8. Respect Both cc and cxx

The port must respect both CC and CXX. What we mean by this is that the port must not set the values of these variables absolutely, overriding existing values; instead, it may append whatever values it needs to the existing values. This is so that build options that affect all ports can be set globally.

If the port does not respect these variables, please add NO_PACKAGE=ignores either cc or cxx to the Makefile.

Here is an example of a Makefile respecting both CC and CXX. Note the ?=:

```
CC?= gcc
```

```
CXX?= g++
```

Here is an example which respects neither CC nor CXX:

```
CC= gcc
```

```
CXX= g++
```

Both CC and CXX can be defined on FreeBSD systems in /etc/make.conf . The first example defines a value if it was not previously set in /etc/make.conf , preserving any system-wide definitions. The second example clobbers anything previously defined.

12.9. Respect cflags

The port must respect CFLAGS. What we mean by this is that the port must not set the value of this variable absolutely, overriding the existing value. Instead, it may append whatever values it needs to the existing value. This is so that build options that affect all ports can be set globally.

If it does not, please add NO_PACKAGE=ignores cflags to the Makefile.

Here is an example of a Makefile respecting CFLAGS. Note the +=:

```
CFLAGS+= -Wall -Werror
```

Here is an example which does not respect CFLAGS :

```
CFLAGS= -Wall -Werror
```

CFLAGS is defined on FreeBSD systems in /etc/make.conf . The first example appends additional flags to CFLAGS , preserving any system-wide definitions. The second example clobbers anything previously defined.

Remove optimization flags from the third party Makefiles. The system CFLAGS contains system-wide optimization flags. An example from an unmodified Makefile:

```
CFLAGS= -O3 -funroll-loops -DHAVE_SOUND
```

Using system optimization flags, the `Makefile` would look similar to this example:

```
CFLAGS+= -DHAVE_SOUND
```

12.10. Verbose Build Logs

Make the port build system display all commands executed during the build stage. Complete build logs are crucial to debugging port problems.

Non-informative build log example (bad):

```
CC      source1.o
CC      source2.o
CCLD    someprogram
```

Verbose build log example (good):

```
cc -O2 -pipe -I/usr/local/include -c -o source1.o source1.c
cc -O2 -pipe -I/usr/local/include -c -o source2.o source2.c
cc -o someprogram source1.o source2.o -L/usr/local/lib -lsomelib
```

Some build systems such as CMake, ninja, and GNU configure are set up for verbose logging by the ports framework. In other cases, ports might need individial tweaks.

12.11. Feedback

Do send applicable changes and patches to the upstream maintainer for inclusion in the next release of the code. This makes updating to the next release that much easier.

12.12. README.html

`README.html` is not part of the port, but generated by `make readme`. Do not include this file in patches or commits.

> **Note**
>
> If `make readme` fails, make sure that the default value of `ECHO_MSG` has not been modified by the port.

12.13. Marking a Port as Architecture Neutral

Ports that do not have any architecture-dependent files or requirements are identified by setting `NO_ARCH=yes` .

12.14. Marking a Port Not Installable with BROKEN, FORBIDDEN, or IGNORE

In certain cases, users must be prevented from installing a port. There are several variables that can be used in a port's `Makefile` to tell the user that the port cannot be installed. The value of these make variables will be the reason that is shown to users for why the port refuses to install itself. Please use the correct make variable. Each variable conveys radically different meanings, both to users and to automated systems that depend on `Makefiles`, such as the ports build cluster, FreshPorts, and portsmon.

12.14.1. Variables

- BROKEN is reserved for ports that currently do not compile, install, deinstall, or run correctly. Use it for ports where the problem is believed to be temporary.

  If instructed, the build cluster will still attempt to try to build them to see if the underlying problem has been resolved. (However, in general, the cluster is run without this.)

  For instance, use BROKEN when a port:

  - does not compile

  - fails its configuration or installation process

  - installs files outside of ${PREFIX}

  - does not remove all its files cleanly upon deinstall (however, it may be acceptable, and desirable, for the port to leave user-modified files behind)

  - has runtime issues on systems where it is supposed to run fine.

- FORBIDDEN is used for ports that contain a security vulnerability or induce grave concern regarding the security of a FreeBSD system with a given port installed (for example, a reputably insecure program or a program that provides easily exploitable services). Mark ports as FORBIDDEN as soon as a particular piece of software has a vulnerability and there is no released upgrade. Ideally upgrade ports as soon as possible when a security vulnerability is discovered so as to reduce the number of vulnerable FreeBSD hosts (we like being known for being secure), however sometimes there is a noticeable time gap between disclosure of a vulnerability and an updated release of the vulnerable software. Do not mark a port FORBIDDEN for any reason other than security.

- IGNORE is reserved for ports that must not be built for some other reason. Use it for ports where the problem is believed to be structural. The build cluster will not, under any circumstances, build ports marked as IGNORE. For instance, use IGNORE when a port:

  - does not work on the installed version of FreeBSD

  - has a distfile which may not be automatically fetched due to licensing restrictions

  - does not work with some other currently installed port (for instance, the port depends on www/apache20 but www/apache22 is installed)

> ### Note
>
> If a port would conflict with a currently installed port (for example, if they install a file in the same place that performs a different function), use CONFLICTS instead. CONFLICTS will set IGNORE by itself.

- To mark a port as IGNOREd only on certain architectures, there are two other convenience variables that will automatically set IGNORE: ONLY_FOR_ARCHS and NOT_FOR_ARCHS . Examples:

```
ONLY_FOR_ARCHS= i386 amd64
```

```
NOT_FOR_ARCHS= ia64 sparc64
```

A custom IGNORE message can be set using ONLY_FOR_ARCHS_REASON and NOT_FOR_ARCHS_REASON . Per architecture entries are possible with ONLY_FOR_ARCHS_REASON_ARCH and NOT_FOR_ARCHS_REASON_ ARCH.

- If a port fetches i386 binaries and installs them, set `IA32_BINARY_PORT`. If this variable is set, `/usr/lib32` must be present for IA32 versions of libraries and the kernel must support IA32 compatibility. If one of these two dependencies is not satisfied, `IGNORE` will be set automatically.

12.14.2. Implementation Notes

Do not quote the values of `BROKEN`, `IGNORE`, and related variables. Due to the way the information is shown to the user, the wording of messages for each variable differ:

```
BROKEN= fails to link with base -lcrypto
```

```
IGNORE= unsupported on recent versions
```

resulting in this output from `make describe`:

```
===>  foobar-0.1 is marked as broken: fails to link with base -lcrypto.
```

```
===>  foobar-0.1 is unsupported on recent versions.
```

12.15. Marking a Port for Removal with DEPRECATED or EXPIRATION_DATE

Do remember that `BROKEN` and `FORBIDDEN` are to be used as a temporary resort if a port is not working. Permanently broken ports will be removed from the tree entirely.

When it makes sense to do so, users can be warned about a pending port removal with `DEPRECATED` and `EXPIRATION_DATE`. The former is a string stating why the port is scheduled for removal; the latter is a string in ISO 8601 format (YYYY-MM-DD). Both will be shown to the user.

It is possible to set `DEPRECATED` without an `EXPIRATION_DATE` (for instance, recommending a newer version of the port), but the converse does not make any sense.

There is no set policy on how much notice to give. Current practice seems to be one month for security-related issues and two months for build issues. This also gives any interested committers a little time to fix the problems.

12.16. Avoid Use of the .error Construct

The correct way for a `Makefile` to signal that the port cannot be installed due to some external factor (for instance, the user has specified an illegal combination of build options) is to set a non-blank value to `IGNORE`. This value will be formatted and shown to the user by `make install`.

It is a common mistake to use `.error` for this purpose. The problem with this is that many automated tools that work with the ports tree will fail in this situation. The most common occurrence of this is seen when trying to build `/usr/ports/INDEX` (see Section 9.1, "Running `make describe`"). However, even more trivial commands such as `make maintainer` also fail in this scenario. This is not acceptable.

> ### Example 12.1. How to Avoid Using .error
>
> The first of the next two `Makefile` snippets will cause `make index` to fail, while the second one will not:
>
> ```
> .error "option is not supported"
> ```
>
> ```
> IGNORE=option is not supported
> ```

12.17. Usage of `sysctl`

The usage of `sysctl` is discouraged except in targets. This is because the evaluation of any `makevars`, such as used during `make index`, then has to run the command, further slowing down that process.

Only use sysctl(8) through `SYSCTL`, as it contains the fully qualified path and can be overridden, if one has such a special need.

12.18. Rerolling Distfiles

Sometimes the authors of software change the content of released distfiles without changing the file's name. Verify that the changes are official and have been performed by the author. It has happened in the past that the distfile was silently altered on the download servers with the intent to cause harm or compromise end user security.

Put the old distfile aside, download the new one, unpack them and compare the content with diff(1). If there is nothing suspicious, update `distinfo`. Be sure to summarize the differences in the PR or commit log, so that other people know that nothing bad has happened.

Contact the authors of the software and confirm the changes with them.

12.19. Use POSIX Standards

FreeBSD ports generally expect POSIX compliance. Some software and build systems make assumptions based on a particular operating system or environment that can cause problems when used in a port.

Do not use `/proc` if there are any other ways of getting the information. For example, `setprogname(argv[0])` in `main()` and then getprogname(3) to know the executable name.

Do not rely on behavior that is undocumented by POSIX.

Do not record timestamps in the critical path of the application if it also works without. Getting timestamps may be slow, depending on the accuracy of timestamps in the OS. If timestamps are really needed, determine how precise they have to be and use an API which is documented to just deliver the needed precision.

A number of simple syscalls (for example gettimeofday(2), getpid(2)) are much faster on Linux® than on any other operating system due to caching and the vsyscall performance optimizations. Do not rely on them being cheap in performance-critical applications. In general, try hard to avoid syscalls if possible.

Do not rely on Linux®-specific socket behavior. In particular, default socket buffer sizes are different (call setsockopt(2) with `SO_SNDBUF` and `SO_RCVBUF`, and while Linux®'s send(2) blocks when the socket buffer is full, FreeBSD's will fail and set `ENOBUFS` in errno.

If relying on non-standard behavior is required, encapsulate it properly into a generic API, do a check for the behavior in the configure stage, and stop if it is missing.

Check the man pages to see if the function used is a POSIX interface (in the "STANDARDS" section of the man page).

Do not assume that `/bin/sh` is bash. Ensure that a command line passed to system(3) will work with a POSIX compliant shell.

A list of common bashisms is available here.

Check that headers are included in the POSIX or man page recommended way. For example, `sys/types.h` is often forgotten, which is not as much of a problem for Linux® as it is for FreeBSD.

12.20. Miscellanea

Always double-check `pkg-descr` and `pkg-plist`. If reviewing a port and a better wording can be achieved, do so.

Do not copy more copies of the GNU General Public License into our system, please.

Please be careful to note any legal issues! Do not let us illegally distribute software!

Chapter 13. A Sample Makefile

Here is a sample `Makefile` that can be used to create a new port. Make sure to remove all the extra comments (ones between brackets).

The format shown is the recommended one for ordering variables, empty lines between sections, and so on. This format is designed so that the most important information is easy to locate. We recommend using portlint to check the `Makefile`.

```
[the header...just to make it easier for us to identify the ports.-]
# Created by: Satoshi Asami <asami@FreeBSD.org>
[The optional Created by: line names the person who originally
created the port.  Note that the ":" is followed by a space
and not a tab character.
If this line is present, future maintainers must
not change or remove it except at the original author's request.-]

# $FreeBSD$
[ ^^^^^^^^^ This will be automatically replaced with RCS ID string by SVN
when it is committed to our repository.  If upgrading a port, do not alter
this line back to "$FreeBSD$".  SVN deals with it automatically.-]

[section to describe the port itself and the master site - PORTNAME
 and PORTVERSION are always first, followed by CATEGORIES,
 and then MASTER_SITES, which can be followed by MASTER_SITE_SUBDIR.
 PKGNAMEPREFIX and PKGNAMESUFFIX, if needed, will be after that.
 Then comes DISTNAME, EXTRACT_SUFX and/or DISTFILES, and then
 EXTRACT_ONLY, as necessary.-]
PORTNAME= xdvi
PORTVERSION= 18.2
CATEGORIES= print
[do not forget the trailing slash ("/")!
 if not using MASTER_SITE_* macros]
MASTER_SITES= ${MASTER_SITE_XCONTRIB}
MASTER_SITE_SUBDIR= applications
PKGNAMEPREFIX= ja-
DISTNAME= xdvi-pl18
[set this if the source is not in the standard ".tar.gz" form]
EXTRACT_SUFX= .tar.Z

[section for distributed patches -- can be empty]
PATCH_SITES= ftp://ftp.sra.co.jp/pub/X11/japanese/
PATCHFILES= xdvi-18.patch1.gz xdvi-18.patch2.gz

[maintainer; *mandatory*!  This is the person who is volunteering to
 handle port updates, build breakages, and to whom a users can direct
 questions and bug reports.  To keep the quality of the Ports Collection
 as high as possible, we no longer accept new ports that are assigned to
 "ports@FreeBSD.org".-]
MAINTAINER= asami@FreeBSD.org
COMMENT= DVI Previewer for the X Window System

[dependencies -- can be empty]
RUN_DEPENDS= gs:print/ghostscript

[this section is for other standard bsd.port.mk variables that do not
 belong to any of the above]
[If it asks questions during configure, build, install...-]
IS_INTERACTIVE= yes
[If it extracts to a directory other than ${DISTNAME}...-]
WRKSRC=  ${WRKDIR}/xdvi-new
[If the distributed patches were not made relative to ${WRKSRC},
 this may need to be tweaked]
PATCH_DIST_STRIP= -p1
```

```
[If it requires a "configure" script generated by GNU autoconf to be run]
GNU_CONFIGURE= yes
[If it requires GNU make, not /usr/bin/make, to build...-]
USES= gmake
[If it is an X application and requires "xmkmf -a" to be run...-]
USES= imake
[et cetera.-]

[non-standard variables to be used in the rules below]
MY_FAVORITE_RESPONSE= "yeah, right"

[then the special rules, in the order they are called]
pre-fetch:
 i go fetch something, yeah

post-patch:
 i need to do something after patch, great

pre-install:
 and then some more stuff before installing, wow

[and then the epilogue]

.include <bsd.port.mk>
```

Chapter 14. Keeping Up

The FreeBSD Ports Collection is constantly changing. Here is some information on how to keep up.

14.1. FreshPorts

One of the easiest ways to learn about updates that have already been committed is by subscribing to FreshPorts. Multiple ports can be monitored. Maintainers are strongly encouraged to subscribe, because they will receive notification of not only their own changes, but also any changes that any other FreeBSD committer has made. (These are often necessary to keep up with changes in the underlying ports framework—although it would be most polite to receive an advance heads-up from those committing such changes, sometimes this is overlooked or impractical. Also, in some cases, the changes are very minor in nature. We expect everyone to use their best judgement in these cases.)

To use FreshPorts, an account is required. Those with registered email addresses at @FreeBSD.org will see the opt-in link on the right-hand side of the web pages. Those who already have a FreshPorts account but are not using a @FreeBSD.org email address can change the email to @FreeBSD.org, subscribe, then change it back again.

FreshPorts also has a sanity test feature which automatically tests each commit to the FreeBSD ports tree. If subscribed to this service, a committer will receive notifications of any errors which FreshPorts detects during sanity testing of their commits.

14.2. The Web Interface to the Source Repository

It is possible to browse the files in the source repository by using a web interface. Changes that affect the entire port system are now documented in the CHANGES file. Changes that affect individual ports are now documented in the UPDATING file. However, the definitive answer to any question is undoubtedly to read the source code of bsd.port.mk, and associated files.

14.3. The FreeBSD Ports Mailing List

As a ports maintainer, consider subscribing to FreeBSD ports mailing list. Important changes to the way ports work will be announced there, and then committed to CHANGES .

If the volume of messages on this mailing list is too high, consider following FreeBSD ports announce mailing list which contains only announcements.

14.4. The FreeBSD Port Building Cluster

One of the least-publicized strengths of FreeBSD is that an entire cluster of machines is dedicated to continually building the Ports Collection, for each of the major OS releases and for each Tier-1 architecture.

Individual ports are built unless they are specifically marked with IGNORE. Ports that are marked with BROKEN will still be attempted, to see if the underlying problem has been resolved. (This is done by passing TRYBROKEN to the port's Makefile.)

14.5. Portscout: the FreeBSD Ports Distfile Scanner

The build cluster is dedicated to building the latest release of each port with distfiles that have already been fetched. However, as the Internet continually changes, distfiles can quickly go missing. Portscout, the FreeBSD Ports distfile scanner, attempts to query every download site for every port to find out if each distfile is still available. Portscout can generate HTML reports and send emails about newly available ports to those who request them. Unless not otherwise subscribed, maintainers are asked to check periodically for changes, either by hand or using the RSS feed.

Portscout's first page gives the email address of the port maintainer, the number of ports the maintainer is responsible for, the number of those ports with new distfiles, and the percentage of those ports that are out-of-date. The search function allows for searching by email address for a specific maintainer, and for selecting whether only out-of-date ports are shown.

Upon clicking on a maintainer's email address, a list of all of their ports is displayed, along with port category, current version number, whether or not there is a new version, when the port was last updated, and finally when it was last checked. A search function on this page allows the user to search for a specific port.

Clicking on a port name in the list displays the FreshPorts port information.

14.6. The FreeBSD Ports Monitoring System

Another handy resource is the FreeBSD Ports Monitoring System (also known as portsmon). This system comprises a database that processes information from several sources and allows it to be browsed via a web interface. Currently, the ports Problem Reports (PRs), the error logs from the build cluster, and individual files from the ports collection are used. In the future, this will be expanded to include the distfile survey, as well as other sources.

To get started, use the Overview of One Port search page to find all the information about a port.

This is the only resource available that maps PR entries to portnames. PR submitters do not always include the portname in their Synopsis, although we would prefer that they did. So, portsmon is a good place to find out whether an existing port has any PRs filed against it, any build errors, or if a new port the porter is considering creating has already been submitted.

Chapter 15. Using USES Macros

15.1. An Introduction to USES

USES macros make it easy to declare requirements and settings for a port. They can add dependencies, change building behavior, add metadata to packages, and so on, all by selecting simple, preset values..

Each section in this chapter describes a possible value for USES, along with its possible arguments. Arguments are appeneded to the value after a colon (:). Multiple arguments are separated by commas (,).

Example 15.1. Using Multiple Values

```
USES= bison perl
```

Example 15.2. Adding an Argument

```
USES= gmake:lite
```

Example 15.3. Adding Multiple Arguments

```
USES= drupal:7,theme
```

Example 15.4. Mixing it All Together

```
USES= pgsql:9.3+ cpe python:2.7,build
```

15.2. 7z

Possible arguments: (none), p7zip, partial

Extract using 7z(1) instead of bsdtar(1) and sets EXTRACT_SUFX=.7z. The p7zip option forces a dependency on the 7z from archivers/p7zip if the one from the base system is not able to extract the files. EXTRACT_SUFX is not changed if the partial option is used, this can be used if the main distribution file does not have a .7z extension.

15.3. ada

Possible arguments: (none), 5, 6

Depends on an Ada-capable compiler, and sets CC accordingly. Defaults to use gcc 5 from ports. Use the :X version option to force building with a different version.

15.4. autoreconf

Possible arguments: (none), build

Runs autoreconf. It encapsulates the aclocal, autoconf, autoheader, automake, autopoint, and libtoolize commands. Each command applies to ${AUTORECONF_WRKSRC}/configure.ac or its old name, ${AUTORECONF_WRKSRC}/configure.in. If configure.ac defines subdirectories with their own configure.ac using AC_CONFIG_SUBDIRS, autoreconf will recursively update those as well. The :build argument only adds build time dependencies on those tools but does not run autoreconf. A port can set AUTORECONF_WRKSRC if WRKSRC does not contain the path to configure.ac.

15.5. blaslapack

Possible arguments: (none), atlas, netlib (default), gotoblas, openblas

Adds dependencies on Blas / Lapack libraries.

15.6. bdb

Possible arguments: (none), 48, 5 (default), 6

Add dependency on the Berkeley DB library. Default to databases/db5. It can also depend on databases/db48 when using the :48 argument or databases/db6 with :6. It is possible to declare a range of acceptable values, :48+ finds the highest installed version, and falls back to 4.8 if nothing else is installed. INVALID_BDB_VER can be used to specify versions which do not work with this port. The framework exposes the following variables to the port:

BDB_LIB_NAME
> The name of the Berkeley DB library. For example, when using databases/db5, it contains db-5.3.

BDB_LIB_CXX_NAME
> The name of the Berkeley DB C++ library. For example, when using databases/db5, it contains db_cxx-5.3 .

BDB_INCLUDE_DIR
> The location of the Berkeley DB include directory. For example, when using databases/db5, it will contain ${LOCALBASE}/include/db5.

BDB_LIB_DIR
> The location of the Berkeley DB library directory. For example, when using databases/db5, it contains ${LOCALBASE}/lib.

BDB_VER
> The detected Berkeley DB version. For example, if using USES=bdb:48+ and Berkeley DB 5 is installed, it contains 5.

Important

databases/db48 is deprecated and unsupported. It must not be used by any port.

15.7. `bison`

Possible arguments: (none), `build`, `run`, `both`

Uses devel/bison By default, with no arguments or with the `build` argument, it implies `bison` is a build-time dependency, `run` implies a run-time dependency, and `both` implies both run-time and build-time dependencies.

15.8. `charsetfix`

Possible arguments: (none)

Prevents the port from installing `charset.alias` . This must be installed only by converters/libiconv. `CHARSET-FIX_MAKEFILEIN` can be set to a path relative to `WRKSRC` if `charset.alias` is not installed by `${WRKSRC}/Makefile.in`.

15.9. `cmake`

Possible arguments: (none), `outsource`, `run`

Uses CMake for configuring and building. With the `outsource` argument, an out-of-source build will be performed. With the `run` argument, a run-time dependency is registered. For more information see Section 6.5.4, "Using cmake".

15.10. `compiler`

Possible arguments: (none), `c++14-lang` , `c++11-lang` , `gcc-c++11-lib` , `c++11-lib` , `c++0x`, `c11`, `openmp`, `nested-fct`, `features`

Determines which compiler to use based on any given wishes. Use `c++14-lang` if the port needs a C++14-capable compiler, `gcc-c++11-lib` if the port needs the g++ compiler with a C++11 library, or `c++11-lib` if the port needs a C++11-ready standard library. If the port needs a compiler understanding C++11, C++0X, C11, OpenMP, or nested functions, the corresponding parameters can be used. Use `features` to request a list of features supported by the default compiler. After including `bsd.port.pre.mk` the port can inspect the results using these variables:

- `COMPILER_TYPE`: the default compiler on the system, either gcc or clang

- `ALT_COMPILER_TYPE`: the alternative compiler on the system, either gcc or clang. Only set if two compilers are present in the base system.

- `COMPILER_VERSION`: the first two digits of the version of the default compiler.

- `ALT_COMPILER_VERSION`: the first two digits of the version of the alternative compiler, if present.

- `CHOSEN_COMPILER_TYPE`: the chosen compiler, either gcc or clang

- `COMPILER_FEATURES`: the features supported by the default compiler. It currently lists the C++ library.

15.11. `cpe`

Possible arguments: (none)

Include Common Platform Enumeration (CPE) information in package manifest as a CPE 2.3 formatted string. See the CPE specification for details. To add CPE information to a port, follow these steps:

1. Search for the official CPE para for the software product either by using the NVD's CPE search engine or in the official CPE dictionary (warning, very large XML file). *Do not ever make up CPE data.*

2. Add `cpe` to `USES` and compare the result of `make -V CPE_STR` to the CPE dictionary para. Continue one step at a time until `make -V CPE_STR` is correct.

3. If the product name (second field, defaults to `PORTNAME`) is incorrect, define `CPE_PRODUCT`.

4. If the vendor name (first field, defaults to `CPE_PRODUCT`) is incorrect, define `CPE_VENDOR`.

5. If the version field (third field, defaults to `PORTVERSION`) is incorrect, define `CPE_VERSION`.

6. If the update field (fourth field, defaults to empty) is incorrect, define `CPE_UPDATE`.

7. If it is still not correct, check `Mk/Uses/cpe.mk` for additional details, or contact the Ports Security Team <ports-secteam@FreeBSD.org>.

8. Derive as much as possible of the CPE name from existing variables such as `PORTNAME` and `PORTVERSION`. Use variable modifiers to extract the relevant portions from these variables rather than hardcoding the name.

9. *Always* run `make -V CPE_STR` and check the output before committing anything that changes `PORTNAME` or `PORTVERSION` or any other variable which is used to derive `CPE_STR`.

15.12. cran

Possible arguments: (none), `auto-plist`

Uses the Comprehensive R Archive Network. Specify `auto-plist` to automatically generate `pkg-plist`.

15.13. desktop-file-utils

Possible arguments: (none)

Uses update-desktop-database from devel/desktop-file-utils. An extra post-install step will be run without interfering with any post-install steps already in the port `Makefile`. A line with `@desktop-file-utils` will be added to the plist.

15.14. desthack

Possible arguments: (none)

Changes the behavior of GNU configure to properly support `DESTDIR` in case the original software does not.

15.15. display

Possible arguments: (none), *ARGS*

Set up a virtual display environment. If the environment variable `DISPLAY` is not set, then Xvfb is added as a build dependency, and `CONFIGURE_ENV` is extended with the port number of the currently running instance of Xvfb. The *ARGS* parameter defaults to `install` and controls the phase around which to start and stop the virtual display.

15.16. dos2unix

Possible arguments: (none)

The port has files with line endings in DOS format which need to be converted. Several variables can be set to control which files will be converted. The default is to convert *all* files, including binaries. See Section 4.4.3, "Simple Automatic Replacements" for examples.

- DOS2UNIX_REGEX : match file names based on a regular expression.

- DOS2UNIX_FILES : match literal file names.

- DOS2UNIX_GLOB : match file names based on a glob pattern.

- DOS2UNIX_WRKSRC : the directory from which to start the conversions. Defaults to ${WRKSRC} .

15.17. drupal

Possible arguments: 6, 7, module, theme

Automate installation of a port that is a Drupal theme or module. Use with the version of Drupal that the port is expecting. For example, USES=drupal:6,module says that this port creates a Drupal 6 module. A Drupal 7 theme can be specified with USES=drupal:7,theme.

15.18. execinfo

Possible arguments: (none)

Add a library dependency on devel/libexecinfo if libexecinfo.so is not present in the base system.

15.19. fakeroot

Possible arguments: (none)

Changes some default behavior of build systems to allow installing as a user. See http://fakeroot.alioth.debian.org/ for more information on fakeroot.

15.20. fam

Possible arguments: (none), fam, gamin

Uses a File Alteration Monitor as a library dependency, either devel/fam or devel/gamin. End users can set WITH_FAM_SYSTEM to specify their preference.

15.21. firebird

Possible arguments: (none), 25

Add a dependency to the client library of the Firebird database.

15.22. fmake

Possible arguments: (none)

Uses devel/fmake as a build-time dependency.

15.23. fonts

Possible arguments: (none), fc, fcfontsdir (default), fontsdir, none

Adds a runtime dependency on tools needed to register fonts. Depending on the argument, add a @fc ${FONTSDIR} line, @fcfontsdir ${FONTSDIR} line, @fontsdir ${FONTSDIR} line, or no line if the argument is none, to the plist. FONTSDIR defaults to ${PREFIX}/share/fonts/${FONTNAME} and FONTNAME to ${PORTNAME}. Add FONTSDIR to PLIST_SUB and SUB_LIST

15.24. fortran

Possible arguments: gcc (default)

Uses the GNU Fortran compiler.

15.25. fuse

Possible arguments: (none)

The port will depend on the FUSE library and handle the dependency on the kernel module depending on the version of FreeBSD.

15.26. gecko

Possible arguments: libxul (default), firefox, seamonkey, thunderbird, build, *XY*, *XY+*

Add a dependency on different gecko based applications. If libxul is used, it is the only argument allowed. When the argument is not libxul, the firefox, seamonkey, or thunderbird arguments can be used, along with optional build and *XY/XY+* version arguments.

15.27. gem

Possible arguments: (none), noautoplist

Handle building with RubyGems. If noautoplist is used, the packing list is not generated automatically.

15.28. gettext

Possible arguments: (none)

Deprecated. Will include both gettext-runtime and gettext-tools.

15.29. gettext-runtime

Possible arguments: (none), lib (default), build, run

Uses devel/gettext-runtime. By default, with no arguments or with the lib argument, implies a library dependency on libintl.so. build and run implies, respectively a build-time and a run-time dependency on gettext.

15.30. gettext-tools

Possible arguments: (none), build (default), run

Uses devel/gettext-tools. By default, with no argument, or with the build argument, a build time dependency on msgfmt is registered. With the run argument, a run-time dependency is registered.

15.31. ghostscript

Possible arguments: *X*, build, run, nox11

A specific version *X* can be used. Possible versions are 7, 8, 9, and agpl (default). nox11 indicates that the -nox11 version of the port is required. build and run add build- and run-time dependencies on Ghostscript. The default is both build- and run-time dependencies.

15.32. gmake

Possible arguments: (none)

Uses devel/gmake as a build-time dependency and sets up the environment to use gmake as the default make for the build.

15.33. gnome

Possible arguments: (none)

Provides an easy way to depend on GNOME components. The components should be listed in USE_GNOME. The available components are:

- atk
- atkmm
- atspi
- cairo
- cairomm
- dconf
- esound
- evolutiondataserver3
- gal2
- gconf2
- gconfmm26
- gdkpixbuf
- gdkpixbuf2
- glib12
- glib20
- glibmm
- gnomecontrolcenter3
- gnomedesktop3

- gnomedocutils

- gnomemenus3

- gnomemimedata

- gnomeprefix

- gnomesharp20

- gnomespeech

- gnomevfs2

- gsound

- gtk-update-icon-cache

- gtk12

- gtk20

- gtk30

- gtkhtml3

- gtkhtml4

- gtkmm20

- gtkmm24

- gtkmm30

- gtksharp10

- gtksharp20

- gtksourceview

- gtksourceview2

- gtksourceview3

- gtksourceviewmm3

- gvfs

- intlhack

- intltool

- introspection

- libartlgpl2

- libbonobo

- libbonoboui

- `libgda4`

- `libgda5`

- `libgda5-ui`

- `libgdamm`

- `libgdamm5`

- `libglade2`

- `libgnome`

- `libgnomecanvas`

- `libgnomekbd`

- `libgnomeprint`

- `libgnomeprintui`

- `libgnomeui`

- `libgsf`

- `libgtkhtml`

- `libgtksourceviewmm`

- `libidl`

- `librsvg2`

- `libsigc++12`

- `libsigc++20`

- `libwnck`

- `libwnck3`

- `libxml++26`

- `libxml2`

- `libxslt`

- `metacity`

- `nautilus3`

- `orbit2`

- `pango`

- `pangomm`

- `pangox-compat`

- `py3gobject3`

- pygnome2

- pygobject

- pygobject3

- pygtk2

- pygtksourceview

- referencehack

- vte

- vte3

The default dependency is build- and run-time, it can be changed with `:build` or `:run`. For example:

```
USES=   gnome
USE_GNOME= gnomemenus3:build intlhack
```

See Section 6.10, "Using GNOME" for more information.

15.34. go

Possible arguments: (none)

Sets default values and targets used to build Go software. A build-time dependency on lang/go is added. The build process is controlled by several variables:

GO_PKGNAME
  The name of the Go package. This is the directory that will be created in `GOPATH/src` . The default value is `${PORTNAME}`.

GO_TARGET
  The name of the packages to build. The default value is `${GO_PKGNAME}`.

CGO_CFLAGS
  Additional `CFLAGS` values to be passed to the C compiler by `go`.

CGO_LDFLAGS
  Additional `LDFLAGS` values to be passed to the C compiler by `go`.

15.35. gperf

Possible arguments: (none)

Add a buildtime dependency on devel/gperf if `gperf` is not present in the base system.

15.36. gssapi

Possible arguments: (none), `base` (default), `heimdal`, `mit`, `flags`, `bootstrap`

Handle dependencies needed by consumers of the GSS-API. Only libraries that provide the Kerberos mechanism are available. By default, or set to `base`, the GSS-API library from the base system is used. Can also be set to `heimdal` to use security/heimdal, or `mit` to use security/krb5.

When the local Kerberos installation is not in LOCALBASE, set HEIMDAL_HOME (for heimdal) or KRB5_HOME (for krb5) to the location of the Kerberos installation.

These variables are exported for the ports to use:

- GSSAPIBASEDIR

- GSSAPICPPFLAGS

- GSSAPIINCDIR

- GSSAPILDFLAGS

- GSSAPILIBDIR

- GSSAPILIBS

- GSSAPI_CONFIGURE_ARGS

The flags option can be given alongside base, heimdal, or mit to automatically add GSSAPICPPFLAGS , GSSAPILD-FLAGS, and GSSAPILIBS to CFLAGS , LDFLAGS, and LDADD, respectively. For example, use base,flags .

The bootstrap option is a special prefix only for use by security/krb5 and security/heimdal. For example, use bootstrap,mit.

Example 15.5. Typical Use

```
OPTIONS_SINGLE= GSSAPI
OPTIONS_SINGLE_GSSAPI= GSSAPI_BASE GSSAPI_HEIMDAL GSSAPI_MIT GSSAPI_NONE

GSSAPI_BASE_USES= gssapi
GSSAPI_BASE_CONFIGURE_ON= --with-gssapi=${GSSAPIBASEDIR} ${GSSAPI_CONFIGURE_ARGS}
GSSAPI_HEIMDAL_USES= gssapi:heimdal
GSSAPI_HEIMDAL_CONFIGURE_ON= --with-gssapi=${GSSAPIBASEDIR} ↵
${GSSAPI_CONFIGURE_ARGS}
GSSAPI_MIT_USES= gssapi:mit
GSSAPI_MIT_CONFIGURE_ON= --with-gssapi=${GSSAPIBASEDIR} ${GSSAPI_CONFIGURE_ARGS}
GSSAPI_NONE_CONFIGURE_ON= --without-gssapi
```

15.37. horde

Possible arguments: (none)

Add buildtime and runtime dependencies on devel/pear-channel-horde. Other Horde dependencies can be added with USE_HORDE_BUILD and USE_HORDE_RUN . See Section 6.15.4.1, "Horde Modules" for more information.

15.38. iconv

Possible arguments: (none), lib, build, patch, translit, wchar_t

Uses iconv functions, either from the port converters/libiconv as a build-time and run-time dependency, or from the base system on 10-CURRENT after a native iconv was committed in 254273. By default, with no arguments or with the lib argument, implies iconv with build-time and run-time dependencies. build implies a build-time dependency, and patch implies a patch-time dependency. If the port uses the WCHAR_T or //TRANSLIT iconv extensions, add the relevant arguments so that the correct iconv is used. For more information see Section 6.23, "Using iconv".

15.39. imake

Possible arguments: (none), env, notall, noman

Add devel/imake as a build-time dependency and run xmkmf -a during the configure stage. If the env argument is given, the configure target is not set. If the -a flag is a problem for the port, add the notall argument. If xmkmf does not generate a install.man target, add the noman argument.

15.40. kde

Possible arguments: 4

Add dependency on KDE components. See Section 6.13, "Using KDE" for more information.

15.41. kmod

Possible arguments: (none)

Fills in the boilerplate for kernel module ports, currently:

• Add kld to CATEGORIES.

• Set SSP_UNSAFE .

• Set IGNORE if the kernel sources are not found in SRC_BASE.

• Define KMODDIR to /boot/modules by default, add it to PLIST_SUB and MAKE_ENV , and create it upon installation. If KMODDIR is set to /boot/kernel , it will be rewritten to /boot/modules . This prevents breaking packages when upgrading the kernel due to /boot/kernel being renamed to /boot/kernel.old in the process.

• Handle cross-referencing kernel modules upon installation and deinstallation, using @kld.

15.42. lha

Possible arguments: (none)

Set EXTRACT_SUFX to .lzh

15.43. libarchive

Possible arguments: (none)

Registers a dependency on archivers/libarchive. Any ports depending on libarchive must include USES=libarchive .

15.44. libedit

Possible arguments: (none)

Registers a dependency on devel/libedit. Any ports depending on libedit must include USES=libedit.

15.45. libtool

Possible arguments: (none), keepla, build

Patches libtool scripts. This must be added to all ports that use libtool. The keepla argument can be used to keep .la files. Some ports do not ship with their own copy of libtool and need a build time dependency on devel/libtool, use the :build argument to add such dependency.

15.46. localbase

Possible arguments: (none)

Ensures that libraries from dependencies in LOCALBASE are used instead of the ones from the base system. Ports that depend on libraries that are also present in the base system should use this. It is also used internally by a few other USES.

15.47. lua

Possible arguments: (none), *XY+*, *XY*, build, run

Adds a dependency on Lua. By default this is a library dependency, unless overridden by the build or run option. The default version is 5.2, unless set by the *XY* parameter (for example, 51 or 52+).

15.48. makeinfo

Possible arguments: (none)

Add a build-time dependency on makeinfo if it is not present in the base system.

15.49. makeself

Possible arguments: (none)

Indicates that the distribution files are makeself archives and sets the appropriate dependencies.

15.50. mate

Possible arguments: (none)

Provides an easy way to depend on MATE components. The components should be listed in USE_MATE. The available components are:

- autogen

- caja

- common

- controlcenter

- desktop

- dialogs

- docutils

- icontheme

- intlhack

- intltool

- libmatekbd

- libmateweather

- marco

- menus

- notificationdaemon

- panel

- pluma

- polkit

- settingsdaemon

The default dependency is build- and run-time, it can be changed with :build or :run. For example:

```
USES=  mate
USE_MATE= menus:build intlhack
```

15.51. metaport

Possible arguments: (none)

Sets the following variables to make it easier to create a metaport: MASTER_SITES , DISTFILES, EXTRACT_ONLY, NO_BUILD , NO_INSTALL, NO_MTREE , NO_ARCH .

15.52. mysql

Possible arguments: (none), *version*, client (default), server, embedded

Provide support for MySQL. If no version is given, try to find the current installed version. Fall back to the default version, MySQL-5.6. The possible versions are 55, 55m, 55p, 56, 56p, 57, 100m, and 101m. The m and p suffixes are for the MariaDB and Percona variants of MySQL. server and embedded add a build- and run-time dependency on the MySQL server. When using server or embedded, add client to also add a dependency on libmysqlclient.so. A port can set IGNORE_WITH_MYSQL if some versions are not supported.

The framework sets MYSQL_VER to the detected MySQL version.

15.53. mono

Possible arguments: (none)

Adds a dependency on the Mono (currently only C#) framework by setting the appropriate dependencies.

15.54. motif

Possible arguments: (none)

Uses x11-toolkits/open-motif as a library dependency. End users can set WANT_LESSTIF for the dependency to be on x11-toolkits/lesstif instead of x11-toolkits/open-motif.

15.55. ncurses

Possible arguments: (none), base, port

Uses ncurses, and causes some useful variables to be set.

15.56. ninja

Possible arguments: (none)

Uses ninja to build the port. End users can set NINJA_VERBOSE for verbose output.

15.57. objc

Possible arguments: (none)

Add objective C dependencies (compiler, runtime library) if the base system does not support it.

15.58. openal

Possible arguments: al, soft (default), si, alut

Uses OpenAL. The backend can be specified, with the software implementation as the default. The user can specify a preferred backend with WANT_OPENAL. Valid values for this knob are soft (default) and si.

15.59. pathfix

Possible arguments: (none)

Look for Makefile.in and configure in PATHFIX_WRKSRC (defaults to WRKSRC) and fix common paths to make sure they respect the FreeBSD hierarchy. For example, it fixes the installation directory of pkgconfig's .pc files to ${PREFIX}/libdata/pkgconfig. If the port uses automake, set PATHFIX_MAKEFILEIN to Makefile.am if needed.

If the port USES=cmake it will look for CMakeLists.txt in PATHFIX_WRKSRC. If needed, that default filename can be changed with PATHFIX_CMAKELISTSTXT.

15.60. pear

Possible arguments: (none)

Adds a dependency on devel/pear. It will setup default behavior for software using the PHP Extension and Application Repository. See Section 6.15.4, "PEAR Modules" for more information.

15.61. perl5

Possible arguments: (none)

Depends on Perl. These variables can be set:

- PERL_VERSION: Full version of Perl to use, or the default if not set

- PERL_ARCH: Directory name of architecture dependent libraries, defaults to mach

- PERL_PORT: Name of the Perl port to be installed, the default is derived from PERL_VERSION

- SITE_PERL : Directory name for site specific Perl packages

- USE_PERL5: Phases in which to use Perl, can be extract, patch, build, install, or run. It can also be configure, modbuild, or modbuildtiny when Makefile.PL, Build.PL , or the Module::Build::Tiny flavor of Build.PL is required. It defaults to build run .

15.62. pgsql

Possible arguments: (none), *X.Y*, *X.Y+*, *X.Y-*

Provide support for PostgreSQL. Maintainer can set version required. Minimum and maximum versions can be specified; for example, 9.0-, 8.4+.

Add PostgreSQL component dependency, using WANT_PGSQL=component[:target]. for example, WANT_PGSQL=server:configure pltcl plperl For the full list use make -V _USE_PGSQL_DEP .

15.63. php

Possible arguments: (none), phpize, ext, zend, build, cli, cgi, mod, web, embed

Provide support for PHP. Add a runtime dependency on the default PHP version, lang/php56.

phpize
    Use to build a PHP extension.

ext
    Use to build, install and register a PHP extension.

zend
    Use to build, install and register a Zend extension.

build
    Set PHP also as a build-time dependency.

cli
    Needs the CLI version of PHP.

cgi
    Needs the CGI version of PHP.

mod
    Needs the Apache module for PHP.

web
    Needs the Apache module or the CGI version of PHP.

embed
> Needs the embedded library version of PHP.

Variables are used to specify which PHP modules are required, as well as which version of PHP are supported.

USE_PHP
> The list of required PHP extensions at run-time. Add :build to the extension name to add a build-time dependency. Example: pcre xml:build gettext

DEFAULT_PHP_VER
> Selects which major version of PHP will be installed as a dependency when no PHP is installed yet. Default is 56. Possible values: 55, 56, and 7.

IGNORE_WITH_PHP
> The port does not work with PHP of the given version. Possible values: 55, 56, and 7.

When building a PHP or Zend extension with :ext or :zend, these variables can be set:

PHP_MODNAME
> The name of the PHP or Zend extension. Default value is ${PORTNAME}.

PHP_HEADER_DIRS
> A list of subdirectories from which to install header files. The framework will always install the header files that are present in the same directory as the extension.

PHP_MOD_PRIO
> The priority at which to load the extension. It is a number between 00 and 99.
>
> For extensions that do not depend on any extension, the priority is automatically set to 20, for extensions that depend on another extension, the priority is automatically set to 30. Some extensions may need to be loaded before every other extension, for example www/php56-opcache. Some may need to be loaded after an extension with a priority of 30. In that case, add PHP_MOD_PRIO=*XX* in the port's Makefile. For example:

```
USES=  php:ext
USE_PHP= wddx
PHP_MOD_PRIO= 40
```

15.64. pkgconfig

Possible arguments: (none), build (default), run, both

Uses devel/pkgconf. With no arguments or with the build argument, it implies pkg-config as a build-time dependency. run implies a run-time dependency and both implies both run-time and build-time dependencies.

15.65. pure

Possible arguments: (none), ffi

Uses lang/pure. Largely used for building related pure ports. With the ffi argument, it implies devel/pure-ffi as a run-time dependency.

15.66. pyqt

Possible arguments: (none), 4, 5

Uses PyQt. If the port is part of PyQT itself, set PYQT_DIST. Use USE_PYQT to select the components the port needs. The available components are:

- core

- dbus

- dbussupport

- demo

- designer

- designerplugin

- doc

- gui

- multimedia

- network

- opengl

- qscintilla2

- sip

- sql

- svg

- test

- webkit

- xml

- xmlpatterns

These components are only available with PyQT4:

- assistant

- declarative

- help

- phonon

- script

- scripttools

These components are only available with PyQT5:

- multimediawidgets

- printsupport

- qml

- serialport

- `webkitwidgets`

- `widgets`

The default dependency for each component is build- and run-time, to select only build or run, add `_build` or `_run` to the component name. For example:

```
USES=  pyqt
USE_PYQT= core doc_build designer_run
```

15.67. python

Possible arguments: (none), *X.Y*, *X.Y+*, *-X.Y*, *X.Y-Z.A*, `build`, `run`, `test`

Uses Python. A supported version or version range can be specified. If Python is only needed at build time, run time or for the tests, it can be set as a build, run or test dependency with `build`, `run`, or `test`. See Section 6.16, "Using Python" for more information.

15.68. qmail

Possible arguments: (none), `build`, `run`, `both`, `vars`

Uses mail/qmail. With the `build` argument, it implies `qmail` as a build-time dependency. `run` implies a run-time dependency. Using no argument or the `both` argument implies both run-time and build-time dependencies. `vars` will only set QMAIL variables for the port to use.

15.69. qmake

Possible arguments: (none), `norecursive`, `outsource`

Uses QMake for configuring. For more information see Section 6.12.3, "Using qmake".

15.70. readline

Possible arguments: (none), `port`

Uses readline as a library dependency, and sets `CPPFLAGS` and `LDFLAGS` as necessary. If the `port` argument is used or if readline is not present in the base system, add a dependency on devel/readline

15.71. scons

Possible arguments: (none)

Provide support for the use of devel/scons

15.72. shared-mime-info

Possible arguments: (none)

Uses update-mime-database from misc/shared-mime-info. This uses will automatically add a post-install step in such a way that the port itself still can specify there own post-install step if needed. It also add an `@shared-mime-info` para to the plist.

15.73. shebangfix

Possible arguments: (none)

A lot of software uses incorrect locations for script interpreters, most notably /usr/bin/perl and /bin/bash. The shebangngfix macro fixes shebang lines in scripts listed in SHEBANG_FILES. The shebangfix macro is run from ${WRKSRC}, so it can contain paths that are relative to ${WRKSRC}. It can also deal with absolute paths if files outside of ${WRKSRC} require patching. For example:

```
USES= shebangfix
SHEBANG_FILES= scripts/foobar.pl scripts/*.sh
```

Currently Bash, Java, Ksh, Lua, Perl, PHP, Python, Ruby, Tcl, and Tk are supported by default.

There are three configuration variables:

SHEBANG_LANG

The list of supported interpreters.

*interp*_CMD

The path to the command interpreter on FreeBSD. The default value is ${LOCALBASE}/bin/*interp*.

*interp*_OLD_CMD

The list of wrong invocations of interpreters. These are typically obsolete paths, or paths used on other operating systems that are incorrect on FreeBSD. They will be replaced by the correct path in *interp*_CMD. This list will always be part of *interp*_OLD_CMD: "/usr/bin/env *interp*" /bin/*interp* /usr/bin/*interp*.

To add another interpreter, set SHEBANG_LANG. For example:

```
SHEBANG_LANG= lua
```

*interp*_OLD_CMD will contain multiple values. Any entry with spaces must be quoted. For example, if it was not already defined, the Ksh entry could be defined as:

```
SHEBANG_LANG= ksh
ksh_OLD_CMD= "/usr/bin/env ksh" /bin/ksh /usr/bin/ksh
ksh_CMD= ${LOCALBASE}/bin/ksh
```

Some software uses strange locations for an interpreter. For example, an application might expect Python to be located in /opt/bin/python2.7. The strange path to be replaced can be declared in the port Makefile:

```
python_OLD_CMD= /opt/bin/python2.7
```

> Note
>
> The fixing of shebangs is done during the patch phase. If scripts are created with incorrect shebangs during the build phase, the build process (for examples, the configure script, or the Makefiles) must be patched to generate the right shebangs. Correct paths for supported interpreters are available in *interp*_CMD.

15.74. sqlite

Possible arguments: (none), 2, 3

Add a dependency on SQLite. The default version used is 3, but version 2 is also possible using the :2 modifier.

15.75. ssl

Possible arguments: (none), build, run

Provide support for OpenSSL. A build- or run-time only dependency can be specified using build or run. These variables are available for the port's use, they are also added to MAKE_ENV :

OPENSSLBASE
Path to the OpenSSL installation base.

OPENSSLDIR
Path to OpenSSL's configuration files.

OPENSSLLIB
Path to the OpenSSL libraries.

OPENSSLINC
Path to the OpenSSL includes.

OPENSSLRPATH
If defined, the path the linker needs to use to find the OpenSSL libraries.

15.76. tar

Possible arguments: (none), Z, bz2, bzip2, lzma, tbz, tbz2, tgz, txz, xz

Set EXTRACT_SUFX to .tar, .tar.Z, .tar.bz2, .tar.bz2, .tar.lzma, .tbz, .tbz2, .tgz, .txz or .tar.xz respectively.

15.77. tcl

Possible arguments: *version*, wrapper, build, run, tea

Add a dependency on Tcl. A specific version can be requested using *version*. The version can be empty, one or more exact version numbers (currently 84, 85, or 86), or a minimal version number (currently 84+, 85+ or 86+). To only request a non version specific wrapper, use wrapper. A build- or run-time only dependency can be specified using build or run. To build the port using the Tcl Extension Architecture, use tea. After including bsd.port.pre.mk the port can inspect the results using these variables:

- TCL_VER : chosen major.minor version of Tcl

- TCLSH: full path of the Tcl interpreter

- TCL_LIBDIR: path of the Tcl libraries

- TCL_INCLUDEDIR: path of the Tcl C header files

- TK_VER : chosen major.minor version of Tk

- WISH: full path of the Tk interpreter

- TK_LIBDIR: path of the Tk libraries

- TK_INCLUDEDIR: path of the Tk C header files

15.78. terminfo

Possible arguments: (none)

Adds @terminfo to the plist. Use when the port installs *.terminfo files in ${PREFIX}/share/misc .

15.79. tk

Same as arguments for tcl

Small wrapper when using both Tcl and Tk. The same variables are returned as when using Tcl.

15.80. twisted

Possible arguments: (none), ARGS

Add a dependency on twistedCore. The list of required components can be specified as a value of this variable. ARGS can be one of:

• build: add twistedCore or any specified component as build dependency.

• run: add twistedCore or any specified component as run dependency.

Besides build and run, one or more other supported twisted components can be specified. Supported values are listed in Uses/twisted.mk.

15.81. uidfix

Possible arguments: (none)

Changes some default behavior (mostly variables) of the build system to allow installing this port as a normal user. Try this in the port before using USES=fakeroot or patching.

15.82. uniquefiles

Possible arguments: (none), dirs

Make files or directories 'unique', by adding a prefix or suffix. If the dirs argument is used, the port needs a prefix (a only a prefix) based on UNIQUE_PREFIX for standard directories DOCSDIR , EXAMPLESDIR, DATADIR , WWWDIR , ETCDIR . These variables are available for ports:

• UNIQUE_PREFIX: The prefix to be used for directories and files. Default: ${PKGNAMEPREFIX}.

• UNIQUE_PREFIX_FILES: A list of files that need to be prefixed. Default: empty.

• UNIQUE_SUFFIX: The suffix to be used for files. Default: ${PKGNAMESUFFIX}.

• UNIQUE_SUFFIX_FILES: A list of files that need to be suffixed. Default: empty.

15.83. webplugin

Possible arguments: (none), ARGS

Automatically create and remove symbolic links for each application that supports the webplugin framework. ARGS can be one of:

• gecko: support plug-ins based on Gecko

- `native`: support plug-ins for Gecko, Opera, and WebKit-GTK

- `linux`: support Linux plug-ins

- `all` (default, implicit): support all plug-in types

- (individual entries): support only the browsers listed

These variables can be adjusted:

- `WEBPLUGIN_FILES`: No default, must be set manually. The plug-in files to install.

- `WEBPLUGIN_DIR`: The directory to install the plug-in files to, default *PREFIX*/lib/browser_plugins/*WEB-PLUGIN_NAME*. Set this if the port installs plug-in files outside of the default directory to prevent broken symbolic links.

- `WEBPLUGIN_NAME`: The final directory to install the plug-in files into, default `PKGBASE`.

15.84. xfce

Possible arguments: (none), `gtk3`

Provide support for Xfce related ports. See Section 6.24, "Using Xfce" for details.

The `gtk3` argument specifies that the port requires GTK3 support. It adds additional features provided by some core components, for example, x11/libxfce4menu and x11-wm/xfce4-panel.

15.85. zip

Possible arguments: (none), `infozip`

Indicates that the distribution files use the ZIP compression algorithm. For files using the InfoZip algorithm the `infozip` argument must be passed to set the appropriate dependencies.

15.86. zope

Possible arguments: (none)

Uses www/zope. Mostly used for building zope related ports. `ZOPE_VERSION` can be used by a port to indicate that a specific version of zope shall be used.

Chapter 16. __FreeBSD_version Values

Here is a convenient list of __FreeBSD_version values as defined in sys/param.h:

Table 16.1. __FreeBSD_version Values

Value	Date	Release
119411		2.0-RELEASE
199501, 199503	March 19, 1995	2.1-CURRENT
199504	April 9, 1995	2.0.5-RELEASE
199508	August 26, 1995	2.2-CURRENT before 2.1
199511	November 10, 1995	2.1.0-RELEASE
199512	November 10, 1995	2.2-CURRENT before 2.1.5
199607	July 10, 1996	2.1.5-RELEASE
199608	July 12, 1996	2.2-CURRENT before 2.1.6
199612	November 15, 1996	2.1.6-RELEASE
199612		2.1.7-RELEASE
220000	February 19, 1997	2.2-RELEASE
(not changed)		2.2.1-RELEASE
(not changed)		2.2-STABLE after 2.2.1-RELEASE
221001	April 15, 1997	2.2-STABLE after texinfo-3.9
221002	April 30, 1997	2.2-STABLE after top
222000	May 16, 1997	2.2.2-RELEASE
222001	May 19, 1997	2.2-STABLE after 2.2.2-RELEASE
225000	October 2, 1997	2.2.5-RELEASE
225001	November 20, 1997	2.2-STABLE after 2.2.5-RELEASE
225002	December 27, 1997	2.2-STABLE after ldconfig -R merge
226000	March 24, 1998	2.2.6-RELEASE
227000	July 21, 1998	2.2.7-RELEASE
227001	July 21, 1998	2.2-STABLE after 2.2.7-RELEASE
227002	September 19, 1998	2.2-STABLE after semctl(2) change
228000	November 29, 1998	2.2.8-RELEASE
228001	November 29, 1998	2.2-STABLE after 2.2.8-RELEASE
300000	February 19, 1996	3.0-CURRENT before mount(2) change
300001	September 24, 1997	3.0-CURRENT after mount(2) change
300002	June 2, 1998	3.0-CURRENT after semctl(2) change
300003	June 7, 1998	3.0-CURRENT after ioctl arg changes
300004	September 3, 1998	3.0-CURRENT after ELF conversion
300005	October 16, 1998	3.0-RELEASE
300006	October 16, 1998	3.0-CURRENT after 3.0-RELEASE
300007	January 22, 1999	3.0-STABLE after 3/4 branch
310000	February 9, 1999	3.1-RELEASE

Value	Date	Release
310001	March 27, 1999	3.1-STABLE after 3.1-RELEASE
310002	April 14, 1999	3.1-STABLE after C++ constructor/destructor order change
320000		3.2-RELEASE
320001	May 8, 1999	3.2-STABLE
320002	August 29, 1999	3.2-STABLE after binary-incompatible IPFW and socket changes
330000	September 2, 1999	3.3-RELEASE
330001	September 16, 1999	3.3-STABLE
330002	November 24, 1999	3.3-STABLE after adding mkstemp(3) to libc
340000	December 5, 1999	3.4-RELEASE
340001	December 17, 1999	3.4-STABLE
350000	June 20, 2000	3.5-RELEASE
350001	July 12, 2000	3.5-STABLE
400000	January 22, 1999	4.0-CURRENT after 3.4 branch
400001	February 20, 1999	4.0-CURRENT after change in dynamic linker handling
400002	March 13, 1999	4.0-CURRENT after C++ constructor/destructor order change
400003	March 27, 1999	4.0-CURRENT after functioning dladdr(3)
400004	April 5, 1999	4.0-CURRENT after __deregister_frame_info dynamic linker bug fix (also 4.0-CURRENT after EGCS 1.1.2 integration)
400005	April 27, 1999	4.0-CURRENT after suser(9) API change (also 4.0-CURRENT after newbus)
400006	May 31, 1999	4.0-CURRENT after cdevsw registration change
400007	June 17, 1999	4.0-CURRENT after the addition of so_cred for socket level credentials
400008	June 20, 1999	4.0-CURRENT after the addition of a poll syscall wrapper to libc_r
400009	July 20, 1999	4.0-CURRENT after the change of the kernel's dev_t type to struct specinfo pointer
400010	September 25, 1999	4.0-CURRENT after fixing a hole in jail(2)
400011	September 29, 1999	4.0-CURRENT after the sigset_t datatype change
400012	November 15, 1999	4.0-CURRENT after the cutover to the GCC 2.95.2 compiler
400013	December 4, 1999	4.0-CURRENT after adding pluggable linux-mode ioctl handlers

Value	Date	Release
400014	January 18, 2000	4.0-CURRENT after importing OpenSSL
400015	January 27, 2000	4.0-CURRENT after the C++ ABI change in GCC 2.95.2 from -fvtable-thunks to -fno-vtable-thunks by default
400016	February 27, 2000	4.0-CURRENT after importing OpenSSH
400017	March 13, 2000	4.0-RELEASE
400018	March 17, 2000	4.0-STABLE after 4.0-RELEASE
400019	May 5, 2000	4.0-STABLE after the introduction of delayed checksums.
400020	June 4, 2000	4.0-STABLE after merging libxpg4 code into libc.
400021	July 8, 2000	4.0-STABLE after upgrading Binutils to 2.10.0, ELF branding changes, and tcsh in the base system.
410000	July 14, 2000	4.1-RELEASE
410001	July 29, 2000	4.1-STABLE after 4.1-RELEASE
410002	September 16, 2000	4.1-STABLE after setproctitle(3) moved from libutil to libc.
411000	September 25, 2000	4.1.1-RELEASE
411001		4.1.1-STABLE after 4.1.1-RELEASE
420000	October 31, 2000	4.2-RELEASE
420001	January 10, 2001	4.2-STABLE after combining libgcc.a and libgcc_r.a, and associated GCC linkage changes.
430000	March 6, 2001	4.3-RELEASE
430001	May 18, 2001	4.3-STABLE after wint_t introduction.
430002	July 22, 2001	4.3-STABLE after PCI powerstate API merge.
440000	August 1, 2001	4.4-RELEASE
440001	October 23, 2001	4.4-STABLE after d_thread_t introduction.
440002	November 4, 2001	4.4-STABLE after mount structure changes (affects filesystem klds).
440003	December 18, 2001	4.4-STABLE after the userland components of smbfs were imported.
450000	December 20, 2001	4.5-RELEASE
450001	February 24, 2002	4.5-STABLE after the usb structure element rename.
450004	April 16, 2002	4.5-STABLE after the sendmail_enable rc.conf(5) variable was made to take the value NONE.

Value	Date	Release
450005	April 27, 2002	4.5-STABLE after moving to XFree86 4 by default for package builds.
450006	May 1, 2002	4.5-STABLE after accept filtering was fixed so that is no longer susceptible to an easy DoS.
460000	June 21, 2002	4.6-RELEASE
460001	June 21, 2002	4.6-STABLE sendfile(2) fixed to comply with documentation, not to count any headers sent against the amount of data to be sent from the file.
460002	July 19, 2002	4.6.2-RELEASE
460100	June 26, 2002	4.6-STABLE
460101	June 26, 2002	4.6-STABLE after MFC of `sed -i'.
460102	September 1, 2002	4.6-STABLE after MFC of many new pkg_install features from the HEAD.
470000	October 8, 2002	4.7-RELEASE
470100	October 9, 2002	4.7-STABLE
470101	November 10, 2002	Start generated __std{in,out,err}p references rather than __sF. This changes std{in,out,err} from a compile time expression to a runtime one.
470102	January 23, 2003	4.7-STABLE after MFC of mbuf changes to replace m_aux mbufs by m_tag's
470103	February 14, 2003	4.7-STABLE gets OpenSSL 0.9.7
480000	March 30, 2003	4.8-RELEASE
480100	April 5, 2003	4.8-STABLE
480101	May 22, 2003	4.8-STABLE after realpath(3) has been made thread-safe
480102	August 10, 2003	4.8-STABLE 3ware API changes to twe.
490000	October 27, 2003	4.9-RELEASE
490100	October 27, 2003	4.9-STABLE
490101	January 8, 2004	4.9-STABLE after e_sid was added to struct kinfo_eproc.
490102	February 4, 2004	4.9-STABLE after MFC of libmap functionality for rtld.
491000	May 25, 2004	4.10-RELEASE
491100	June 1, 2004	4.10-STABLE
491101	August 11, 2004	4.10-STABLE after MFC of revision 20040629 of the package tools
491102	November 16, 2004	4.10-STABLE after VM fix dealing with unwiring of fictitious pages
492000	December 17, 2004	4.11-RELEASE

Value	Date	Release
492100	December 17, 2004	4.11-STABLE
492101	April 18, 2006	4.11-STABLE after adding libdata/ld-config directories to mtree files.
500000	March 13, 2000	5.0-CURRENT
500001	April 18, 2000	5.0-CURRENT after adding addition ELF header fields, and changing our ELF binary branding method.
500002	May 2, 2000	5.0-CURRENT after kld metadata changes.
500003	May 18, 2000	5.0-CURRENT after buf/bio changes.
500004	May 26, 2000	5.0-CURRENT after binutils upgrade.
500005	June 3, 2000	5.0-CURRENT after merging libxpg4 code into libc and after TASKQ interface introduction.
500006	June 10, 2000	5.0-CURRENT after the addition of AGP interfaces.
500007	June 29, 2000	5.0-CURRENT after Perl upgrade to 5.6.0
500008	July 7, 2000	5.0-CURRENT after the update of KAME code to 2000/07 sources.
500009	July 14, 2000	5.0-CURRENT after ether_ifattach() and ether_ifdetach() changes.
500010	July 16, 2000	5.0-CURRENT after changing mtree defaults back to original variant, adding -L to follow symlinks.
500011	July 18, 2000	5.0-CURRENT after kqueue API changed.
500012	September 2, 2000	5.0-CURRENT after setproctitle(3) moved from libutil to libc.
500013	September 10, 2000	5.0-CURRENT after the first SMPng commit.
500014	January 4, 2001	5.0-CURRENT after <sys/select.h> moved to <sys/selinfo.h>.
500015	January 10, 2001	5.0-CURRENT after combining libgcc.a and libgcc_r.a, and associated GCC linkage changes.
500016	January 24, 2001	5.0-CURRENT after change allowing libc and libc_r to be linked together, deprecating -pthread option.
500017	February 18, 2001	5.0-CURRENT after switch from struct ucred to struct xucred to stabilize kernel-exported API for mountd et al.
500018	February 24, 2001	5.0-CURRENT after addition of CPUTYPE make variable for controlling CPU-specific optimizations.
500019	June 9, 2001	5.0-CURRENT after moving machine/ioctl_fd.h to sys/fdcio.h

Value	Date	Release
500020	June 15, 2001	5.0-CURRENT after locale names renaming.
500021	June 22, 2001	5.0-CURRENT after Bzip2 import. Also signifies removal of S/Key.
500022	July 12, 2001	5.0-CURRENT after SSE support.
500023	September 14, 2001	5.0-CURRENT after KSE Milestone 2.
500024	October 1, 2001	5.0-CURRENT after d_thread_t, and moving UUCP to ports.
500025	October 4, 2001	5.0-CURRENT after ABI change for descriptor and creds passing on 64 bit platforms.
500026	October 9, 2001	5.0-CURRENT after moving to XFree86 4 by default for package builds, and after the new libc strnstr() function was added.
500027	October 10, 2001	5.0-CURRENT after the new libc strcasestr() function was added.
500028	December 14, 2001	5.0-CURRENT after the userland components of smbfs were imported.
(not changed)		5.0-CURRENT after the new C99 specific-width integer types were added.
500029	January 29, 2002	5.0-CURRENT after a change was made in the return value of sendfile(2).
500030	February 15, 2002	5.0-CURRENT after the introduction of the type fflags_t, which is the appropriate size for file flags.
500031	February 24, 2002	5.0-CURRENT after the usb structure element rename.
500032	March 16, 2002	5.0-CURRENT after the introduction of Perl 5.6.1.
500033	April 3, 2002	5.0-CURRENT after the sendmail_enable rc.conf(5) variable was made to take the value NONE.
500034	April 30, 2002	5.0-CURRENT after mtx_init() grew a third argument.
500035	May 13, 2002	5.0-CURRENT with Gcc 3.1.
500036	May 17, 2002	5.0-CURRENT without Perl in /usr/src
500037	May 29, 2002	5.0-CURRENT after the addition of dlfunc(3)
500038	July 24, 2002	5.0-CURRENT after the types of some struct sockbuf members were changed and the structure was reordered.
500039	September 1, 2002	5.0-CURRENT after GCC 3.2.1 import. Also after headers stopped using _BSD_FOO_T_ and started using _FOO_T_DECLARED. This value can

Value	Date	Release
		also be used as a conservative estimate of the start of bzip2(1) package support.
500040	September 20, 2002	5.0-CURRENT after various changes to disk functions were made in the name of removing dependency on disklabel structure internals.
500041	October 1, 2002	5.0-CURRENT after the addition of getopt_long(3) to libc.
500042	October 15, 2002	5.0-CURRENT after Binutils 2.13 upgrade, which included new FreeBSD emulation, vec, and output format.
500043	November 1, 2002	5.0-CURRENT after adding weak pthread_XXX stubs to libc, obsoleting libXThrStub.so. 5.0-RELEASE.
500100	January 17, 2003	5.0-CURRENT after branching for RELENG_5_0
500101	February 19, 2003	<sys/dkstat.h> is empty. Do not include it.
500102	February 25, 2003	5.0-CURRENT after the d_mmap_t interface change.
500103	February 26, 2003	5.0-CURRENT after taskqueue_swi changed to run without Giant, and taskqueue_swi_giant added to run with Giant.
500104	February 27, 2003	cdevsw_add() and cdevsw_remove() no longer exists. Appearance of MAJOR_AUTO allocation facility.
500105	March 4, 2003	5.0-CURRENT after new cdevsw initialization method.
500106	March 8, 2003	devstat_add_entry() has been replaced by devstat_new_entry()
500107	March 15, 2003	Devstat interface change; see sys/sys/param.h 1.149
500108	March 15, 2003	Token-Ring interface changes.
500109	March 25, 2003	Addition of vm_paddr_t.
500110	March 28, 2003	5.0-CURRENT after realpath(3) has been made thread-safe
500111	April 9, 2003	5.0-CURRENT after usbhid(3) has been synced with NetBSD
500112	April 17, 2003	5.0-CURRENT after new NSS implementation and addition of POSIX.1 getpw*_r, getgr*_r functions
500113	May 2, 2003	5.0-CURRENT after removal of the old rc system.
501000	June 4, 2003	5.1-RELEASE.
501100	June 2, 2003	5.1-CURRENT after branching for RELENG_5_1.

Value	Date	Release
501101	June 29, 2003	5.1-CURRENT after correcting the semantics of sigtimedwait(2) and sigwaitinfo(2).
501102	July 3, 2003	5.1-CURRENT after adding the lockfunc and lockfuncarg fields to bus_dma_tag_create(9).
501103	July 31, 2003	5.1-CURRENT after GCC 3.3.1-pre 20030711 snapshot integration.
501104	August 5, 2003	5.1-CURRENT 3ware API changes to twe.
501105	August 17, 2003	5.1-CURRENT dynamically-linked /bin and /sbin support and movement of libraries to /lib.
501106	September 8, 2003	5.1-CURRENT after adding kernel support for Coda 6.x.
501107	September 17, 2003	5.1-CURRENT after 16550 UART constants moved from `<dev/sio/sioreg.h>` to `<dev/ic/ns16550.h>`. Also when libmap functionality was unconditionally supported by rtld.
501108	September 23, 2003	5.1-CURRENT after PFIL_HOOKS API update
501109	September 27, 2003	5.1-CURRENT after adding kiconv(3)
501110	September 28, 2003	5.1-CURRENT after changing default operations for open and close in cdevsw
501111	October 16, 2003	5.1-CURRENT after changed layout of cdevsw
501112	October 16, 2003	5.1-CURRENT after adding kobj multiple inheritance
501113	October 31, 2003	5.1-CURRENT after the if_xname change in struct ifnet
501114	November 16, 2003	5.1-CURRENT after changing /bin and /sbin to be dynamically linked
502000	December 7, 2003	5.2-RELEASE
502010	February 23, 2004	5.2.1-RELEASE
502100	December 7, 2003	5.2-CURRENT after branching for RELENG_5_2
502101	December 19, 2003	5.2-CURRENT after __cxa_atexit/__cxa_finalize functions were added to libc.
502102	January 30, 2004	5.2-CURRENT after change of default thread library from libc_r to libpthread.
502103	February 21, 2004	5.2-CURRENT after device driver API megapatch.

Value	Date	Release
502104	February 25, 2004	5.2-CURRENT after getopt_long_only() addition.
502105	March 5, 2004	5.2-CURRENT after NULL is made into ((void *)0) for C, creating more warnings.
502106	March 8, 2004	5.2-CURRENT after pf is linked to the build and install.
502107	March 10, 2004	5.2-CURRENT after time_t is changed to a 64-bit value on sparc64.
502108	March 12, 2004	5.2-CURRENT after Intel C/C++ compiler support in some headers and execve(2) changes to be more strictly conforming to POSIX.
502109	March 22, 2004	5.2-CURRENT after the introduction of the bus_alloc_resource_any API
502110	March 27, 2004	5.2-CURRENT after the addition of UTF-8 locales
502111	April 11, 2004	5.2-CURRENT after the removal of the getvfsent(3) API
502112	April 13, 2004	5.2-CURRENT after the addition of the .warning directive for make.
502113	June 4, 2004	5.2-CURRENT after ttyioctl() was made mandatory for serial drivers.
502114	June 13, 2004	5.2-CURRENT after import of the ALTQ framework.
502115	June 14, 2004	5.2-CURRENT after changing sema_timedwait(9) to return 0 on success and a non-zero error code on failure.
502116	June 16, 2004	5.2-CURRENT after changing kernel dev_t to be pointer to struct cdev *.
502117	June 17, 2004	5.2-CURRENT after changing kernel udev_t to dev_t.
502118	June 17, 2004	5.2-CURRENT after adding support for CLOCK_VIRTUAL and CLOCK_PROF to clock_gettime(2) and clock_getres(2).
502119	June 22, 2004	5.2-CURRENT after changing network interface cloning overhaul.
502120	July 2, 2004	5.2-CURRENT after the update of the package tools to revision 20040629.
502121	July 9, 2004	5.2-CURRENT after marking Bluetooth code as non-i386 specific.
502122	July 11, 2004	5.2-CURRENT after the introduction of the KDB debugger framework, the conversion of DDB into a backend and the introduction of the GDB backend.

Value	Date	Release
502123	July 12, 2004	5.2-CURRENT after change to make VFS_ROOT take a struct thread argument as does vflush. Struct kinfo_proc now has a user data pointer. The switch of the default X implementation to xorg was also made at this time.
502124	July 24, 2004	5.2-CURRENT after the change to separate the way ports rc.d and legacy scripts are started.
502125	July 28, 2004	5.2-CURRENT after the backout of the previous change.
502126	July 31, 2004	5.2-CURRENT after the removal of kmem_alloc_pageable() and the import of gcc 3.4.2.
502127	August 2, 2004	5.2-CURRENT after changing the UMA kernel API to allow ctors/inits to fail.
502128	August 8, 2004	5.2-CURRENT after the change of the vfs_mount signature as well as global replacement of PRISON_ROOT with SUSER_ALLOWJAIL for the suser(9) API.
503000	August 23, 2004	5.3-BETA/RC before the pfil API change
503001	September 22, 2004	5.3-RELEASE
503100	October 16, 2004	5.3-STABLE after branching for RELENG_5_3
503101	December 3, 2004	5.3-STABLE after addition of glibc style strftime(3) padding options.
503102	February 13, 2005	5.3-STABLE after OpenBSD's nc(1) import MFC.
503103	February 27, 2005	5.4-PRERELEASE after the MFC of the fixes in <src/include/stdbool.h> and <src/sys/i386/include/_types.h> for using the GCC-compatibility of the Intel C/C++ compiler.
503104	February 28, 2005	5.4-PRERELEASE after the MFC of the change of ifi_epoch from wall clock time to uptime.
503105	March 2, 2005	5.4-PRERELEASE after the MFC of the fix of EOVERFLOW check in vswprintf(3).
504000	April 3, 2005	5.4-RELEASE.
504100	April 3, 2005	5.4-STABLE after branching for RELENG_5_4
504101	May 11, 2005	5.4-STABLE after increasing the default thread stacksizes

Value	Date	Release
504102	June 24, 2005	5.4-STABLE after the addition of sha256
504103	October 3, 2005	5.4-STABLE after the MFC of if_bridge
504104	November 13, 2005	5.4-STABLE after the MFC of bsdiff and portsnap
504105	January 17, 2006	5.4-STABLE after MFC of ldconfig_lo-cal_dirs change.
505000	May 12, 2006	5.5-RELEASE.
505100	May 12, 2006	5.5-STABLE after branching for RE-LENG_5_5
600000	August 18, 2004	6.0-CURRENT
600001	August 27, 2004	6.0-CURRENT after permanently enabling PFIL_HOOKS in the kernel.
600002	August 30, 2004	6.0-CURRENT after initial addition of ifi_epoch to struct if_data. Backed out after a few days. Do not use this value.
600003	September 8, 2004	6.0-CURRENT after the re-addition of the ifi_epoch member of struct if_data.
600004	September 29, 2004	6.0-CURRENT after addition of the struct inpcb argument to the pfil API.
600005	October 5, 2004	6.0-CURRENT after addition of the "-d DESTDIR" argument to newsyslog.
600006	November 4, 2004	6.0-CURRENT after addition of glibc style strftime(3) padding options.
600007	December 12, 2004	6.0-CURRENT after addition of 802.11 framework updates.
600008	January 25, 2005	6.0-CURRENT after changes to VOP_*VOBJECT() functions and introduction of MNTK_MPSAFE flag for Giantfree filesystems.
600009	February 4, 2005	6.0-CURRENT after addition of the cpufreq framework and drivers.
600010	February 6, 2005	6.0-CURRENT after importing Open-BSD's nc(1).
600011	February 12, 2005	6.0-CURRENT after removing semblance of SVID2 matherr() support.
600012	February 15, 2005	6.0-CURRENT after increase of default thread stacks' size.
600013	February 19, 2005	6.0-CURRENT after fixes in <src/include/stdbool.h> and <src/sys/i386/include/_types.h> for using the GCC-compatibility of the Intel C/C++ compiler.
600014	February 21, 2005	6.0-CURRENT after EOVERFLOW checks in vswprintf(3) fixed.

Value	Date	Release
600015	February 25, 2005	6.0-CURRENT after changing the struct if_data member, ifi_epoch, from wall clock time to uptime.
600016	February 26, 2005	6.0-CURRENT after LC_CTYPE disk format changed.
600017	February 27, 2005	6.0-CURRENT after NLS catalogs disk format changed.
600018	February 27, 2005	6.0-CURRENT after LC_COLLATE disk format changed.
600019	February 28, 2005	Installation of acpica includes into /usr/include.
600020	March 9, 2005	Addition of MSG_NOSIGNAL flag to send(2) API.
600021	March 17, 2005	Addition of fields to cdevsw
600022	March 21, 2005	Removed gtar from base system.
600023	April 13, 2005	LOCAL_CREDS, LOCAL_CONNWAIT socket options added to unix(4).
600024	April 19, 2005	hwpmc(4) and related tools added to 6.0-CURRENT.
600025	April 26, 2005	struct icmphdr added to 6.0-CURRENT.
600026	May 3, 2005	pf updated to 3.7.
600027	May 6, 2005	Kernel libalias and ng_nat introduced.
600028	May 13, 2005	POSIX ttyname_r(3) made available through unistd.h and libc.
600029	May 29, 2005	6.0-CURRENT after libpcap updated to v0.9.1 alpha 096.
600030	June 5, 2005	6.0-CURRENT after importing NetBSD's if_bridge(4).
600031	June 10, 2005	6.0-CURRENT after struct ifnet was broken out of the driver softcs.
600032	July 11, 2005	6.0-CURRENT after the import of libpcap v0.9.1.
600033	July 25, 2005	6.0-STABLE after bump of all shared library versions that had not been changed since RELENG_5.
600034	August 13, 2005	6.0-STABLE after credential argument is added to dev_clone event handler. 6.0-RELEASE.
600100	November 1, 2005	6.0-STABLE after 6.0-RELEASE
600101	December 21, 2005	6.0-STABLE after incorporating scripts from the local_startup directories into the base rcorder(8).
600102	December 30, 2005	6.0-STABLE after updating the ELF types and constants.

Value	Date	Release
600103	January 15, 2006	6.0-STABLE after MFC of pidfile(3) API.
600104	January 17, 2006	6.0-STABLE after MFC of ldconfig_local_dirs change.
600105	February 26, 2006	6.0-STABLE after NLS catalog support of csh(1).
601000	May 6, 2006	6.1-RELEASE
601100	May 6, 2006	6.1-STABLE after 6.1-RELEASE.
601101	June 22, 2006	6.1-STABLE after the import of csup.
601102	July 11, 2006	6.1-STABLE after the iwi(4) update.
601103	July 17, 2006	6.1-STABLE after the resolver update to BIND9, and exposure of reentrant version of netdb functions.
601104	August 8, 2006	6.1-STABLE after DSO (dynamic shared objects) support has been enabled in OpenSSL.
601105	September 2, 2006	6.1-STABLE after 802.11 fixups changed the api for the IEEE80211_IOC_STA_INFO ioctl.
602000	November 15, 2006	6.2-RELEASE
602100	September 15, 2006	6.2-STABLE after 6.2-RELEASE.
602101	December 12, 2006	6.2-STABLE after the addition of Wi-Spy quirk.
602102	December 28, 2006	6.2-STABLE after pci_find_extcap() addition.
602103	January 16, 2007	6.2-STABLE after MFC of dlsym change to look for a requested symbol both in specified dso and its implicit dependencies.
602104	January 28, 2007	6.2-STABLE after MFC of ng_deflate(4) and ng_pred1(4) netgraph nodes and new compression and encryption modes for ng_ppp(4) node.
602105	February 20, 2007	6.2-STABLE after MFC of BSD licensed version of gzip(1) ported from NetBSD.
602106	March 31, 2007	6.2-STABLE after MFC of PCI MSI and MSI-X support.
602107	April 6, 2007	6.2-STABLE after MFC of ncurses 5.6 and wide character support.
602108	April 11, 2007	6.2-STABLE after MFC of CAM 'SG' peripheral device, which implements a subset of Linux SCSI SG passthrough device API.
602109	April 17, 2007	6.2-STABLE after MFC of readline 5.2 patchset 002.
602110	May 2, 2007	6.2-STABLE after MFC of pmap_invalidate_cache(), pmap_change_at-

Value	Date	Release
		tr(), pmap_mapbios(), pmap_mapdev_attr(), and pmap_unmapbios() for amd64 and i386.
602111	June 11, 2007	6.2-STABLE after MFC of BOP_BD-FLUSH and caused breakage of the filesystem modules KBI.
602112	September 21, 2007	6.2-STABLE after libutil(3) MFC's.
602113	October 25, 2007	6.2-STABLE after MFC of wide and single byte ctype separation. Newly compiled binary that references to ctype.h may require a new symbol, _mb_sb_limit, which is not available on older systems.
602114	October 30, 2007	6.2-STABLE after ctype ABI forward compatibility restored.
602115	November 21, 2007	6.2-STABLE after back out of wide and single byte ctype separation.
603000	November 25, 2007	6.3-RELEASE
603100	November 25, 2007	6.3-STABLE after 6.3-RELEASE.
603101	December 7, 2007	6.3-STABLE after fixing multibyte type support in bit macro.
603102	April 24, 2008	6.3-STABLE after adding l_sysid to struct flock.
603103	May 27, 2008	6.3-STABLE after MFC of the memrchr function.
603104	June 15, 2008	6.3-STABLE after MFC of support for :u variable modifier in make(1).
604000	October 4, 2008	6.4-RELEASE
604100	October 4, 2008	6.4-STABLE after 6.4-RELEASE.
700000	July 11, 2005	7.0-CURRENT.
700001	July 23, 2005	7.0-CURRENT after bump of all shared library versions that had not been changed since RELENG_5.
700002	August 13, 2005	7.0-CURRENT after credential argument is added to dev_clone event handler.
700003	August 25, 2005	7.0-CURRENT after memmem(3) is added to libc.
700004	October 30, 2005	7.0-CURRENT after solisten(9) kernel arguments are modified to accept a backlog parameter.
700005	November 11, 2005	7.0-CURRENT after IFP2ENADDR() was changed to return a pointer to IF_LLADDR().
700006	November 11, 2005	7.0-CURRENT after addition of if_addr member to struct ifnet and IFP2ENADDR() removal.

Value	Date	Release
700007	December 2, 2005	7.0-CURRENT after incorporating scripts from the local_startup directories into the base rcorder(8).
700008	December 5, 2005	7.0-CURRENT after removal of MNT_NODEV mount option.
700009	December 19, 2005	7.0-CURRENT after ELF-64 type changes and symbol versioning.
700010	December 20, 2005	7.0-CURRENT after addition of hostb and vgapci drivers, addition of pci_find_extcap(), and changing the AGP drivers to no longer map the aperture.
700011	December 31, 2005	7.0-CURRENT after tv_sec was made time_t on all platforms but Alpha.
700012	January 8, 2006	7.0-CURRENT after ldconfig_local_dirs change.
700013	January 12, 2006	7.0-CURRENT after changes to /etc/rc.d/abi to support /compat/linux/etc/ld.so.cache being a symlink in a readonly filesystem.
700014	January 26, 2006	7.0-CURRENT after pts import.
700015	March 26, 2006	7.0-CURRENT after the introduction of version 2 of hwpmc(4)'s ABI.
700016	April 22, 2006	7.0-CURRENT after addition of fcloseall(3) to libc.
700017	May 13, 2006	7.0-CURRENT after removal of ip6fw.
700018	July 15, 2006	7.0-CURRENT after import of snd_emu10kx.
700019	July 29, 2006	7.0-CURRENT after import of OpenSSL 0.9.8b.
700020	September 3, 2006	7.0-CURRENT after addition of bus_dma_get_tag function
700021	September 4, 2006	7.0-CURRENT after libpcap 0.9.4 and tcpdump 3.9.4 import.
700022	September 9, 2006	7.0-CURRENT after dlsym change to look for a requested symbol both in specified dso and its implicit dependencies.
700023	September 23, 2006	7.0-CURRENT after adding new sound IOCTLs for the OSSv4 mixer API.
700024	September 28, 2006	7.0-CURRENT after import of OpenSSL 0.9.8d.
700025	November 11, 2006	7.0-CURRENT after the addition of libelf.
700026	November 26, 2006	7.0-CURRENT after major changes on sound sysctls.

Value	Date	Release
700027	November 30, 2006	7.0-CURRENT after the addition of Wi-Spy quirk.
700028	December 15, 2006	7.0-CURRENT after the addition of sctp calls to libc
700029	January 26, 2007	7.0-CURRENT after the GNU gzip(1) implementation was replaced with a BSD licensed version ported from NetBSD.
700030	February 7, 2007	7.0-CURRENT after the removal of IPIP tunnel encapsulation (VIF-F_TUNNEL) from the IPv4 multicast forwarding code.
700031	February 23, 2007	7.0-CURRENT after the modification of bus_setup_intr() (newbus).
700032	March 2, 2007	7.0-CURRENT after the inclusion of ipw(4) and iwi(4) firmware.
700033	March 9, 2007	7.0-CURRENT after the inclusion of ncurses wide character support.
700034	March 19, 2007	7.0-CURRENT after changes to how insmntque(), getnewvnode(), and vfs_hash_insert() work.
700035	March 26, 2007	7.0-CURRENT after addition of a notify mechanism for CPU frequency changes.
700036	April 6, 2007	7.0-CURRENT after import of the ZFS filesystem.
700037	April 8, 2007	7.0-CURRENT after addition of CAM 'SG' peripheral device, which implements a subset of Linux SCSI SG passthrough device API.
700038	April 30, 2007	7.0-CURRENT after changing getenv(3), putenv(3), setenv(3) and unsetenv(3) to be POSIX conformant.
700039	May 1, 2007	7.0-CURRENT after the changes in 700038 were backed out.
700040	May 10, 2007	7.0-CURRENT after the addition of flopen(3) to libutil.
700041	May 13, 2007	7.0-CURRENT after enabling symbol versioning, and changing the default thread library to libthr.
700042	May 19, 2007	7.0-CURRENT after the import of gcc 4.2.0.
700043	May 21, 2007	7.0-CURRENT after bump of all shared library versions that had not been changed since RELENG_6.
700044	June 7, 2007	7.0-CURRENT after changing the argument for vn_open()/VOP_OPEN() from file descriptor index to the struct file *.

Value	Date	Release
700045	June 10, 2007	7.0-CURRENT after changing pam_nologin(8) to provide an account management function instead of an authentication function to the PAM framework.
700046	June 11, 2007	7.0-CURRENT after updated 802.11 wireless support.
700047	June 11, 2007	7.0-CURRENT after adding TCP LRO interface capabilities.
700048	June 12, 2007	7.0-CURRENT after RFC 3678 API support added to the IPv4 stack. Legacy RFC 1724 behavior of the IP_MULTICAST_IF ioctl has now been removed; 0.0.0.0/8 may no longer be used to specify an interface index. Use struct ipmreqn instead.
700049	July 3, 2007	7.0-CURRENT after importing pf from OpenBSD 4.1
(not changed)		7.0-CURRENT after adding IPv6 support for FAST_IPSEC, deleting KAME IPSEC, and renaming FAST_IPSEC to IPSEC.
700050	July 4, 2007	7.0-CURRENT after converting setenv/putenv/etc. calls from traditional BSD to POSIX.
700051	July 4, 2007	7.0-CURRENT after adding new mmap/lseek/etc syscalls.
700052	July 6, 2007	7.0-CURRENT after moving I4B headers to include/i4b.
700053	September 30, 2007	7.0-CURRENT after the addition of support for PCI domains
700054	October 25, 2007	7.0-CURRENT after MFC of wide and single byte ctype separation.
700055	October 28, 2007	7.0-RELEASE, and 7.0-CURRENT after ABI backwards compatibility to the FreeBSD 4/5/6 versions of the PCIOCGETCONF, PCIOCREAD and PCIOCWRITE IOCTLs was MFCed, which required the ABI of the PCIOCGETCONF IOCTL to be broken again
700100	December 22, 2007	7.0-STABLE after 7.0-RELEASE
700101	February 8, 2008	7.0-STABLE after the MFC of m_collapse().
700102	March 30, 2008	7.0-STABLE after the MFC of kdb_enter_why().
700103	April 10, 2008	7.0-STABLE after adding l_sysid to struct flock.
700104	April 11, 2008	7.0-STABLE after the MFC of procstat(1).

Value	Date	Release
700105	April 11, 2008	7.0-STABLE after the MFC of umtx features.
700106	April 15, 2008	7.0-STABLE after the MFC of write(2) support to psm(4).
700107	April 20, 2008	7.0-STABLE after the MFC of F_DUP2FD command to fcntl(2).
700108	May 5, 2008	7.0-STABLE after some lockmgr(9) changes, which makes it necessary to include sys/lock.h to use lockmgr(9).
700109	May 27, 2008	7.0-STABLE after MFC of the memrchr function.
700110	August 5, 2008	7.0-STABLE after MFC of kernel NFS lockd client.
700111	August 20, 2008	7.0-STABLE after addition of physically contiguous jumbo frame support.
700112	August 27, 2008	7.0-STABLE after MFC of kernel DTrace support.
701000	November 25, 2008	7.1-RELEASE
701100	November 25, 2008	7.1-STABLE after 7.1-RELEASE.
701101	January 10, 2009	7.1-STABLE after strndup merge.
701102	January 17, 2009	7.1-STABLE after cpuctl(4) support added.
701103	February 7, 2009	7.1-STABLE after the merge of multi-/no-IPv4/v6 jails.
701104	February 14, 2009	7.1-STABLE after the store of the suspension owner in the struct mount, and introduction of vfs_susp_clean method into the struct vfsops.
701105	March 12, 2009	7.1-STABLE after the incompatible change to the kern.ipc.shmsegs sysctl to allow allocating larger SysV shared memory segments on 64bit architectures.
701106	March 14, 2009	7.1-STABLE after the merge of a fix for POSIX semaphore wait operations.
702000	April 15, 2009	7.2-RELEASE
702100	April 15, 2009	7.2-STABLE after 7.2-RELEASE.
702101	May 15, 2009	7.2-STABLE after ichsmb(4) was changed to use left-adjusted slave addressing to match other SMBus controller drivers.
702102	May 28, 2009	7.2-STABLE after MFC of the fdopendir function.
702103	June 06, 2009	7.2-STABLE after MFC of PmcTools.

Value	Date	Release
702104	July 14, 2009	7.2-STABLE after MFC of the close-from system call.
702105	July 31, 2009	7.2-STABLE after MFC of the SYSVIPC ABI change.
702106	September 14, 2009	7.2-STABLE after MFC of the x86 PAT enhancements and addition of d_mmap_single() and the scatter/gather list VM object type.
703000	February 9, 2010	7.3-RELEASE
703100	February 9, 2010	7.3-STABLE after 7.3-RELEASE.
704000	December 22, 2010	7.4-RELEASE
704100	December 22, 2010	7.4-STABLE after 7.4-RELEASE.
800000	October 11, 2007	8.0-CURRENT. Separating wide and single byte ctype.
800001	October 16, 2007	8.0-CURRENT after libpcap 0.9.8 and tcpdump 3.9.8 import.
800002	October 21, 2007	8.0-CURRENT after renaming kthread_create() and friends to kproc_create() etc.
800003	October 24, 2007	8.0-CURRENT after ABI backwards compatibility to the FreeBSD 4/5/6 versions of the PCIOCGETCONF, PCIOCREAD and PCIOCWRITE IOCTLs was added, which required the ABI of the PCIOCGETCONF IOCTL to be broken again
800004	November 12, 2007	8.0-CURRENT after agp(4) driver moved from src/sys/pci to src/sys/dev/agp
800005	December 4, 2007	8.0-CURRENT after changes to the jumbo frame allocator (rev 174247).
800006	December 7, 2007	8.0-CURRENT after the addition of callgraph capture functionality to hwpmc(4).
800007	December 25, 2007	8.0-CURRENT after kdb_enter() gains a "why" argument.
800008	December 28, 2007	8.0-CURRENT after LK_EXCLUPGRADE option removal.
800009	January 9, 2008	8.0-CURRENT after introduction of lockmgr_disown(9)
800010	January 10, 2008	8.0-CURRENT after the vn_lock(9) prototype change.
800011	January 13, 2008	8.0-CURRENT after the VOP_LOCK(9) and VOP_UNLOCK(9) prototype changes.
800012	January 19, 2008	8.0-CURRENT after introduction of lockmgr_recursed(9), BUF_RECURSED(9) and BUF_ISLOCKED(9) and the removal of BUF_REFCNT().

Value	Date	Release
800013	January 23, 2008	8.0-CURRENT after introduction of the "ASCII" encoding.
800014	January 24, 2008	8.0-CURRENT after changing the prototype of lockmgr(9) and removal of lockcount() and LOCKMGR_ASSERT().
800015	January 26, 2008	8.0-CURRENT after extending the types of the fts(3) structures.
800016	February 1, 2008	8.0-CURRENT after adding an argument to MEXTADD(9)
800017	February 6, 2008	8.0-CURRENT after the introduction of LK_NODUP and LK_NOWITNESS options in the lockmgr(9) space.
800018	February 8, 2008	8.0-CURRENT after the addition of m_collapse.
800019	February 9, 2008	8.0-CURRENT after the addition of current working directory, root directory, and jail directory support to the kern.proc.filedesc sysctl.
800020	February 13, 2008	8.0-CURRENT after introduction of lockmgr_assert(9) and BUF_ASSERT functions.
800021	February 15, 2008	8.0-CURRENT after introduction of lockmgr_args(9) and LK_INTERNAL flag removal.
800022	(backed out)	8.0-CURRENT after changing the default system ar to BSD ar(1).
800023	February 25, 2008	8.0-CURRENT after changing the prototypes of lockstatus(9) and VOP_ISLOCKED(9), more specifically retiring the struct thread argument.
800024	March 1, 2008	8.0-CURRENT after axing out the lockwaiters and BUF_LOCKWAITERS functions, changing the return value of brelvp from void to int and introducing new flags for lockinit(9).
800025	March 8, 2008	8.0-CURRENT after adding F_DUP2FD command to fcntl(2).
800026	March 12, 2008	8.0-CURRENT after changing the priority parameter to cv_broadcastpri such that 0 means no priority.
800027	March 24, 2008	8.0-CURRENT after changing the bpf monitoring ABI when zerocopy bpf buffers were added.
800028	March 26, 2008	8.0-CURRENT after adding l_sysid to struct flock.
800029	March 28, 2008	8.0-CURRENT after reintegration of the BUF_LOCKWAITERS function and the addition of lockmgr_waiters(9).

Value	Date	Release
800030	April 1, 2008	8.0-CURRENT after the introduction of the rw_try_rlock(9) and rw_try_wlock(9) functions.
800031	April 6, 2008	8.0-CURRENT after the introduction of the lockmgr_rw and lockmgr_args_rw functions.
800032	April 8, 2008	8.0-CURRENT after the implementation of the openat and related syscalls, introduction of the O_EXEC flag for the open(2), and providing the corresponding linux compatibility syscalls.
800033	April 8, 2008	8.0-CURRENT after added write(2) support for psm(4) in native operation level. Now arbitrary commands can be written to /dev/psm%d and status can be read back from it.
800034	April 10, 2008	8.0-CURRENT after introduction of the memrchr function.
800035	April 16, 2008	8.0-CURRENT after introduction of the fdopendir function.
800036	April 20, 2008	8.0-CURRENT after switchover of 802.11 wireless to multi-bss support (aka vaps).
800037	May 9, 2008	8.0-CURRENT after addition of multi routing table support (aka setfib(1), setfib(2)).
800038	May 26, 2008	8.0-CURRENT after removal of netatm and ISDN4BSD. Also, the addition of the Compact C Type (CTF) tools.
800039	June 14, 2008	8.0-CURRENT after removal of sgtty.
800040	June 26, 2008	8.0-CURRENT with kernel NFS lockd client.
800041	July 22, 2008	8.0-CURRENT after addition of arc4random_buf(3) and arc4random_uniform(3).
800042	August 8, 2008	8.0-CURRENT after addition of cpuctl(4).
800043	August 13, 2008	8.0-CURRENT after changing bpf(4) to use a single device node, instead of device cloning.
800044	August 17, 2008	8.0-CURRENT after the commit of the first step of the vimage project renaming global variables to be virtualized with a V_ prefix with macros to map them back to their global names.
800045	August 20, 2008	8.0-CURRENT after the integration of the MPSAFE TTY layer, including

Value	Date	Release
		changes to various drivers and utilities that interact with it.
800046	September 8, 2008	8.0-CURRENT after the separation of the GDT per CPU on amd64 architecture.
800047	September 10, 2008	8.0-CURRENT after removal of VSVTX, VSGID and VSUID.
800048	September 16, 2008	8.0-CURRENT after converting the kernel NFS mount code to accept individual mount options in the nmount() iovec, not just one big struct nfs_args.
800049	September 17, 2008	8.0-CURRENT after the removal of suser(9) and suser_cred(9).
800050	October 20, 2008	8.0-CURRENT after buffer cache API change.
800051	October 23, 2008	8.0-CURRENT after the removal of the MALLOC(9) and FREE(9) macros.
800052	October 28, 2008	8.0-CURRENT after the introduction of accmode_t and renaming of VOP_ACCESS 'a_mode' argument to 'a_accmode'.
800053	November 2, 2008	8.0-CURRENT after the prototype change of vfs_busy(9) and the introduction of its MBF_NOWAIT and MBF_MNTLSTLOCK flags.
800054	November 22, 2008	8.0-CURRENT after the addition of buf_ring, memory barriers and ifnet functions to facilitate multiple hardware transmit queues for cards that support them, and a lockless ring-buffer implementation to enable drivers to more efficiently manage queuing of packets.
800055	November 27, 2008	8.0-CURRENT after the addition of Intel™ Core, Core2, and Atom support to hwpmc(4).
800056	November 29, 2008	8.0-CURRENT after the introduction of multi-/no-IPv4/v6 jails.
800057	December 1, 2008	8.0-CURRENT after the switch to the ath hal source code.
800058	December 12, 2008	8.0-CURRENT after the introduction of the VOP_VPTOCNP operation.
800059	December 15, 2008	8.0-CURRENT incorporates the new arp-v2 rewrite.
800060	December 19, 2008	8.0-CURRENT after the addition of makefs.
800061	January 15, 2009	8.0-CURRENT after TCP Appropriate Byte Counting.

Value	Date	Release
800062	January 28, 2009	8.0-CURRENT after removal of minor(), minor2unit(), unit2minor(), etc.
800063	February 18, 2009	8.0-CURRENT after GENERIC config change to use the USB2 stack, but also the addition of fdevname(3).
800064	February 23, 2009	8.0-CURRENT after the USB2 stack is moved to and replaces dev/usb.
800065	February 26, 2009	8.0-CURRENT after the renaming of all functions in libmp(3).
800066	February 27, 2009	8.0-CURRENT after changing USB devfs handling and layout.
800067	February 28, 2009	8.0-CURRENT after adding getdelim(), getline(), stpncpy(), strnlen(), wcsnlen(), wcscasecmp(), and wcsncasecmp().
800068	March 2, 2009	8.0-CURRENT after renaming the ushub devclass to uhub.
800069	March 9, 2009	8.0-CURRENT after libusb20.so.1 was renamed to libusb.so.1.
800070	March 9, 2009	8.0-CURRENT after merging IGMPv3 and Source-Specific Multicast (SSM) to the IPv4 stack.
800071	March 14, 2009	8.0-CURRENT after gcc was patched to use C99 inline semantics in c99 and gnu99 mode.
800072	March 15, 2009	8.0-CURRENT after the IFF_NEEDSGIANT flag has been removed; non-MPSAFE network device drivers are no longer supported.
800073	March 18, 2009	8.0-CURRENT after the dynamic string token substitution has been implemented for rpath and needed paths.
800074	March 24, 2009	8.0-CURRENT after tcpdump 4.0.0 and libpcap 1.0.0 import.
800075	April 6, 2009	8.0-CURRENT after layout of structs vnet_net, vnet_inet and vnet_ipfw has been changed.
800076	April 9, 2009	8.0-CURRENT after adding delay profiles in dummynet.
800077	April 14, 2009	8.0-CURRENT after removing VOP_LEASE() and vop_vector.vop_lease.
800078	April 15, 2009	8.0-CURRENT after struct rt_weight fields have been added to struct rt_metrics and struct rt_metrics_lite, changing the layout of struct rt_metrics_lite. A bump to RTM_VERSION was made, but backed out.

Value	Date	Release
800079	April 15, 2009	8.0-CURRENT after struct llentry pointers are added to struct route and struct route_in6.
800080	April 15, 2009	8.0-CURRENT after layout of struct inpcb has been changed.
800081	April 19, 2009	8.0-CURRENT after the layout of struct malloc_type has been changed.
800082	April 21, 2009	8.0-CURRENT after the layout of struct ifnet has changed, and with if_ref() and if_rele() ifnet refcounting.
800083	April 22, 2009	8.0-CURRENT after the implementation of a low-level Bluetooth HCI API.
800084	April 29, 2009	8.0-CURRENT after IPv6 SSM and MLDv2 changes.
800085	April 30, 2009	8.0-CURRENT after enabling support for VIMAGE kernel builds with one active image.
800086	May 8, 2009	8.0-CURRENT after adding support for input lines of arbitrarily length in patch(1).
800087	May 11, 2009	8.0-CURRENT after some VFS KPI changes. The thread argument has been removed from the FSD parts of the VFS. VFS_* functions do not need the context any more because it always refers to curthread. In some special cases, the old behavior is retained.
800088	May 20, 2009	8.0-CURRENT after net80211 monitor mode changes.
800089	May 23, 2009	8.0-CURRENT after adding UDP control block support.
800090	May 23, 2009	8.0-CURRENT after virtualizing interface cloning.
800091	May 27, 2009	8.0-CURRENT after adding hierarchical jails and removing global securelevel.
800092	May 29, 2009	8.0-CURRENT after changing sx_init_flags() KPI. The SX_ADAPTIVESPIN is retired and a new SX_NOADAPTIVE flag is introduced to handle the reversed logic.
800093	May 29, 2009	8.0-CURRENT after adding mnt_xflag to struct mount.
800094	May 30, 2009	8.0-CURRENT after adding VOP_ACCESSX(9).
800095	May 30, 2009	8.0-CURRENT after changing the polling KPI. The polling handlers

Value	Date	Release
		now return the number of packets processed. A new IFCAP_POLLING_NOCOUNT is also introduced to specify that the return value is not significant and the counting should be skipped.
800096	June 1, 2009	8.0-CURRENT after updating to the new netisr implementation and after changing the way we store and access FIBs.
800097	June 8, 2009	8.0-CURRENT after the introduction of vnet destructor hooks and infrastructure.
800097	June 11, 2009	8.0-CURRENT after the introduction of netgraph outbound to inbound path call detection and queuing, which also changed the layout of struct thread.
800098	June 14, 2009	8.0-CURRENT after OpenSSL 0.9.8k import.
800099	June 22, 2009	8.0-CURRENT after NGROUPS update and moving route virtualization into its own VImage module.
800100	June 24, 2009	8.0-CURRENT after SYSVIPC ABI change.
800101	June 29, 2009	8.0-CURRENT after the removal of the /dev/net/* per-interface character devices.
800102	July 12, 2009	8.0-CURRENT after padding was added to struct sackhint, struct tcpcb, and struct tcpstat.
800103	July 13, 2009	8.0-CURRENT after replacing struct tcpopt with struct toeopt in the TOE driver interface to the TCP syncache.
800104	July 14, 2009	8.0-CURRENT after the addition of the linker-set based per-vnet allocator.
800105	July 19, 2009	8.0-CURRENT after version bump for all shared libraries that do not have symbol versioning turned on.
800106	July 24, 2009	8.0-CURRENT after introduction of OBJT_SG VM object type.
800107	August 2, 2009	8.0-CURRENT after making the newbus subsystem Giant free by adding the newbus sxlock and 8.0-RELEASE.
800108	November 21, 2009	8.0-STABLE after implementing EVFILT_USER kevent filter.
800500	January 7, 2010	8.0-STABLE after __FreeBSD_version bump to make pkg_add -r use packages-8-stable.

Value	Date	Release
800501	January 24, 2010	8.0-STABLE after change of the scandir(3) and alphasort(3) prototypes to conform to SUSv4.
800502	January 31, 2010	8.0-STABLE after addition of sigpause(3).
800503	February 25, 2010	8.0-STABLE after addition of SIOCGIFDESCR and SIOCSIFDESCR ioctls to network interfaces. These ioctl can be used to manipulate interface description, as inspired by OpenBSD.
800504	March 1, 2010	8.0-STABLE after MFC of importing x86emu, a software emulator for real mode x86 CPU from OpenBSD.
800505	May 18, 2010	8.0-STABLE after MFC of adding liblzma, xz, xzdec, and lzmainfo.
801000	June 14, 2010	8.1-RELEASE
801500	June 14, 2010	8.1-STABLE after 8.1-RELEASE.
801501	November 3, 2010	8.1-STABLE after KBI change in struct sysentvec, and implementation of PL_FLAG_SCE/SCX/EXEC/SI and pl_siginfo for ptrace(PT_LWPINFO).
802000	December 22, 2010	8.2-RELEASE
802500	December 22, 2010	8.2-STABLE after 8.2-RELEASE.
802501	February 28, 2011	8.2-STABLE after merging DTrace changes, including support for userland tracing.
802502	March 6, 2011	8.2-STABLE after merging log2 and log2f into libm.
802503	May 1, 2011	8.2-STABLE after upgrade of the gcc to the last GPLv2 version from the FSF gcc-4_2-branch.
802504	May 28, 2011	8.2-STABLE after introduction of the KPI and supporting infrastructure for modular congestion control.
802505	May 28, 2011	8.2-STABLE after introduction of Hhook and Khelp KPIs.
802506	May 28, 2011	8.2-STABLE after addition of OSD to struct tcpcb.
802507	June 6, 2011	8.2-STABLE after ZFS v28 import.
802508	June 8, 2011	8.2-STABLE after removal of the schedtail event handler and addition of the sv_schedtail method to struct sysvec.
802509	July 14, 2011	8.2-STABLE after merging the SSSE3 support into binutils.
802510	July 19, 2011	8.2-STABLE after addition of RFTSIGZMB flag for rfork(2).

Value	Date	Release
802511	September 9, 2011	8.2-STABLE after addition of automatic detection of USB mass storage devices which do not support the no synchronize cache SCSI command.
802512	September 10, 2011	8.2-STABLE after merging of re-factoring of auto-quirk.
802513	October 25, 2011	8.2-STABLE after merging of the MAP_PREFAULT_READ flag to mmap(2).
802514	November 16, 2011	8.2-STABLE after merging of addition of posix_fallocate(2) syscall.
802515	January 6, 2012	8.2-STABLE after merging of addition of the posix_fadvise(2) system call.
802516	January 16, 2012	8.2-STABLE after merging gperf 3.0.3
802517	February 15, 2012	8.2-STABLE after introduction of the new extensible sysctl(3) interface NET_RT_IFLISTL to query address lists (rev 231769).
803000	March 3, 2012	8.3-RELEASE.
803500	March 3, 2012	8.3-STABLE after branching releng/8.3 (RELENG_8_3).
804000	March 28, 2013	8.4-RELEASE.
804500	March 28, 2013	8.4-STABLE after 8.4-RELEASE.
804504	September 9, 2014	8.4-STABLE after FreeBSD-SA-14:18 (rev 271305).
804505	September 16, 2014	8.4-STABLE after FreeBSD-SA-14:19 (rev 271668).
804506	October 21, 2014	8.4-STABLE after FreeBSD-SA-14:21 (rev 273413).
804507	November 4, 2014	8.4-STABLE after FreeBSD-SA-14:23, FreeBSD-SA-14:24, and FreeBSD-SA-14:25 (rev 274162).
804508	February 25, 2015	8-STABLE after FreeBSD-EN-15:01.vt, FreeBSD-EN-15:02.openssl, FreeBSD-EN-15:03.freebsd-update, FreeBSD-SA-15:04.igmp, and FreeBSD-SA-15:05.bind (rev 279287).
900000	August 22, 2009	9.0-CURRENT.
900001	September 8, 2009	9.0-CURRENT after importing x86emu, a software emulator for real mode x86 CPU from OpenBSD.
900002	September 23, 2009	9.0-CURRENT after implementing the EVFILT_USER kevent filter functionality.
900003	December 2, 2009	9.0-CURRENT after addition of sigpause(3) and PIE support in csu.

Value	Date	Release
900004	December 6, 2009	9.0-CURRENT after addition of libulog and its libutempter compatibility interface.
900005	December 12, 2009	9.0-CURRENT after addition of `sleepq_sleepcnt()`, which can be used to query the number of waiters on a specific waiting queue.
900006	January 4, 2010	9.0-CURRENT after change of the `scandir(3)` and `alphasort(3)` prototypes to conform to SUSv4.
900007	January 13, 2010	9.0-CURRENT after the removal of utmp(5) and the addition of utmpx (see `getutxent(3)`) for improved logging of user logins and system events.
900008	January 20, 2010	9.0-CURRENT after the import of BSDL bc/dc and the deprecation of GNU bc/dc.
900009	January 26, 2010	9.0-CURRENT after the addition of SIOCGIFDESCR and SIOCSIFDESCR ioctls to network interfaces. These ioctl can be used to manipulate interface description, as inspired by OpenBSD.
900010	March 22, 2010	9.0-CURRENT after the import of zlib 1.2.4.
900011	April 24, 2010	9.0-CURRENT after adding soft-updates journalling.
900012	May 10, 2010	9.0-CURRENT after adding liblzma, xz, xzdec, and lzmainfo.
900013	May 24, 2010	9.0-CURRENT after bringing in USB fixes for linux(4).
900014	June 10, 2010	9.0-CURRENT after adding Clang.
900015	July 22, 2010	9.0-CURRENT after the import of BSD grep.
900016	July 28, 2010	9.0-CURRENT after adding mti_zone to struct malloc_type_internal.
900017	August 23, 2010	9.0-CURRENT after changing back default grep to GNU grep and adding WITH_BSD_GREP knob.
900018	August 24, 2010	9.0-CURRENT after the `pthread_kill(3)` -generated signal is identified as SI_LWP in si_code. Previously, si_code was SI_USER.
900019	August 28, 2010	9.0-CURRENT after addition of the MAP_PREFAULT_READ flag to `mmap(2)`.
900020	September 9, 2010	9.0-CURRENT after adding drain functionality to sbufs, which also changed the layout of struct sbuf.

Value	Date	Release
900021	September 13, 2010	9.0-CURRENT after DTrace has grown support for userland tracing.
900022	October 2, 2010	9.0-CURRENT after addition of the BSDL man utilities and retirement of GNU/GPL man utilities.
900023	October 11, 2010	9.0-CURRENT after updating xz to git 20101010 snapshot.
900024	November 11, 2010	9.0-CURRENT after libgcc.a was replaced by libcompiler_rt.a.
900025	November 12, 2010	9.0-CURRENT after the introduction of the modularised congestion control.
900026	November 30, 2010	9.0-CURRENT after the introduction of Serial Management Protocol (SMP) passthrough and the XPT_SMP_IO and XPT_GDEV_ADVINFO CAM CCBs.
900027	December 5, 2010	9.0-CURRENT after the addition of log2 to libm.
900028	December 21, 2010	9.0-CURRENT after the addition of the Hhook (Helper Hook), Khelp (Kernel Helpers) and Object Specific Data (OSD) KPIs.
900029	December 28, 2010	9.0-CURRENT after the modification of the TCP stack to allow Khelp modules to interact with it via helper hook points and store per-connection data in the TCP control block.
900030	January 12, 2011	9.0-CURRENT after the update of libdialog to version 20100428.
900031	February 7, 2011	9.0-CURRENT after the addition of pthread_getthreadid_np(3).
900032	February 8, 2011	9.0-CURRENT after the removal of the uio_yield prototype and symbol.
900033	February 18, 2011	9.0-CURRENT after the update of binutils to version 2.17.50.
900034	March 8, 2011	9.0-CURRENT after the struct sysvec (sv_schedtail) changes.
900035	March 29, 2011	9.0-CURRENT after the update of base gcc and libstdc++ to the last GPLv2 licensed revision.
900036	April 18, 2011	9.0-CURRENT after the removal of libobjc and Objective-C support from the base system.
900037	May 13, 2011	9.0-CURRENT after importing the libprocstat(3) library and fuser(1) utility to the base system.
900038	May 22, 2011	9.0-CURRENT after adding a lock flag argument to VFS_FHTOVP(9).

Value	Date	Release
900039	June 28, 2011	9.0-CURRENT after importing pf from OpenBSD 4.5.
900040	July 19, 2011	Increase default MAXCPU for FreeBSD to 64 on amd64 and ia64 and to 128 for XLP (mips).
900041	August 13, 2011	9.0-CURRENT after the implementation of Capsicum capabilities; fget(9) gains a rights argument.
900042	August 28, 2011	Bump shared libraries' version numbers for libraries whose ABI has changed in preparation for 9.0.
900043	September 2, 2011	Add automatic detection of USB mass storage devices which do not support the no synchronize cache SCSI command.
900044	September 10, 2011	Re-factor auto-quirk. 9.0-RELEASE.
900045	January 2, 2012	9-CURRENT after MFC of true/false from 1000002.
900500	January 2, 2012	9.0-STABLE.
900501	January 6, 2012	9.0-STABLE after merging of addition of the posix_fadvise(2) system call.
900502	January 16, 2012	9.0-STABLE after merging gperf 3.0.3
900503	February 15, 2012	9.0-STABLE after introduction of the new extensible sysctl(3) interface NET_RT_IFLISTL to query address lists (rev 231768).
900504	March 3, 2012	9.0-STABLE after changes related to mounting of filesystem inside a jail (rev 232728).
900505	March 13, 2012	9.0-STABLE after introduction of new tcp(4) socket options: TCP_KEEPINIT, TCP_KEEPIDLE, TCP_KEEPINTVL, and TCP_KEEPCNT (rev 232945).
900506	May 22, 2012	9.0-STABLE after introduction of the quick_exit function and related changes required for C++11 (rev 235786).
901000	August 5, 2012	9.1-RELEASE.
901500	August 6, 2012	9.1-STABLE after branching releng/9.1 (RELENG_9_1).
901501	November 11, 2012	9.1-STABLE after LIST_PREV() added to queue.h (rev 242893) and KBI change in USB serial devices (rev 240659).
901502	November 28, 2012	9.1-STABLE after USB serial jitter buffer requires rebuild of USB serial device modules.
901503	February 21, 2013	9.1-STABLE after USB moved to the driver structure requiring a rebuild

Value	Date	Release
		of all USB modules. Also indicates the presence of nmtree.
901504	March 15, 2013	9.1-STABLE after install gained -l, -M, -N and related flags and cat gained the -l option.
901505	June 13, 2013	9.1-STABLE after fixes in ctfmerge bootstrapping (rev 249243).
902001	August 3, 2013	releng/9.2 branched from stable/9 (rev 253912).
902501	August 2, 2013	9.2-STABLE after creation of releng/9.2 branch (rev 253913).
902502	August 26, 2013	9.2-STABLE after inclusion of the PIM_RESCAN CAM path inquiry flag (rev 254938).
902503	August 27, 2013	9.2-STABLE after inclusion of the SI_UNMAPPED cdev flag (rev 254979).
902504	October 22, 2013	9.2-STABLE after inclusion of support for "first boot" rc(8) scripts (rev 256917).
902505	December 12, 2013	9.2-STABLE after Heimdal encoding fix (rev 259448).
902506	December 31, 2013	9-STABLE after MAP_STACK fixes (rev 260082).
902507	March 5, 2014	9-STABLE after upgrade of libc++ to 3.4 release (rev 262801).
902508	March 14, 2014	9-STABLE after merge of the Radeon KMS driver (rev 263170).
902509	March 21, 2014	9-STABLE after upgrade of llvm/clang to 3.4 release (rev 263509).
902510	March 27, 2014	9-STABLE after merge of the vt(4) driver (rev 263818).
902511	March 27, 2014	9-STABLE after FreeBSD-SA-14:06.openssl (rev 264289).
902512	April 30, 2014	9-STABLE after FreeBSD-SA-14:08.tcp (rev 265123).
903000	June 20, 2014	9-RC1 releng/9.3 branch (rev 267656).
903500	June 20, 2014	9.3-STABLE releng/9.3 branch (rev 267657).
903501	July 8, 2014	9-STABLE after FreeBSD-SA-14:17.kmem (rev 268433).
903502	August 19, 2014	9-STABLE after SOCK_DGRAM bug fix (rev 269789).
903503	September 9, 2014	9-STABLE after FreeBSD-SA-14:18 (rev 269687).
903504	September 16, 2014	9-STABLE after FreeBSD-SA-14:19 (rev 271668).

Value	Date	Release
903505	October 21, 2014	9-STABLE after FreeBSD-SA-14:20, FreeBSD-SA-14:21, and Free-BSD-SA-14:22 (rev 273412).
903506	November 4, 2014	9-STABLE after FreeBSD-SA-14:23, FreeBSD-SA-14:24, and Free-BSD-SA-14:25 (rev 274162).
903507	December 13, 2014	9-STABLE after merging an important fix to the LLVM vectorizer, which could lead to buffer overruns in some cases (rev 275742).
903508	February 25, 2015	9-STABLE after FreeBSD-EN-15:01.vt, FreeBSD-EN-15:02.openssl, Free-BSD-EN-15:03.freebsd-update, Free-BSD-SA-15:04.igmp, and Free-BSD-SA-15:05.bind (rev 279287).
903509	February 29, 2016	9-STABLE after bumping the default value of `compat.linux.osrelease` to `2.6.18` to support the linux-c6-* ports out of the box (rev 296219).
1000000	September 26, 2011	10.0-CURRENT.
1000001	November 4, 2011	10-CURRENT after addition of the posix_fadvise(2) system call.
1000002	December 12, 2011	10-CURRENT after defining boolean true/false in sys/types.h, size-of(bool) may have changed (rev 228444). 10-CURRENT after xlocale.h was introduced (rev 227753).
1000003	December 16, 2011	10-CURRENT after major changes to carp(4), changing size of struct in_aliasreq, struct in6_aliasreq (rev 228571) and straitening arguments check of SIOCAIFADDR (rev 228574).
1000004	January 1, 2012	10-CURRENT after the removal of skpc(9) and the addition of memc-chr(9) (rev 229200).
1000005	January 16, 2012	10-CURRENT after the removal of support for SIOCSIFADDR, SIOCSIFNETMASK, SIOCSIFBRDAD-DR, SIOCSIFDSTADDR ioctls (rev 230207).
1000006	January 26, 2012	10-CURRENT after introduction of read capacity data asynchronous notification in the cam(4) layer (rev 230590).
1000007	February 5, 2012	10-CURRENT after introduction of new tcp(4) socket options: TCP_KEEPINIT, TCP_KEEPIDLE, TCP_KEEPINTVL, and TCP_KEEPCNT (rev 231025).

Value	Date	Release
1000008	February 11, 2012	10-CURRENT after introduction of the new extensible sysctl(3) interface NET_RT_IFLISTL to query address lists (rev 231505).
1000009	February 25, 2012	10-CURRENT after import of libarchive 3.0.3 (rev 232153).
1000010	March 31, 2012	10-CURRENT after xlocale cleanup (rev 233757).
1000011	April 16, 2012	10-CURRENT import of LLVM/Clang 3.1 trunk r154661 (rev 234353).
1000012	May 2, 2012	10-CURRENT jemalloc import (rev 234924).
1000013	May 22, 2012	10-CURRENT after byacc import (rev 235788).
1000014	June 27, 2012	10-CURRENT after BSD sort becoming the default sort (rev 237629).
1000015	July 12, 2012	10-CURRENT after import of OpenSSL 1.0.1c (rev 238405).
(not changed)	July 13, 2012	10-CURRENT after the fix for LLVM/Clang 3.1 regression (rev 238429).
1000016	August 8, 2012	10-CURRENT after KBI change in ucom(4) (rev 239179).
1000017	August 8, 2012	10-CURRENT after adding streams feature to the USB stack (rev 239214).
1000018	September 8, 2012	10-CURRENT after major rewrite of pf(4) (rev 240233).
1000019	October 6, 2012	10-CURRENT after pfil(9) KBI/KPI changed to supply packets in net byte order to AF_INET filter hooks (rev 241245).
1000020	October 16, 2012	10-CURRENT after the network interface cloning KPI changed and struct if_clone becoming opaque (rev 241610).
1000021	October 22, 2012	10-CURRENT after removal of support for non-MPSAFE filesystems and addition of support for FUSEFS (rev 241519, 241897).
1000022	October 22, 2012	10-CURRENT after the entire IPv4 stack switched to network byte order for IP packet header storage (rev 241913).
1000023	November 5, 2012	10-CURRENT after jitter buffer in the common USB serial driver code, to temporarily store characters if the TTY buffer is full. Add flow stop and start signals when this happens (rev 242619).

Value	Date	Release
1000024	November 5, 2012	10-CURRENT after clang was made the default compiler on i386 and amd64 (rev 242624).
1000025	November 17, 2012	10-CURRENT after the sin6_scope_id member variable in struct sockaddr_in6 was changed to being filled by the kernel before passing the structure to the userland via sysctl or routing socket. This means the KAME-specific embedded scope id in sin6_addr.s6_addr[2] is always cleared in userland application (rev 243443).
1000026	January 11, 2013	10-CURRENT after install gained the -N flag (rev 245313). May also be used to indicate the presence of nmtree.
1000027	January 29, 2013	10-CURRENT after cat gained the -l flag (rev 246083).
1000028	February 13, 2013	10-CURRENT after USB moved to the driver structure requiring a rebuild of all USB modules (rev 246759).
1000029	March 4, 2013	10-CURRENT after the introduction of tickless callout facility which also changed the layout of struct callout (rev 247777).
1000030	March 12, 2013	10-CURRENT after KPI breakage introduced in the VM subsystem to support read/write locking (rev 248084).
1000031	April 26, 2013	10-CURRENT after the dst parameter of the ifnet if_output method was changed to take const qualifier (rev 249925).
1000032	May 1, 2013	10-CURRENT after the introduction of the accept4 (rev 250154) and pipe2 (rev 250159) system calls.
1000033	May 21, 2013	10-CURRENT after flex 2.5.37 import (rev 250881).
1000034	June 3, 2013	10-CURRENT after the addition of these functions to libm: cacos, cacosf, cacosh, cacoshf, casin, casinf, casinh, casinhf, catan, catanf, catanh, catanhf, logl, log2l, log10l, log1pl, expm1l (rev 251294).
1000035	June 8, 2013	10-CURRENT after the introduction of the aio_mlock system call (rev 251526).
1000036	July 9, 2013	10-CURRENT after the addition of a new function to the kernel GSSAPI module's function call interface (rev 253049).

Value	Date	Release
1000037	July 9, 2013	10-CURRENT after the migration of statistics structures to PCPU counters. Changed structures include: `ahstat`, `arpstat`, `espstat`, `icmp6_ifstat`, `icmp6stat`, `in6_ifstat`, `ip6stat`, `ipcompstat`, `ipipstat`, `ipsecstat`, `mrt6stat`, `mrtstat`, `pfkeystat`, `pim6stat`, `pimstat`, `rip6stat`, `udpstat` (rev 253081).
1000038	July 16, 2013	10-CURRENT after making `ARM EABI` the default ABI on arm, armeb, armv6, and armv6eb architectures (rev 253396).
1000039	July 22, 2013	10-CURRENT after `CAM` and mps(4) driver scanning changes (rev 253549).
1000040	July 24, 2013	10-CURRENT after addition of libusb pkgconf files (rev 253638).
1000041	August 5, 2013	10-CURRENT after change from `time_second` to `time_uptime` in `PF_INET6` (rev 253970).
1000042	August 9, 2013	10-CURRENT after VM subsystem change to unify soft and hard busy mechanisms (rev 254138).
1000043	August 13, 2013	10-CURRENT after `WITH_ICONV` is enabled by default. A new src.conf(5) option, `WITH_LIBICONV_COMPAT` (disabled by default) adds `libiconv_open` to provide compatibility with the libiconv port (rev 254273).
1000044	August 15, 2013	10-CURRENT after `libc.so` conversion to an ld(1) script (rev 251668, 254358).
1000045	August 15, 2013	10-CURRENT after devfs programming interface change by replacing the cdevsw flag `D_UNMAPPED_IO` with the struct cdev flag `SI_UNMAPPED` (rev 254389).
1000046	August 19, 2013	10-CURRENT after addition of `M_PROTO[9-12]` and removal of `M_FRAG|M_FIRSTFRAG|M_LASTFRAG` mbuf flags (rev 254524, 254526).
1000047	August 21, 2013	10-CURRENT after stat(2) update to allow storing some Windows/DOS and CIFS file attributes as stat(2) flags (rev 254627).
1000048	August 22, 2013	10-CURRENT after modification of structure `xsctp_inpcb` (rev 254672).
1000049	August 24, 2013	10-CURRENT after physio(9) support for devices that do not function properly with split I/O, such as sa(4) (rev 254760).

Value	Date	Release
1000050	August 24, 2013	10-CURRENT after modifications of structure mbuf (rev 254780, 254799, 254804, 254807 254842).
1000051	August 25, 2013	10-CURRENT after Radeon KMS driver import (rev 254885, 254887).
1000052	September 3, 2013	10-CURRENT after import of NetBSD libexecinfo is connected to the build (rev 255180).
1000053	September 6, 2013	10-CURRENT after API and ABI changes to the Capsicum framework (rev 255305).
1000054	September 6, 2013	10-CURRENT after gcc and libstdc++ are no longer built by default (rev 255321).
1000055	September 6, 2013	10-CURRENT after addition of MMAP_32BIT mmap(2) flag (rev 255426).
1000100	December 7, 2013	releng/10.0 branched from stable/10 (rev 259065).
1000500	October 10, 2013	10-STABLE after branch from head/ (rev 256283).
1000501	October 22, 2013	10-STABLE after addition of first-boot rc(8) support (rev 256916).
1000502	November 20, 2013	10-STABLE after removal of iconv symbols from libc.so.7 (rev 258398).
1000510	December 7, 2013	releng/10.0 __FreeBSD_version update to prevent the value from going backwards (rev 259067).
1000700	December 7, 2013	10-STABLE after releng/10.0 branch (rev 259069).
1000701	December 15, 2013	10.0-STABLE after Heimdal encoding fix (rev 259447).
1000702	December 31, 2013	10-STABLE after MAP_STACK fixes (rev 260135).
1000703	March 5, 2014	10-STABLE after upgrade of libc++ to 3.4 release (rev 262801).
1000704	March 7, 2014	10-STABLE after MFC of the vt(4) driver (rev 262861).
1000705	March 21, 2014	10-STABLE after upgrade of llvm/clang to 3.4 release (rev 263508).
1000706	April 6, 2014	10-STABLE after GCC support for __block definition (rev 264214).
1000707	April 8, 2014	10-STABLE after FreeBSD-SA-14:06.openssl (rev 264289).
1000708	April 30, 2014	10-STABLE after FreeBSD-SA-14:07.devfs, FreeBSD-SA-14:08.tcp, and FreeBSD-SA-14:09.openssl (rev 265122).

Value	Date	Release
1000709	May 13, 2014	10-STABLE after support for UDP-Lite protocol (RFC 3828) (rev 265946).
1000710	June 13, 2014	10-STABLE after changes to strcasecmp(3), moving strcasecmp_l() and strncasecmp_l() from <string.h> to <strings.h> for POSIX 2008 compliance (rev 267465).
1000711	July 8, 2014	10-STABLE after FreeBSD-SA-14:17.kmem (rev 268432).
1000712	August 1, 2014	10-STABLE after nfsd(8) 4.1 merge (rev 269398).
1000713	August 3, 2014	10-STABLE after regex(3) library update to add ">" and "<" delimiters (rev 269484).
1000714	August 3, 2014	10-STABLE after SOCK_DGRAM bug fix (rev 269490).
1000715	September 9, 2014	10-STABLE after FreeBSD-SA-14:18 (rev 269686).
1000716	September 16, 2014	10-STABLE after FreeBSD-SA-14:19 (rev 271667).
1000717	September 18, 2014	10-STABLE after i915 HW context support (rev 271816).
1001000	October 2, 2014	10.1-RC1 after releng/10.1 branch (rev 272463).
1001500	October 2, 2014	10-STABLE after releng/10.1 branch (rev 272464).
1001501	October 21, 2014	10-STABLE after FreeBSD-SA-14:20, FreeBSD-SA-14:22, and FreeBSD-SA-14:23 (rev 273411).
1001502	November 4, 2014	10-STABLE after FreeBSD-SA-14:23, FreeBSD-SA-14:24, and FreeBSD-SA-14:25 (rev 274162).
1001503	November 25, 2014	10-STABLE after merging new libraries/utilities (dpv and figpar) for data throughput visualization (rev 275040).
1001504	December 13, 2014	10-STABLE after merging an important fix to the LLVM vectorizer, which could lead to buffer overruns in some cases (rev 275742).
1001505	January 3, 2015	10-STABLE after merging some arm constants in r276312 (rev 276633).
1001506	January 12, 2015	10-STABLE after merging max table size update for yacc (rev 277087).
1001507	January 27, 2015	10-STABLE after changes to the UDP tunneling callback to provide a context pointer and the source sockaddr (rev 277790).

Value	Date	Release
1001508	February 18, 2015	10-STABLE after addition of the `CDAI_TYPE_EXT_INQ` request type (rev 278974).
1001509	February 25, 2015	10-STABLE after Free-BSD-EN-15:01.vt, Free-BSD-EN-15:02.openssl, Free-BSD-EN-15:03.freebsd-update, Free-BSD-SA-15:04.igmp, and Free-BSD-SA-15:05.bind (rev 279287).
1001511	19 March, 2015	10-STABLE after `sys/capability.h` is renamed to `sys/capsicum.h` (rev 280224/).
1001512	24 March, 2015	10-STABLE after addition of new mtio(4), sa(4) ioctls (rev 281954).
1001513	24 April, 2015	10-STABLE after starting the process of removing the use of the deprecated "M_FLOWID" flag from the network code (rev 281955).
1002000	24 July, 2015	`releng/10.2` branched from 10-STABLE (rev 285830).
1002500	24 July, 2015	10-STABLE after `releng/10.2` branched from 10-STABLE (rev 285831).
1002501	8 October, 2015	10-STABLE after merge of ZFS changes that affected the internal interface of zfeature_info structure (rev 288572).
1002502	24 November, 2015	10-STABLE after merge of dump device changes that affected the arguments of g_dev_setdumpdev() (rev 291215).
1002503	14 December, 2015	10-STABLE after merge of changes to the internal interface between the nfsd.ko and nfscommon.ko modules, requiring them to be upgraded together (rev 292223).
1002504	22 December, 2015	10-STABLE after merge of xz 5.2.2 merge (multithread support) (rev 292588).
1002505	30 December, 2015	10-STABLE after merge of changes to pci(4) (rev 292907).
1002506	9 January, 2016	10-STABLE after merge of utimensat(5) (rev 293473).
1002507	9 January, 2016	10-STABLE after merge of changes to linux(4) (rev 293477 through 293609).
1002508	9 January, 2016	10-STABLE after merge of changes to figbar(3) types/macros (rev 290275).
1002509	1 February, 2016	10-STABLE after merge of API change to dpv(3) (rev 295107).

Value	Date	Release
1003000	4 March, 2016	releng/10.3 branched from 10-STABLE (rev 296373).
1003500	4 March, 2016	10-STABLE after releng/10.3 branched from 10-STABLE (rev 296374).
1003501	19 June, 2016	10-STABLE after adding kdbcontrol's -P option (rev 298297).
1003502	19 June, 2016	10-STABLE after libcrypto.so was made position independent (rev 299966).
1003503	19 June, 2016	10-STABLE after allowing MK_ overrides (rev 300233).
1003504	21 June, 2016	10-STABLE after MFC of filemon changes from 11-CURRENT (rev 302066).
1003505	27 June, 2016	10-STABLE after converting sed to use REG_STARTEND, fixing a Mesa issue (rev 302228).
1100000	October 10, 2013	11.0-CURRENT (rev 256284).
1100001	October 19, 2013	11.0-CURRENT after addition of support for "first boot" rc.d scripts, so ports can make use of this (rev 256776).
1100002	November 5, 2013	11.0-CURRENT after dropping support for historic ioctls (rev 257696).
1100003	November 17, 2013	11.0-CURRENT after iconv changes (rev 258284).
1100004	December 15, 2013	11.0-CURRENT after the behavior change of gss_pseudo_random introduced in r259286 (rev 259424).
1100005	December 28, 2013	11.0-CURRENT after r259951 - Do not coalesce entries in vm_map_stack() (rev 260010).
1100006	January 28, 2014	11.0-CURRENT after upgrades of libelf and libdwarf (rev 261246).
1100007	January 30, 2014	11.0-CURRENT after upgrade of libc++ to 3.4 release (rev 261283).
1100008	February 14, 2014	11.0-CURRENT after libc++ 3.4 ABI compatibility fix (rev 261801).
1100009	February 16, 2014	11.0-CURRENT after upgrade of llvm/clang to 3.4 release (rev 261991).
1100010	February 28, 2014	11.0-CURRENT after upgrade of ncurses to 5.9 release (rev 262629).
1100011	March 13, 2014	11.0-CURRENT after ABI change in struct if_data (rev 263102).
1100012	March 14, 2014	11.0-CURRENT after removal of Novell IPX protocol support (rev 263140).

Value	Date	Release
1100013	March 14, 2014	11.0-CURRENT after removal of AppleTalk protocol support (rev 263152).
1100014	March 16, 2014	11.0-CURRENT after renaming `<sys/capability.h>` to `<sys/capsicum.h>` to avoid a clash with similarly named headers in other operating systems. A compatibility header is left in place to limit build breakage, but will be deprecated in due course (rev 263235).
1100015	March 22, 2014	11.0-CURRENT after `cnt` rename to `vm_cnt` (rev 263620).
1100016	March 23, 2014	11.0-CURRENT after addition of `armv6hf` `TARGET_ARCH` (rev 263660).
1100017	April 4, 2014	11.0-CURRENT after GCC support for `__block` definition (rev 264121).
1100018	April 6, 2014	11.0-CURRENT after support for UDP-Lite protocol (RFC 3828) (rev 264212).
1100019	April 8, 2014	11.0-CURRENT after FreeBSD-SA-14:06.openssl (rev 264265).
1100020	May 1, 2014	11.0-CURRENT after removing lindev in favor of having /dev/full by default (rev 265212).
1100021	May 6, 2014	11.0-CURRENT after `src.opts.mk` changes, decoupling make.conf(5) from `buildworld` (rev 265419).
1100022	May 30, 2014	11.0-CURRENT after changes to strcasecmp(3), moving `strcasecmp_l()` and `strncasecmp_l()` from `<string.h>` to `<strings.h>` for POSIX 2008 compliance (rev 266865).
1100023	June 13, 2014	11.0-CURRENT after the CUSE library and kernel module have been attached to the build by default (rev 267440).
1100024	June 27, 2014	11.0-CURRENT after sysctl(3) API change (rev 267992).
1100025	June 30, 2014	11.0-CURRENT after regex(3) library update to add ">" and "<" delimiters (rev 268066).
1100026	July 1, 2014	11.0-CURRENT after the internal interface between the NFS modules, including the krpc, was changed by (rev 268115).
1100027	July 8, 2014	11.0-CURRENT after FreeBSD-SA-14:17.kmem (rev 268431).

Value	Date	Release
1100028	July 21, 2014	11.0-CURRENT after hdestroy() compliance fix changed ABI (rev 268945).
1100029	August 3, 2014	11.0-CURRENT after SOCK_DGRAM bug fix (rev 269489).
1100030	September 1, 2014	11.0-CURRENT after SOCK_RAW sockets were changed to not modify packets at all (rev 270929).
1100031	September 9, 2014	11.0-CURRENT after Free-BSD-SA-14:18.openssl (rev 269686).
1100032	September 11, 2014	11.0-CURRENT after API changes to ifa_ifwithbroadaddr, ifa_ifwithdstaddr, ifa_ifwithnet, and ifa_ifwithroute (rev 271438).
1100033	September 9, 2014	11.0-CURRENT after changing access, eaccess, and faccessat to validate the mode argument (rev 271657).
1100034	September 16, 2014	11.0-CURRENT after Free-BSD-SA-14:19.tcp (rev 271666).
1100035	September 17, 2014	11.0-CURRENT after i915 HW context support (rev 271705).
1100036	September 17, 2014	Version bump to have ABI note distinguish binaries ready for strict mmap(2) flags checking (rev 271724).
1100037	October 6, 2014	11.0-CURRENT after addition of explicit_bzero(3) (rev 272673).
1100038	October 11, 2014	11.0-CURRENT after cleanup of TCP wrapper headers (rev 272951).
1100039	October 18, 2014	11.0-CURRENT after removal of MAP_RENAME and MAP_NORESERVE (rev 273250).
1100040	October 21, 2014	11.0-CURRENT after Free-BSD-SA-14:23 (rev 273146).
1100041	October 30, 2014	11.0-CURRENT after API changes to syscall_register, syscall32_register, syscall_register_helper and syscall32_register_helper (rev 273707).
1100042	November 3, 2014	11.0-CURRENT after a change to struct tcpcb (rev 274046).
1100043	November 4, 2014	11.0-CURRENT after enabling vt(4) by default (rev 274085).
1100044	November 4, 2014	11.0-CURRENT after adding new libraries/utilities (dpv and figpar) for data throughput visualization (rev 274116).
1100045	November 4, 2014	11.0-CURRENT after Free-BSD-SA-14:23, FreeBSD-SA-14:24, and FreeBSD-SA-14:25 (rev 274162).

Value	Date	Release
1100046	November 13, 2014	11.0-CURRENT after `kern_poll` signature change (rev 274462).
1100047	November 13, 2014	11.0-CURRENT after removal of no-at version of VFS syscalls helpers, like `kern_open` (rev 274476).
1100048	December 1, 2014	11.0-CURRENT after starting the process of removing the use of the deprecated "M_FLOWID" flag from the network code (rev 275358).
1100049	December 9, 2014	11.0-CURRENT after importing an important fix to the LLVM vectorizer, which could lead to buffer overruns in some cases (rev 275633).
1100050	December 12, 2014	11.0-CURRENT after adding AES-ICM and AES-GCM to OpenCrypto (rev 275732).
1100051	December 23, 2014	11.0-CURRENT after removing old NFS client and server code from the kernel (rev 276096).
1100052	December 31, 2014	11.0-CURRENT after upgrade of clang, llvm and lldb to 3.5.0 release (rev 276479).
1100053	January 7, 2015	11.0-CURRENT after MCLGET() gained a return value (rev 276750).
1100054	January 15, 2015	11.0-CURRENT after rewrite of call-out subsystem (rev 277213).
1100055	January 22, 2015	11.0-CURRENT after reverting call-out changes in r277213 (rev 277528).
1100056	January 23, 2015	11.0-CURRENT after addition of `futimens` and `utimensat` system calls (rev 277610).
1100057	January 29, 2015	11.0-CURRENT after removal of d_thread_t (rev 277897).
1100058	February 5, 2015	11.0-CURRENT after addition of support for probing the SCSI VPD Extended Inquiry page (0x86) (rev 278228).
1100059	February 9, 2015	11.0-CURRENT after import of xz 5.2.0, which added multi-threaded compression and lzma gained libthr dependency (rev 278433).
1100060	February 16, 2015	11.0-CURRENT after forwarding `FBIO_BLANK` to framebuffer clients (rev 278846).
1100061	February 18, 2015	11.0-CURRENT after `CDAI_FLAG_NONE` addition (rev 278964).
1100062	February 23, 2015	11.0-CURRENT after mtio(4) and sa(4) API and ioctl(2) additions (rev 279221).

Value	Date	Release
1100063	March 7, 2015	11.0-CURRENT after adding mutex support to the pps_ioctl() API in the kernel (rev 279728).
1100064	March 7, 2015	11.0-CURRENT after adding PPS support to USB serial drivers (rev 279729).
1100065	March 15, 2015	11.0-CURRENT after upgrading clang, llvm and lldb to 3.6.0 (rev 280031).
1100066	March 20, 2015	11.0-CURRENT after removal of SSLv2 support from OpenSSL (rev 280306).
1100067	March 25, 2015	11.0-CURRENT after removal of SSLv2 support from fetch(1) and fetch(3) (rev 280630).
1100068	April 6, 2015	11.0-CURRENT after change to net.inet6.ip6.mif6table sysctl (rev 281172).
1100069	April 15, 2015	11.0-CURRENT after removal of const qualifier from iconv(3) (rev 281550).
1100071	April 29, 2015	11.0-CURRENT after API/ABI change to smb(4) (rev 281985).
1100072	May 1, 2015	11.0-CURRENT after adding reallocarray(3) in libc (rev 282314).
1100073	May 8, 2015	11.0-CURRENT after extending the maximum number of allowed PCM channels in a PCM stream to 127 and decreasing the maximum number of sub-channels to 1 (rev 282650).
1100074	May 25, 2015	11.0-CURRENT after adding preliminary support for x86-64 Linux binaries (rev 283424), and upgrading clang and llvm to 3.6.1 (rev 283526).
1100075	May 27, 2015	11.0-CURRENT after dounmount() requiring a reference on the passed struct mount (rev 283602).
1100076	June 4, 2015	11.0-CURRENT after disabled generation of legacy formatted password databases entries by default. (rev 283983).
1100077	June 10, 2015	11.0-CURRENT after API changes to lim_cur, lim_max, and lim_rlimit (rev 284215).
1100079	August 18, 2015	11.0-CURRENT after import of jemalloc 4.0.0 (rev 286866).
1100080	October 5, 2015	11.0-CURRENT after upgrading clang, llvm, lldb, compiler-rt and libc ++ to 3.7.0 (rev 288943).

Value	Date	Release
1100081	October 16, 2015	11.0-CURRENT after undating ZFS to support resumable send/receive (rev r289362).
1100085	October 30, 2015	11.0-CURRENT after import of OpenSSL 1.0.2d (rev 290207).
1100088	November 7, 2015	11.0-CURRENT after string collation and locales rework (rev 290495).
1100089	November 7, 2015	11.0-CURRENT after API change to sysctl_add_oid(9) (rev 290475 and r290505).
1100090	November 10, 2015	11.0-CURRENT after API change to callout_stop macro; (rev 290664).
1100092	December 19, 2015	11.0-CURRENT after removal of vm_pageout_grow_cache (rev 292469).
1100093	December 30, 2015	11.0-CURRENT after removal of sys/crypto/sha2.h (rev 292782).
1100094	January 15, 2016	11.0-CURRENT after LinuxKPI PCI changes (rev 294086).
1100095	January 19, 2016	11.0-CURRENT after LRO optimizations (rev 294327).
1100096	January 21, 2016	11.0-CURRENT after LinuxKPI idr_* additions (rev 294505).
1100097	January 26, 2016	11.0-CURRENT after API change to dpv(3) (rev 294860).
1100098	February 16, 2016	11.0-CURRENT after API change to rman (rev 294883).
1100100	February 26, 2016	11.0-CURRENT after bus_alloc_resource_anywhere() API addition (rev 296136).
1100116	May 31, 2016	11.0-CURRENT after SHA-512t256 (rev 300903) and Skein (rev 300966) where added to libmd, libcrypt, the kernel, and ZFS (rev 301010).
1100117	June 6, 2016	11.0-CURRENT after libpam was synced with stock 301602, bumping library version.
1100118	June 21, 2016	11.0-CURRENT after breaking binary compatibility of struct disk 302069.
1100119	June 23, 2016	11.0-CURRENT after switching geom_disk to using a pool mutex 302150.
1100120	June 23, 2016	11.0-CURRENT after adding spares to struct ifnet 302153.
1100500	August 12, 2016	11.0-STABLE adding branched 303976.
1100121	August 12, 2015	11-STABLE after releng/11.0 branched from 11-STABLE (rev 303975).

Value	Date	Release
1200000	July 7, 2016	12.0-CURRENT (rev 302409).
1200004	August 24, 2016	12.0-CURRENT after fixing LC_*_MASK for newlocale(3) and querylocale(3) (rev 304703).

Note

Note that 2.2-STABLE sometimes identifies itself as "2.2.5-STABLE" after the 2.2.5-RELEASE. The pattern used to be year followed by the month, but we decided to change it to a more straightforward major/minor system starting from 2.2. This is because the parallel development on several branches made it infeasible to classify the releases merely by their real release dates. Do not worry about old -CURRENTs; they are listed here just for reference.

www.ingramcontent.com/pod-product-compliance
Lightning Source LLC
Chambersburg PA
CBHW080404060326
40689CB00019B/4131